SU
ON DEMAND

*The dust jacket image from the original
hardcover edition published in 1945*

# SURRENDER ON DEMAND

## VARIAN FRY

### Preface by Warren Christopher

### Published in conjunction with the
### United States Holocaust Memorial Museum

**JOHNSON BOOKS**
**Boulder**

Published in conjunction with the United States Holocaust Memorial Museum.

Published in the United States by Johnson Books, a division of Johnson Publishing Company, 1880 South 57th Court, Boulder, Colorado 80301.

9   8   7   6   5   4   3

Cover design by Debra B. Topping
Front cover photograph of Varian Fry in the office on the rue Grignan, Marseilles, Fall 1940, by Lipnitski, courtesy of Varian Fry Papers, Rare Book and Manuscript Library, Columbia University.

Library of Congress Cataloging-in-Publication Data
Fry, Varian.
    Surrender on demand / Varian Fry.
        p.      cm.
    Originally presented: New York: Random House, 1945.
    Includes index.
    ISBN 1-55566-209-9 (pbk.: alk. paper)
    1. World War, 1939–1945—Refugees.   2. World War, 1939–1945—France.   3. World War, 1939–1945—Personal narrative, American.
4. Emergency Rescue Committee—History.   I. Title.
D809.F7F79    1997
940.53ʹ08691—dc21                                                    97-25624
                                                                                CIP

Printed in the United States by
Johnson Printing
1880 South 57th Court
Boulder, Colorado 80301

 Printed on recycled paper with soy ink

FOR
ANNA CAPLES AND PAUL HAGEN,
WHO BEGAN IT;
FOR FRANK KINGDON,
WHO LENT IT HIS SUPPORT;
FOR INGRID WARBURG
AND HAROLD ORAM,
WHO MADE IT POSSIBLE;
AND FOR ALL THOSE WHO, IN
SWITZERLAND, FRANCE, SPAIN,
PORTUGAL AND AFRICA,
FORGETFUL OF SELF,
AND SOMETIMES AT RISK OF
THEIR LIVES,
CARRIED IT OUT

"I've always thought that what we did for the refugees in France resembled the obligation of soldiers to bring back their wounded from the battlefield, even at the risk of their own lives. Some may die. Some will be crippled for life. Some will recover and be the better soldiers for having had experience of battle. But one must bring them *all* back. At least one must try."

Beamish, in conversation

# CONTENTS

PREFACE, by Warren Christopher     ix

FOREWORD     xi

I. Conspiracy in the Hotel Splendide     3

II. I Find Confederates     19

III. Forgery Is a Fine Art     39

IV. I Become a British Agent     56

V. The Door Swings Shut     79

VI. The Ship That Didn't Sail     94

VII. The Villa Air-Bel     113

VIII. Journey Into the Night     122

IX. The Marshal Comes to Town     130

X. The Kidnapping at Cannes     150

XI. Delivery to Death     163

XII. Spring in Provence     178

XIII. Underground Through Spain     185

XIV. "Because You Have Protected Jews and Anti-Nazis"     206

XV. Good-bye to All That     224

XVI. After Much Suffering     236

ORIGINAL UNPUBLISHED FOREWORD     241

AFTERWORD     245

GLOSSARY OF FOREIGN TERMS     261

INDEX     269

# *PREFACE*

I wish to pay tribute to Varian Fry—a remarkable man and a remarkable American. Regretfully, during his lifetime, his heroic actions never received the support they deserved from the United States government, particularly the State Department. Even today, Varian Fry's tale of courage and compassion is too little known by his own countrymen. It was therefore with pride, but also with humility, that I, as America's Secretary of State, had the opportunity to speak on behalf of this extraordinary humanitarian at Israel's Yad Vashem Holocaust Memorial Museum when Fry was honored as one of the "Righteous Among the Nations."

The Holocaust is a haunting reminder of man's capacity for evil. One cannot ponder it without experiencing a profound sadness about the human condition. The measure of our faith is only restored by the knowledge that, in the face of such evil, there were also men and women like Varian Fry— otherwise ordinary individuals who were capable of summoning up extraordinary moral courage to confront and defy overwhelming brutality. There were thousands of such people. Some have no doubt been lost to history. Thankfully, many others are remembered, at such places as Yad Vashem, and also the United States Holocaust Memorial Museum. Varian Fry was such a person, and it is hoped that Americans will remember him always.

Varian Fry arrived in Marseilles in August 1940, a young, thirty-two-year-old representative of the Emergency Rescue Committee. His assignment was supposed to last three weeks.

He remained in France thirteen months. His initial orders were to help two hundred individuals escape the coming Nazi onslaught. He ended up rescuing close to four thousand.

Operating under constant threat, without regard for his personal safety, Varian Fry worked tirelessly, using every means available, to secure safe passage for those who came to him, desperate for help. He remained in France long after the dangers to his own life became apparent. His explanation was simple: "I stayed," he wrote, "because the refugees needed me." And because he knew that he was truly their last hope; that without his personal intervention, thousands more would have been lost to the death machines in places like Dachau and Buchenwald.

Every life that Varian Fry rescued was precious. But among those he saved were some of the greatest artists and intellectuals of our time: Marc Chagall, Hannah Arendt, Jacques Lipchitz, and many others whose works have made lasting contributions to world civilization.

We owe Varian Fry our deepest gratitude. But we also owe him a promise—a promise never to forget the horrors that he struggled against so heroically; and a promise to do whatever is necessary to ensure that such horrors can never happen again.

Allow me once again to say how pleased I am to have had the wonderful opportunity to honor and commemorate the remarkable life of Varian Fry. May his example guide us always.

—WARREN CHRISTOPHER
U.S. Secretary of State, 1993–97

# FOREWORD

This is the story of an experiment in democratic solidarity. The fall of France, in June, 1940, meant not merely the defeat of the French nation; it meant also the creation of the most gigantic man-trap in history. Ever since the Russian Revolution—in fact, even before—France had been the haven of Europe's exiles. Whenever a change of government in another land, or invasion by a foreign power, had obliged men to flee for their lives, France had opened her arms to them. White Russians and Russian Mensheviks; Italian liberals, republicans and socialists; Germans of all parties but the Nazi; Austrians ranging in their political views from monarchists to communists; Spaniards of every republican and leftist view; Czechs, Poles, Dutch, Belgians—one after another they had found refuge in France.

Hitler's invasion of France eliminated the French army as a barrier against Germany and Italy, and the armistice left the German refugees at the mercy of their most relentless foes. Nor had democrats and leftists of any nationality much reason to trust the new, reactionary government which had been brought to power in the wake of the defeat.

When it was learned that the armistice which France made with Germany in June, 1940, contained a clause providing for the "surrender on demand" of German refugees,[1] a group of

[1] Article 19. The full text, as cabled from Berlin by the Associated Press, read as follows: "All German war and civil prisoners in French

xi

American citizens, who were deeply shocked by this violation of the right of asylum and who believed that democrats
must help democrats, regardless of nationality, immediately
formed the Emergency Rescue Committee. The sole purpose of the Committee was to bring the political and intellectual refugees out of France before the Gestapo and the
Ovra and the Seguridad got them.

After several weeks of fruitless searching for a suitable agent
to send to France, the Committee selected me. I had had no
experience in refugee work, and none in underground work.
But I accepted the assignment because, like the members of
the Committee, I believed in the importance of democratic
solidarity. I had seen the democratic governments of Europe
go down one by one: first Italy; then Germany; then Austria;
then Spain; then Czechoslovakia; then Norway, Holland, Belgium, France; and I was convinced that if democracy was to
endure at all it would have to become internationally minded.
Thus, quite apart from any sentimental reasons, I accepted
the assignment out of deep political convictions.

But the sentimental reasons were also there; and they were

custody, including those under arrest and convicted who were seized
and sentenced because of acts in favor of the German Reich, shall be
surrendered immediately to German troops.
"*The French Government is obliged to surrender upon demand all
Germans named by the German Government in France, as well as in
French possessions, Colonies, Protectorate Territories and Mandates.*
"The French Government binds itself to prevent removal of German war and civil prisoners from France into French possessions or
into foreign countries. Regarding prisoners already taken outside
France, as well as sick and wounded German prisoners who cannot be
transported, exact lists with the places of residence are to be produced.
The German High Command assumes care of sick and wounded German war prisoners."
The paragraph in italics is the one which applied to political refugees. "Germans" originally meant all inhabitants of the Greater Reich,
i.e., Germans, Austrians, Czechs and many Poles, but was later stretched
to include everybody the German government wanted to get its
hands on.

strong. Among the refugees who were caught in France were many writers and artists whose work I had enjoyed: novelists like Franz Werfel and Lion Feuchtwanger; painters like Marc Chagall and Max Ernst; sculptors like Jacques Lipchitz. For some of these men, although I knew them only through their work, I had a deep love; and to them all I owed a heavy debt of gratitude for the pleasure they had given me. Now that they were in danger, I felt obliged to help them, if I could; just as they, without knowing it, had often in the past helped me.

Most of all, it was a feeling of sympathy for the German and Austrian Socialist Parties which led me to go to France in the summer of 1940, a sympathy born of long familiarity with their principles and their works—particularly the excellent workers' housing projects they built in the twenties. I had not always agreed with their ideas or their methods, but I knew when I saw those housing projects that their hearts were in the right place.

Finally, I knew, from first-hand experience, what defeat at the hands of Hitler could mean. In 1935 I visited Germany and tasted the atmosphere of oppression which the Hitler regime had brought. I talked to many anti-Nazis and Jews, shared their anxiety and their sense of helplessness, felt with them the tragic hopelessness of their situation. And while I was in Berlin I witnessed on the Kurfuerstendamm the first great pogrom against the Jews, saw with my own eyes young Nazi toughs gather and smash up Jewish-owned cafés, watched with horror as they dragged Jewish patrons from their seats, drove hysterical, crying women down the street, knocked over an elderly man and kicked him in the face. Now that that same oppression had spread to France, I could not remain idle as long as I had any chance at all of saving even a few of its intended victims.

Thus, for a variety of reasons, and through a series of acci-

dents, I left New York in August, 1940, on a secret mission
to France, a mission which many of my friends thought a very
dangerous one, and which some of them warned me against
undertaking. I left with my pockets full of lists of men and
women I was to rescue, and my head full of suggestions on
how to do it. Altogether, there were more than two hundred
names on my lists, and many hundreds more were added later.

I also left believing that my job could be done in one
month. I stayed thirteen, and, when I finally came back,
against my will, the work was still far from finished.

This is the story of those thirteen months, and of what followed them. Those of my readers who have been impatient
to know the truth about the work of the Emergency Rescue
Committee in France will understand now why that story
could not have been told sooner. For it is a story of illegal
work under the nose of the Gestapo, and many of those who
participated in it remained in France, at the mercy of the
Gestapo, long after I had returned to the safety of America.
To have written about that work while the Gestapo was still
in France would have been to betray comrades and friends to
imprisonment and possibly to death.

VARIAN FRY

NEW YORK
JANUARY, 1945

*Surrender on Demand*

# I. *Conspiracy in the Hotel Splendide*

THERE were no taxis outside the station, but there were plenty of porters. One of them took my suitcases.

"What hotel?" he asked.

"The Splendide," I said.

"Have you a reservation?"

"No."

"Then you won't get a room there," he said. "Better try the Hotel Suisse. It's the only one in town where you'll find a room. The refugees have taken everything in Marseille."

"I'd like to try the Splendide, nevertheless," I said.

We crossed the street and went down the great staircase to the boulevard d'Athènes. The Splendide was the first large building on the right. There were no rooms, but I left my name and asked them to save me one as soon as they had it. Then I gave in to the insistence of the porter and went to the Hotel Suisse. It was obvious that he had an arrangement with the management.

The Hotel Suisse was one of those "family" hotels with which France abounds. It smelled strongly of drains and garlic. But there was a room vacant, and I took it. It was on the front of the hotel, facing the Gare St. Charles, Marseille's principal railway station. The most conspicuous thing in the room was a large, flushable *bidet*, stark and white against the dark-green walls and the hexagonal red-tile floor. From the window I had a fine view of the station's monumental stairway, the little park which nestles beside it, and the one-man

3

*pissotière* under the station embankment, with its inevitable *Amer Picon* advertisement.

After lunch I went to the American Consulate. The woman behind the desk on the second floor had bleached hair, deep-blue eyelids, and an unnatural sparkle in her eyes. When I said I had come to see the Consul about visas, she handed me a slip of paper with an address typed on it and told me to go downstairs and take a trolley marked Montrédon. She smirked and squirmed coquettishly as she talked.

The trolley was already full when I got in. I showed the slip of paper to the conductor.

"You'll know when we come to it," he said. "Everybody gets off there."

Glancing around, I could see from their bewildered looks and the condition of their clothes that more than half the passengers were refugees.

The trolley took us along the broad avenue du Prado to the sea, then turned left and followed the Mediterranean coast for fifteen or twenty minutes. It was a hot August afternoon. Landscape and climate reminded me of the coast near Athens —arid gray limestone hills, closely packed beach houses, umbrella pines, date palms, dry heat, dust. It was so hot that I had difficulty keeping awake.

At Montrédon the car stopped and everybody got off. The way to the visa division led up a long drive lined with plane trees; under the trees were narrow irrigation ditches. The refugees hurried ahead, stirring up a cloud of choking dust as they walked. I lagged behind, glad of the shade and the comforting, cool sound of the water running down the ditches to the sea.

When I reached the big brick house at the end of the drive, a large crowd of refugees was already gathered there. They occupied all the benches in the waiting room and spilled out onto the porch; some of them were sitting on the parapet, dangling their legs over the edge.

I went inside and stood at the open door of the big center room. A dog-faced young man came up and frowned at me.

"What do you mean, trying to get ahead of the others?" he barked in French. "Go back to your place and wait your turn."

But when I explained that I was an American citizen come to inquire about the visas of some refugees my committee was interested in, his manner changed abruptly.

"Oh, excuse me, sir," he said. He was speaking English now, and sweetly. "I didn't know you were an American."

I gave him my card.

"If you'll come inside," he said, leading me into the office and offering me a chair in front of a large American office desk, "I'll take your card to the Consul."

I sat down and began to wait. There were five or six mahogany desks in the room and rows of green-metal filing cases behind them. Through the great bay windows I could see the lawns and trees of the Chateau Pastré and the mountains and sea beyond them. From the waiting room came the murmur of a hundred voices, speaking French and German.

I had waited ten minutes when a young vice-consul came up to the desk.

"What are you doing here?" he fairly shouted. "Get back to the waiting room, where you belong!"

I got up without saying a word. In the waiting room I sat for two hours. Then I went back to Marseille.

-2-

That evening I had dinner with the Franz Werfels. I had met Werfel's sister in Lisbon and gotten their address from her. They were living at the Hotel du Louvre et de la Paix, on the Canebière, under the name of one of Mrs. Werfel's previous husbands, Gustav Mahler, the composer. There was a good deal of mystery about them at the hotel, and I had to wait quite a while before I was finally allowed to go up to their rooms. But when I got upstairs I found they had been expecting me for some time.

Werfel looked exactly like his photographs: large, dumpy

and pallid, like a half-filled sack of flour. His hair was thin on top and too long on the sides. He was wearing a silk dressing gown and soft slippers, and was sitting all over a small gilt chair. He seemed very glad to see me, but very anxious not to have anyone else know he was there.

Mrs. Werfel was much calmer. She brought out boxes of chocolates and a bottle of Benedictine, poured the Benedictine into tumblers and offered them to her husband and me.

They had fled from Paris to Lourdes, where they had sought the protection of the Church, they said. While waiting there Werfel had begun a new novel, *The Song of Bernadette*. When they realized that they would never be able to leave France from Lourdes, they came to Marseille to get the American visas which were ready for them at the Consulate.

Having got the visas, they were at a loss to know what to do next. They had applied for exit visas, but there had been no answer. Should they leave without them, or should they wait? Werfel was inclined to think that, in spite of the general ban, he would be able to get exit visas. Mrs. Werfel was for trying their luck without exit visas, as others were doing. They appealed to me for advice and help.

"You must save us, Mr. Fry," Werfel said, speaking English with a strong Austrian accent.

"Oh, ja, you must save us," Mrs. Werfel echoed. And then, with a radiant smile, and "A little more Benedictine, ja?" she half-filled my glass before I had time to protest.

We had dinner at Basso's, a large and expensive restaurant on the Vieux Port. All during dinner the Werfels talked about the horrors of the retreat. After dinner we went back to the hotel, where they insisted on ordering a bottle of champagne. Over the champagne we discussed ways of escaping from France.

I explained that I had just arrived and hadn't yet had time to find out what the possibilities were. They had heard of refugees going down to the frontier and getting over safely, but they didn't know what happened to them in Spain. They thought most of them were probably arrested there and handed over to the Gestapo. There was also the risk of being arrested for traveling without permission in France. And there was real danger that the police would arrest them and deport them to Germany if they stayed in Marseille. It was all very confusing. What were they to do?

I had to admit that I didn't know, but I advised them to stay in hiding at the hotel until I could find out what the chances of escape really were.

The truth was that I was at a complete loss about how to begin, and where. My job was to save certain refugees. But how was I to do it? How was I to get in touch with them? What could I do for them when I found them?

-3-

I had to find the answers before it was too late, and the first person to consult was Frank Bohn. A few weeks after the French defeat, the American Federation of Labor had succeeded in persuading the State Department to grant emergency visitors' visas to a long list of European labor leaders, and had sent Bohn over to Marseille to help them escape. He was one of two or three Americans already in France whose names had been given me, in the strictest confidence, just before I left New York.

I called on Bohn the morning of my second day in Marseille. I found him in his small room on the third floor of the Hotel Splendide. When he opened the door to my knock, and I told him who I was and why I had come to France, he grabbed my hand in a great big friendly clutch and fairly yanked me across the threshold into the room.

"Oh, I'm so glad you've come," he said, in the tones of an itinerant revivalist, pumping my arm up and down vigorously. "We need all the help we can get. Come in, come in. I'm so glad you've come."

Inside the little room there were several German refugees, all standing. Bohn introduced me to them.

"This is Comrade Fry," he said, speaking German. "Genossin *Bierman, Genosse Fry. Genosse Heine*, this is Comrade Fry."

I was somewhat alarmed to hear myself called "comrade," especially in Vichy France, but I shook hands all around without protesting the title. Then one of the refugees said, "Please, take place," and we all sat down.

"Is it all right to talk here?" I whispered to Bohn, looking around at the people in the room.

"Yes, indeed, my boy," Bohn said aloud. "Everybody here's a good comrade. You can say anything you please."

"Well, then," I said, "perhaps you can tell me just what the situation is and what I have to do to get my people out."

"Certainly, old man," Bohn said. "For most of them it's very simple. The disorder is working in our favor, you see. The French aren't giving any exit visas to refugees at all, and it's even very hard for them to get safe conduct to come to Marseille and get their American visas. But the police don't seem to be paying much attention to them, and the Gestapo doesn't seem to have gotten around to them either. This has been a lucky thing for the refugees. It's given them time to get away. So far we've found that the ordinary refugee can travel pretty safely without a safe conduct. If they have overseas visas they can get Portuguese and Spanish transit visas, and once they have these they can go down to the frontier and cross on foot."

"Don't they ever get arrested?" I asked.

"So far nobody has," Heine answered. "The police seem to sympathize with us. Some of the *commissaires* at the frontier have even been known to take pity on refugees without exit visas and let them go through on the train—provided no other *commissaire* is around to see what's going on. It seems to be a question of luck. If you happen to strike the right man you can go through on the train. If you strike the wrong one, you have to walk."

"You have a better chance of going through on the train if you are a young male who looks as though he was thinking of joining de Gaulle," Mrs. Bierman said, with what I thought was a trace of bitterness in her voice.

"Well," I said, "if it's as simple as all that, why hasn't everybody left by now?"

"For various reasons, old man," Bohn said. "In the first place, many of them are still waiting for overseas visas. Many are still in concentration camps. Then the leaders don't dare go through Spain. They're afraid they'd be arrested there and deported to Germany."

"Why can't they use false passports?" I asked. "Can't they get them?"

"Oh, yes, we can get them all right," Bohn said, "but the trouble is the men who're in the greatest danger don't dare use them. They're afraid they'd be recognized and exposed. Now you take a man like Rudolph Breitscheid, for instance. For years he was one of the most important men in Germany, leader of the Social Democratic bloc in the Reichstag, and he's convinced he couldn't get five miles in Spain without being recognized. The same thing is true of Hilferding and Modigliani and many others."

"Let's see, now," I said, getting out my list of European labor leaders. "Just who are Hilferding and Modigliani?"

"Hilferding was German Minister of Finance and Modigliani was the leader of the Italian Socialist Party."

"He's the brother of the painter. You know, the one who did the oval-faced females," someone added.

"Are they all here in Marseille?" I asked.

"Yes," Bohn said. "They're all here, and all waiting for me to get them out."

"Any idea how you're going to do it?"

Bohn leaned forward in his chair until his face was close to mine.

"By boat," he said, in a loud stage whisper. "I'm working out a scheme now. It's too early for me to tell you more than that. But I'll keep you posted, old man. I expect to have the thing cinched in a few days."

"That's fine," I said. "Now, tell me, what do you use for

cover operations? I mean, before I left New York, Paul Hagen and some of the others who've had experience with underground work told me you needed some sort of cover operations, something that would provide an innocent explanation for what you had to do on the surface. What do you recommend?"

"You need them in Germany, all right," Bohn said, "but not here. At least not yet. I've been operating right from this room, and I haven't had any trouble with the police at all."

"You mean you operate openly?" I asked. The tone of my voice must have betrayed my disappointment, because everybody started to answer at once. In the end it was Heine who won out.

"Not quite openly," he said. "Great secrecy is necessary on such matters as escapes over the mountains, false passports and boats. What Dr. Bohn means is that we've been seeing the refugees right here in this room. If anyone asks us what we're doing we say we're helping them get their visas and giving them money to live on."

"As that is quite legal, the French police can hardly object," Bohn explained. "Of course what we're really doing is getting the poor devils away. But we keep that a dark secret."

"How do you find the Consulate?" I asked. "Have they co-operated?"

"Splendidly!" Bohn said. "Splendidly! Don't you worry. If anything *should* happen to us, the Consulate and the Embassy would back us up to the hilt."

"That surprises me," I said. "I didn't exactly get that impression yesterday." And I told him what had happened at Montrédon.

"Accidents will happen, old man," Bohn said. "The office boy probably mislaid your card. Or maybe Harry Bingham was out. He's the Vice-Consul in charge of visas, and the son of the late Senator from Connecticut. I believe his brother's the editor of *Common Sense*. Anyway, he has a heart of gold. He does everything he can to help us, within American law. On the other hand the Consul-General is pretty nervous, although I think he sympathizes with what we're trying to do."

"In general, I gather that things aren't as bad over here as people back in the States think they are," I said.

"Not quite," Bohn said. "But we have to hurry, just the same. You never can tell when things will change, old man. And when they do, it won't be for the better."

"Well," I said, "how shall we work? I mean we'll have to work out a way of co-operating, so as not to both be seeing the same people all the time, won't we?"

"You're right, my boy," Bohn said. "Suppose you take the writers and artists and all the young members of the various left-wing groups you're interested in, and we'll go on handling the trade-union people and the older socialists. Bedrich Heine here is a member of the Executive of the Social Democratic Party, and Erika Bierman is Breitscheid's secretary. We three work together. You'll always find one of us in this room, and you're welcome to come in whenever you want to."

"That's fine," I said. "That means that men like Breitscheid and Hilferding and Modigliani are your babies, and Werfel and Feuchtwanger and Heiden are mine. By the way, have you any idea what's become of Feuchtwanger and Heiden?"

"I believe that Konrad Heiden is in Montauban," Heine said, "but I haven't heard what's become of Feuchtwanger. Some say he's in Switzerland. He was interned in the camp of St. Nicolas last spring, but after the armistice he escaped, and nobody's heard of him since."

"Huh-hmm," Bohn said, clearing his throat. "Perhaps you and I had better talk privately about this, old man."

He got up and led me into the bathroom.

"I've promised Harry Bingham not to breathe a word of this to anybody," he said, after he had closed the door, "but I'm sure he wouldn't mind my telling you. It was Harry who got Feuchtwanger out of that camp. He arranged it all with Mrs. Feuchtwanger in advance, and she got word of their plans to her husband. Luckily she wasn't interned, you see. A few days after the armistice Harry drove his car out to a place near the camp where the men were allowed to go and swim, and Feuchtwanger met him there. Harry had brought some women's clothes along, and Feuchtwanger put them on and Harry drove him back to Marseille."

"Gosh," I said, "he really *is* a prince, isn't he! Where is Feuchtwanger now?"

"Hiding in Harry's villa," Bohn said.

"Have you any plans for getting him out of France?"

"No," Bohn said, "I haven't. He's your responsibility, not mine. But you can put him on my boat if you want to."

"Okay," I said. "I'll put the Werfels and the Feuchtwangers on your boat."

-4-

After talking to Bohn, I decided to alter my plans. Instead of traveling around Southern France on a bicycle, pretending to be a relief worker investigating the needs of the French people, but really locating refugees on my lists and helping them escape, I'd set up headquarters at the Splendide, as Bohn had done, and have the refugees come to me. Bohn got me a room at the Splendide like his own, and I moved down from the Suisse that same day. Then I wrote letters to all the refugees on my lists whose addresses I had, telling them I had just arrived from the States with messages for them, and asking them to come to Marseille to see me if they could. I got more addresses from Bohn. Some of the people on my lists he had already seen himself. About others he or his assistants, Erika Bierman and Bedrich Heine, had some information. But most of them were still missing. Nobody knew where they were or what had become of them.

The refugees began coming to my room the next day. Many of them had been through hell; their nerves were shattered and their courage gone. Many had been herded into concentration camps at the outbreak of the war, then released, then interned again when the Germans began their great offensive in May. In the concentration camps they had waited fearfully while the *Wehrmacht* drew nearer and nearer. It was often literally at the last moment that they had had a chance to save themselves. Then they had joined the great exodus to the south, sometimes walking hundreds of miles to get away from the Nazis.

Many of them, especially the Germans and Austrians, believed that every ring of the doorbell, every step on the stair, every knock on the door might be the police come to get them and deliver them to the Gestapo. They sought frantically for some means of escape from the net which had suddenly been dropped over their heads. In their eagerness to get away, they easily became prey to every sort of swindler and blackmailer. Sometimes, under the incessant pounding of wild rumors and fantastic horror stories, their already badly frayed nerves gave way altogether, and they had nervous breakdowns.

Some of them believed the Germans were going to take over unoccupied France at a given hour of a given day, usually some time during the following week. They generally knew not only when the occupation was to take place, but exactly how many divisions had been assigned to the job. They heard and believed that the Spanish frontier had just been closed by Senegalese troops, to keep the refugees from getting out. They knew for a fact that the Gestapo was roaming all over the unoccupied zone, and had handed a list of several hundred wanted men and women to M. Laval, who had given orders for the immediate arrest of everyone on it.

Nor was it only the Germans and the Austrians who were worried. Luis Compañys, the Catalan trade-union leader, had been picked up by the Nazis in Belgium or the occupied part of France and sent down to Spain, where he was promptly garroted. And the French police were treating foreigners with a combination of muddle and brutality which left very few of them with any desire to stay in France longer than they had to.

The situation was especially bad in big cities like Marseille, where there was a large and constantly changing refugee population which kept the police nervous and occasionally stirred them to arrest large numbers on the streets. These sudden mass arrests were called râfles. You never knew when one was coming, or where. It might be on the Canebière in broad daylight, or it might be in a café or hotel after dark. Only one thing was certain: if you were picked up in a râfle you would spend several days in jail, even if you were found to be *en règle* in the end; if you weren't *en règle*, you would go from jail to a concentration camp.

-5-

Fortunately for me, the first of the refugees to come to the Splendide in response to my summons were Paul Hagen's German socialist friends and some of the younger Austrian socialists. They were all young and vigorous and not at all lacking in courage. Most of them had already received American visas. All they needed, they said, was money. With enough money in their pockets for the trip to Lisbon, they would take their chances with the French and Spanish police and the Gestapo in Spain. They would get Portuguese and Spanish transit visas and go down to the frontier and cross over on foot.

I gave them money and they went. All of them got to Lisbon. It was as simple as that.

One of them gave me a map of the frontier showing just how they planned to cross it. The map showed the cemetery at Cerbère and the path along the cemetery wall. The international boundary was indicated by a series of crosses, and the route to avoid the French border control was shown by arrows. I kept the map behind the mirror of my wardrobe, to show to others who didn't know the way.

The important thing, once you got across into Spain, was to present yourself to the Spanish border authorities, and not go farther into Spain until you had the Spanish *entrada* stamp on your passport, Paul's friends said. Otherwise, you would be arrested for illegal entry. But if you presented yourself to the first border post you came to, and declared your money, you were all right. The Spanish seemed to take no interest at all in the presence or absence of a French exit visa on a passport. They were interested only in Spanish transit visas, and, above all, in money. If you had a valid Spanish transit visa and declared your money, you could enter and cross Spain. No one knew of any arrests occurring in Spain. There were rumors of them, but no authenticated cases.

The Spanish Consulates in Marseille, Toulouse and Perpignan were all giving transit visas on presentation of passports with valid Portuguese transit visas. And the Portuguese Consulates were giving transit visas on almost anything which seemed to mean that the holder could go on from Portugal. Refugees who hadn't yet received United States visas were taking Chinese or Siamese visas and getting Portuguese transit visas on them, with the intention of waiting for their United States visas in Lisbon rather than in France.

The Chinese visas were all in Chinese, except for two words: "100 francs." The Chinese and those who could read Chinese said that the "visa" really read: "This person shall not, under any circumstances, be allowed to enter China." I don't know whether this was true or not, but it didn't matter so long as the Portuguese were accepting the visa as a valid one. The Siamese visas were real enough, only there was absolutely no way of going from Portugal to Siam without getting numerous unobtainable transit visas. Yet, at the time, the Portuguese Consuls gave the holders of these Siamese visas Portuguese transit visas exactly as though there were ships from Lisbon to Bangkok. Once they had the Portuguese and Spanish transit visas, most of the refugees were able to go to Lisbon with little or no difficulty.

As for the police control at the railroad station at Marseille, it was only for arriving passengers. If you had to come to Marseille by train, you could avoid the police check-up by going into the station restaurant through a service corridor to the Hotel Terminus. If anyone asked you what you were doing (something which never happened), you could say you were going to telephone, or to wash your hands. Once you were in the hotel you could walk out onto the street exactly like any guest.

Of course, there were risks. There was the fact that foreigners weren't supposed to travel in France without safe conducts issued by the military authorities. Except at Marseille, there wasn't any regular inspection of papers, but there might be a chance inspection anywhere, at any time, in the stations, on the trains, even on the streets. Any foreigner caught traveling without such a safe conduct was likely to be sent to a concentration camp. Once he was in a concentration camp, there was no telling how long it would be before he could get out again—if ever. Meanwhile the Gestapo would be able to lay its hands on him very handily, if it wanted him. Whereas, as long as he was living in a hotel, he might have some chance of slipping through the Gestapo's fingers. Even in a hotel he had to make out a form, which was immediately turned over to the police. The best place to hide was with friends or in a brothel.

There was also the danger of being arrested at the frontier for trying to leave France without an exit visa. That, too, was a grave offense, and would almost certainly land foreigners in concentration camps. So far it hadn't happened; but there was no assurance that it wouldn't.

All in all, the perils of leaving France without an exit visa were considerable, and some of the refugees refused to do it, preferring the risks of staying to the risks of leaving. One of my hardest jobs in those early weeks was to persuade them to go. Some of the intellectuals were particularly difficult. They were jittery with fear at the idea of staying, and paralyzed with fear at the idea of leaving. You would get them prepared with their passports and all their visas in order, and a month later they would still be sitting in the Marseille cafés, waiting for the police to come and get them.

-6-

But these were the exceptions. Most of the refugees were eager to get away. I sat in my little room on the back of the fourth floor of the Hotel Splendide and they came to me. I gave them money and advice and tried to give them hope. Those who already had visas I instructed how to cross the frontier. When they were ready to leave, I shook their hands, and said, "I'll see you soon in New York." Many of them were incredulous, hardly daring to hope. But that short sentence, spoken with conviction, seemed to do more than anything else to restore their faith in the future. If the American is so sure he will see us soon in New York, they must have thought, then maybe there *is* some hope.

Those who hadn't yet received their visas were more of a problem. Some of them could afford to wait for American visas, because there wasn't any particular reason why they should be wanted by the Gestapo. When that was the case, I cabled their names to New York and asked the committee there to get them emergency visas as quickly as possible. Others couldn't wait; they had to get out of France right away. When they had passports, I helped them get Chinese, Siamese or sometimes Belgian Congo visas and advised them to go as far as Lisbon, where they could wait, in comparative safety, for their American visas to be authorized. But some of the refugees had neither visas nor passports to put them on, and even some of those who had passports needed new ones, under false names, for fear they would be arrested in Spain if they tried to go through under their own names.

The saddest cases were the *apatrides*, the men and women who had been deprived of their nationality by decree of the Nazi government. Not only could they not get legal passports, but they were presumably in the greatest danger of being picked up by the Gestapo, for they had already been singled out as enemies of the Nazi state. The French had given most of them green, accordion-folded documents called *titres de voyage*—a kind of refugee passport—but the Spanish didn't recognize these, and everyone who went down to the frontier with one had to come back again.

Luckily, when an American visa had been authorized for an *apatride*, or man without a country, the American Consulate usually gave him a paper called an "affidavit in lieu of passport." For a while this worked, provided the man was willing to take the chance of going through Spain under his own name. In fact, many minor French and Spanish officials obviously took the bearers of such documents for American citizens, and treated them with the special deference European under-officials somehow almost always reserve for Americans—or used to. I was not inclined to correct the false impression.

But if a refugee's American visa hadn't yet been authorized, or he wasn't willing to travel under his own name even if it had been, there was usually only one solution—a false passport. It was the Czech Consul at Marseille who solved that problem, and it was Donald Lowrie who put me in touch with him. Lowrie was one of the representatives of the Y.M.C.A. in France, and also the delegate of the American Friends of Czechoslovakia. He had been in Prague when the Germans came in, and he had helped a good many German and Czech anti-Nazis escape. When he got to Marseille he was already known to the Czech Consul as a good friend of the Czechs. I met him very soon after my arrival, and he took me down to the Czech Consulate and introduced me to the Consul.

Vladimir Vochoč was a diplomat of the old school. He had been chief of the European personnel division of the Czech Foreign Office before the fall of Prague, and a professor at the University of Prague. I don't think he liked the idea of handing out false passports, but he was wise enough to realize that his country had been invaded by the Nazis, and that it wouldn't be liberated by legal means alone. He was willing to help any anti-Nazi save his life if there was any chance at all that, once saved, the man would be useful in overthrowing the Nazis and so restoring the independence of Czechoslovakia. Vochoč's own job consisted in smuggling the Czech volunteers out of France so they could fight again with the British.

At Lowrie's suggestion, I made a deal with Vochoč. He agreed to grant Czech passports to any anti-Nazis I recommended to him. In return I gave him enough money to have new passports printed when his limited supply had run out.

He couldn't get any more from Prague, obviously, but as a Consul he had the right to have them printed in France. The work was actually done at Bordeaux, in the occupied zone, under the noses of the Germans. It was a very nice job. The covers were pink, whereas the old Prague passports had been green, but otherwise you couldn't tell one from the other.

After that there was nothing left to do but work out a safe way to receive the passports. Lowrie was living at the Hotel Terminus, and I used to go over to his room and have breakfast with him twice a week. Each time I went I would take him an envelope of photographs and descriptions of my candidates for Czech passports, and he would give me an envelope of the passports Vochoč had already prepared for the previous lot. Then I'd go back to my room at the Splendide and hand the passports to the refugees as they came in to get them.

## II. *I Find Confederates*

MY ROOM at the Splendide overlooked the courtyard of a girls' school, and, beyond it, the city. In the distance you could see, silhouetted against the sky, or half-hidden by mist, the tower and dome of Notre Dame de la Garde, which crowns the hill to the south of the Vieux Port as the Sacré Coeur crowns Montmartre.

In the daytime, during recess periods, when the girls came out to play in the courtyard of the school, the noise could be heard in my room. But the city itself was almost hushed. Vichy still obviously thought that the war would soon be over. It had proclaimed the interval between the armistice and the definitive peace a period of mourning and had forbidden dancing, the playing of jazz, and certain other, more peculiarly French, amusements once available in the *maisons closes*. But there was no attempt to ration food, and the only conspicuous shortages were of razor blades, soap and gasoline.

Marseille was filled with refugees, French as well as others. But all those who could were going home again as fast as they could get there. Even many French Jews were returning to the occupied zone. They wanted to get back and they quieted whatever anxieties they may have felt about life under the Nazis by telling themselves that Hitler would never dare do to the French what he was doing to the Poles. In fact, everyone but the anti-fascist refugees and the intellectuals seemed intent on straightening out the confusion which followed the defeat and getting back to "normalcy" as quickly as possible.

The newspapers, reduced to two or at most four pages, carried column after column of classified advertisements in which people tried to reunite families scattered by the war and the retreat. The notices often reflected poignant and even tragic situations: "Mother seeks baby daughter, age two, lost on the road between Tours and Poitiers in the retreat," or, "Generous reward for information leading to the recovery of my son Jacques, age ten, last seen at Bordeaux, June 17th." But life in Marseille was very different from what I had imagined it would be. There was no disorder. There were no children starving on the streets. There were very few signs of war of any kind. The people of Marseille seemed to have resigned themselves to defeat, even to take it lightly, as they take everything.

The French refugees were rapidly being sent home—all, that is, except those whose homes were in the so-called "forbidden zone," and those who wouldn't go back to the occupied zone to live under the Nazis—but every day brought trainloads of soldiers on their way to be demobilized, either in Southern France or in Africa. Marseille was as crowded with soldiers as it was with refugees. There were men from every branch of the French army: colonials, with bright-red fezzes, or *chéchias*, on their heads; volunteers of the Foreign Legion, wearing their *képis* in dust covers; Zouaves, in baggy, Turkish-style trousers; Spahis, with broad black sashes around their waists; Alpine *chasseurs*, in olive-green uniforms and enormous berets, worn well down over the left ear; dusty moles from the tunnels of the Maginot Line, in gray jumpers; cavalry officers, smartly dressed in khaki tunics and doe-colored riding breeches, and wearing rakish, brown-velour caps instead of *képis* or helmets; the black Senegalese, their heads done up in turbans pinned together with a single gilt star; members of the tank corps, in padded leather helmets; and ordinary infantrymen by the tens of thousands, weary, dirty and bedraggled. All day long soldiers and refugees flowed to and from the Gare St. Charles, up and down the boulevard Dugommier and the Canebière, in and out of the cafés and restaurants of the Canebière and the Vieux Port, spilling into the streets, like crowds coming from a football game, packing the front and rear platforms of the street cars, pushing, shoving, jostling. But quiet—the living flotsam and jetsam left over from a great disaster.

I added two words to my French vocabulary during those first days. They were *pagaille* and *débrouiller*.

*Pagaille* means utter confusion. It was a word on everyone's lips in France, the only word which seemed adequately to sum up the situation.

"*Quelle pagaille!*" people said when they talked about the defeat and the retreat.

The other word means look out for yourself, out-smart the other fellow. In a *pagaille* like that which reigned in France after the armistice, the only thing anyone could do was *se débrouiller*. It was the philosophy of each man for himself and the devil take the hindmost.

"*Faut se débrouiller,*" they said, when they boarded the trains, considered the food situation, or talked of the defeat.

-2-

A few days after I met him, Bohn and I had breakfast with Breitscheid and Hilferding at a sidewalk café. Mrs. Breitscheid and her husband's secretary, Mrs. Bierman, were with them. Mrs. Hilferding was still in Paris, hiding from the Gestapo. Breitscheid, tall and handsome, sat bolt upright in his chair. His face looked yellow and waxen under his snow-white hair, and he kept his hands folded on the edge of the small round metal table or tapped his fingers nervously on the table top as he talked. He had a disconcerting way of looking past you into space as he spoke. Hilferding, shorter and stouter, with sandy gray hair and mustache, was more relaxed, and seemed more at ease than the others. Mrs. Breitscheid was very nervous, and so was Mrs. Bierman.

Bohn tried to cheer them up by telling them his boat plans were making good progress and urging them to wait calmly until he was ready to send them away. Then he went off to the Consulate. As soon as he had gone, Breitscheid asked me what I thought of Bohn's plan, and he and Hilferding began to argue about whether they should wait for the boat or risk crossing the frontier into Spain on foot. Both had American visitors' visas, and Hilferding seemed to think they should try their luck through Spain. But Breitscheid thought otherwise. He wasn't sure of Bohn's boat, but he wasn't sure of Spain either. He had an imperious manner, to which Hilferding seemed to defer. I left them still discussing the boat versus Spain and went back to the Splendide to keep an appointment with Giuseppe Modigliani.

Modigliani and his wife were waiting for me in the lobby when I arrived. If the difficulty with Breitscheid and Hilferding was to get them to make up their minds, the trouble with Modigliani was that he had already made up his. He wanted to leave France, but he absolutely refused to do anything illegal.

"Suppose I should be caught and exposed in the act of sneaking out of the country on a false passport," he snorted.

"Why, it would disgrace the entire Italian labor movement!"

"Giuseppe!" his wife remonstrated. "Giuseppe! Please be reasonable!"

But Giuseppe retaliated by beginning to shout, and she had to stop for fear he would gather a crowd.

"If only he would shave off his beard and leave his fur coat behind," she sighed, "he could go as easily as the others. But every time I mention it he begins to shout."

"Shave off my beard, indeed!" Modigliani exclaimed. "No, my dear, I have always worn a beard and I always shall! As for the coat, you know perfectly well . . ."

"Yes," Mrs. Modigliani interrupted, "I know perfectly well that nothing will ever induce you to part with it, even to save your life.

"You see," she explained, "Local 89 of the Garment Workers' Union presented it to him when he visited the United States, and he's so proud of it he wears it winter and summer, regardless of the weather. I've tried everything I can think of to persuade him to leave it behind, but he won't hear of it."

"Certainly not!" Modigliani said, with the air of a man who is closing a discussion once and for all.

Mrs. Modigliani shrugged.

"What can you do?" she asked resignedly.

I had to admit I didn't know.

Bohn had told me that Modigliani had agreed to leave on his boat, but even that seemed doubtful after my conversation with him. I found him, if possible, even more of a problem than Breitscheid and Hilferding, and I was glad that all three men were primarily Bohn's responsibility and not mine. My hands were already quite full enough.

-3-

Before the end of my first week in Marseille, word had apparently spread all over the unoccupied zone that an American had arrived from New York, like an angel from heaven, with his pockets stuffed with money and passports and a direct connection with the State Department enabling him to get any kind of visa at a moment's notice. I even heard that at Toulouse an enterprising merchant was selling my name and address to the refugees for fifty francs. It wasn't true, of course, that I could get visas quickly—I wish it had been— but the refugees believed it, and they began coming in droves. I was no longer seeing just the people on my lists, but scores who thought they ought to be on them. I had to get help, not only to handle the crowds, but also to advise me on the political views and intellectual merits of the candidates. Most of them were complete strangers to me, and I had to be careful not to help a police spy or a fifth columnist, or a communist masquerading as a democrat.

The first person to work for me in France was "Beamish." He was a young political refugee from Germany, very intelligent and eternally good-natured and cheerful. I began to call him Beamish because of his impish eyes and perennial pout, which would turn into a broad grin in an instant. I had only one fault to find with him, and that was his absent-mindedness. When you spoke to him, it was sometimes five or ten seconds before he would show any sign of having heard you. As he himself said, he was *un peu dans la lune*—a little in the clouds. To an impatient person like myself, it was sometimes rather annoying.

Beamish had had a good deal of experience with underground work already, and, despite his youth (he was only twenty-five), he was a veteran anti-fascist with two wars to his credit. He had fought in the Spanish Republican army for nearly a year, and had then signed up for service in the French army.

When the defeat came, Beamish and all the other German, Austrian and Italian volunteers in the French army were in a very nasty situation. If the Nazis or the Italians got them, they would shoot them as traitors. Luckily, Beamish had a lieutenant who was very *compréhensif*. Just before the armistice, the lieutenant called all the Germans, Austrians and Italians in the company into his headquarters and told them he was going to make them French citizens, to save them from the vengeance of the Boches. Each man was to pick his new name and the place and date of his birth. Beamish picked the name Albert Hermant, after the French romantic poet, and decided to have been born in Philadelphia, of French parents. His lieutenant made out a new *livret militaire* for him under the new name, and signed and stamped it. Then he told him to beat it.

"*Sauve qui peut, faut se débrouiller,*" I remember Beamish quoting the lieutenant as saying.

The next day the Germans caught up with the company at Niort. Beamish buried his real papers in a tin can in the back yard of the house where he was billeted and made for the south of France on his bicycle, passing columns of German soldiers on the way. In the unoccupied zone he got a *feuille de démobilisation,* a *carte d'identité,* and numerous other papers, all in his new name. Instead of a birth certificate he had something called a "certificate of life." Given him by the Mayor of Nîmes, it said simply that, "We, mayor of Nîmes, certify that Mr. Albert Hermant, born, etc., is alive because he appeared before us today."

When I met Beamish, he was just Albert Hermant, *de Philadelphie.* You could have searched him from head to foot, but you wouldn't have found any trace of his real name. He had papers under his new name in every pocket. When I asked him why he had picked Philadelphia to be born in, he said it was one of the few American cities he knew the name of and he thought it would be much harder to check up in America than it would be in France. He was quite disappointed when I told him that Philadelphia was one of the first cities in the United States to keep careful vital records and statistics.

Beamish used to say he had too many false papers to be really plausible.

"There's such a thing as being too *en règle,*" he explained. "It's like a criminal who has too many alibis."

Besides his *livret militaire,* his demobilization order, his identity card and his "certificate of life," he had cards of membership in the *Auberges de Jeunesse* (the French youth hostels), the *Club des Sans Club* (a kind of tourists' association) and half a dozen other ordinary, non-political French organizations.

"I've overdone it a little, I guess," he used to chuckle. "I ought to get rid of some of these. The police would suspect me right away if they found all this stuff on me."

But I don't think he ever destroyed a single one of his cards and papers. He loved them too much, just because they were false—so beautifully fraudulent, so outrageously *en règle*.

Beamish soon became my specialist on illegal questions. It was he who found new sources of false passports when the Czech passports were exposed and couldn't be used any more. It was he who arranged to change and transfer money on the black bourse when my original stock of dollars gave out. And it was he who organized the guide service over the frontier when it was no longer possible for people to go down to Cerbère on the train and cross over on foot. But of this more later.

-4-

Beamish had never been a member of any political party, but his sympathies were with the socialists. The second person to join my staff was an Austrian Catholic and monarchist named Franz von Hildebrand. Beamish spoke English with a slight but undeniable German accent. Franzi spoke it like an upper-class Englishman. He had also gone to Williams College, and had picked up a rich vocabulary of American slang there. I don't know why he went back to Austria afterward, but he was there when the fighting broke out between the Heimwehr and the socialists, and he fought with the Heimwehr.

Some of the Austrian socialists were distressed to see him working in my room. But I was representing a committee which was just as much interested in Catholics as it was in socialists; and in fairness to the Catholics I had to give them representation at Marseille. Besides, Franzi had changed his views since 1934, and had dropped his old hostility to the socialists, and, as it seemed to me to be a good idea not to have too many leftists around, I kept him. I didn't want the police to be able to say I was running an illegal office of the outlawed Socialist Party.

Franzi had a Swiss passport, and so he ranked as a national of a neutral country—a big help. Switzerland had given his family honorary Swiss citizenship generations before. After the armistice, it seemed wise to forget that he was also an Austrian. In Marseille he went by the name of Monsieur Richard (which everybody pronounced Re-sharr, with the accent on the second syllable). With his blue eyes, blond hair, and neatly trimmed mustache, he looked like one of the Germanic knights who accompanied the Emperor Henry IV to Canossa to make peace with Franzi's namesake, Pope Gregory VII, né Hildebrand. And his language was probably just about as profane as theirs. "Well, for God's sake," he'd say when I'd been out on an errand and had gotten back later than I expected to, "where the hell have you been? I thought you'd fallen through." Or, "Goddamn it, Fry, how the hell do you expect us to go on working when you don't come back after lunch? We thought you'd been pinched."

Franzi's father, Professor Dietrich von Hildebrand, formerly of the University of Vienna, was hiding with his wife in an apartment on the corner of the rue Breteuil and the rue Grignan. As one of the most prominent of the Austrian refugees, Professor von Hildebrand was in danger of extradition under Article 19, Swiss passport or no Swiss passport, and I had agreed to help him escape. Franzi and his charming Irish wife and pretty infant daughter were living with him, and planning to leave with him.

Franzi had two other useful qualities besides being a Catholic. He had worked with an Austrian committee in Paris, and so he knew how a relief committee should be run. He also knew many of the non-socialist refugees and could advise me about them. I could get all the advice I needed about the socialists from Beamish and Paul Hagen's friends, but I

depended on Franzi and his father to tell me about many of
the others.

-5-

For a while Beamish, Franzi and I handled all the work.
There was a small writing table and a flat-topped dressing
table, with mirror attached, in my room. We used the writing
table as an interviewer's desk and unscrewed the mirror from
the dressing table and used it as a second interviewer's desk.
Beamish sat at one table and Franzi at the other. I usually
sat on the edge of the bed, or stood up. The refugees waited
in the corridor outside my door, and we let them in one at a
time. I'd talk to them a little first, and then, if there seemed
to be any chance at all that they were one of "our cases," I'd
pass them on to Beamish or Franzi, who would take down
their names and addresses and other information about
them on ordinary white file cards. Sometimes, when Beamish
or Franzi was out, I'd do the whole interview myself.

Our days began at about eight o'clock in the morning,
when the first of the refugees arrived, and went on until
twelve or one the following morning. In the afternoon, when
the sun fell full on the back of the hotel, it would be so hot
in the little room that we would take off our ties and roll up
our sleeves and order iced coffee. We also let down the
jalousie to keep out the sun, but it didn't do much good.

In the evenings, after the last of the refugees had gone, we
would have a kind of conference, going over all the cards we
had made out during the day and trying to decide what action
to take on each case. As we were always afraid the police might
put a microphone in the room, or install an agent in the next
room to listen through the locked connecting door, we used
to discuss secret subjects only in the bathroom, with all the
taps turned on. The idea came from a story of Beamish's that,
just before the war, the Polish Ambassador in Berlin used to
hold all his secret conferences in one of the bathrooms of the
Embassy. The noise of water rushing into the bathtub creates
vibrations which sound like claps of thunder on the dictaphone

record of a conversation picked up by microphone, and not a word can be made out, Beamish said.

Our final job was to write the daily cable to New York. Generally it consisted of the names and references of applicants for United States visas. When it was finished, we would take it down the dark and narrow rue des Dominicaines to the little police station which stands in a crooked alley back of the rue Colbert. Rats abandoned their feasts of garbage dumped in the gutters and scurried for cover as we passed. Overhead, the street lights burned so faintly that they might almost as well have been put out altogether. When we reached the police station, identified by blue lights on both sides of the entrance, we went into a room marked *visas de télégrammes* and interrupted a game of *belote* or woke a slumbering *gendarme*, depending on how late it was, to get the cable stamped. Some of the men stamped the cable without even trying to read it, while others insisted on having us translate it word for word. None could read a word of English. But the real censorship came later anyway. All the police had to do was look at your passport and certify that the person who presented the cable was the one who signed it.

After the cable had been stamped, we had to take it to the post office off the big barren square back of the stock exchange. The night window was a small opening in a temporary wooden partition in a room which looked as though it was being rebuilt after a bombing. We would pull a bell like an old-fashioned doorbell and the little window would open and we would push the telegram through. All we could see of the post-office clerk was his hairy hands as he filled his thin scratchy pen with violet ink, counted the words, calculated the charge and made out the receipt.

Sometimes he also made us sign a declaration that the cable said what it seemed to say and had no hidden meaning. But generally he overlooked this. I guess he realized as well as we did that anyone who wanted to send a cable with a double meaning wouldn't be stopped by the necessity of signing a small slip of paper.

When the cable had been sent we would go out onto the square and shake hands with Franzi and say good night. Beamish would walk back to the Splendide with me before going to his own room in the Hotel Lux. Before I left New York, someone had warned me not to go out alone at night, and I always remembered the advice.

One night we made our trip to the police station and post office even later than usual. Beamish and I had just turned the corner of the rue des Dominicaines and were walking wearily up the boulevard d'Athènes toward the entrance of the Hotel Splendide when a large car with a German license plate stopped in front of the marquee. The chauffeur opened the door of the car and five German army officers got out. They were wearing long gray overcoats, peaked caps turned up in front, like the wrong end of a decoy duck, black-kid gloves and shiny black-leather boots. Under the peaks of their caps we could make out the gilt eagles and swastikas of the Nazi empire.

We stood in the shadow of the building under the taped windows of the dining room and watched them as they acknowledged the salute of the chauffeur and passed through the hotel's revolving door. We gave them time to get up to their rooms before we moved. Then we followed them into the hotel, and made the concierge get us a couple of brandies to steady our nerves before we said good night to one another.

But usually we saw nothing more menacing on our nightly promenades than the rats feasting on Marseille's garbage.

-6-

Every morning at eight o'clock the grind would begin again, and each day it would be a little worse than the day before, with more people asking for help, more harrowing stories to listen to, more impossible decisions to make. Deciding who should be helped and who not was one of the toughest jobs of all. My lists were obviously arbitrary. They had been made up quickly and from memory by people who were thousands of miles away and had little or no idea of what was really going on in France. Some names had been put on them which ought not to have been there. Others had been left off which ought to have been on.

But how could we decide whom to help and whom not, except by sticking to the lists? We couldn't help everybody in France who needed help. We couldn't even help every intellectual and political refugee who really needed help, or said he did. And we had no way of knowing who was really in danger and who wasn't. We had to guess, and the only safe way to guess was to give each refugee the full benefit of the doubt. Otherwise we might refuse help to someone who was really in danger and learn later that he had been dragged away to Dachau or Buchenwald because we had turned him down. But we had one fixed rule from which we never varied: we refused to help anybody who wasn't known to people we could trust. We weren't taking any chances with police stooges.

Whenever a refugee came to me whose name was on one of my lists, I would show him the lists and ask him if he could help us find any of the others on it. We got a pretty grim picture of what had happened to the refugees that way. We learned, for instance, that Ernst Weiss, the Czech novelist, had taken poison in his room in Paris when the Germans entered the city; that Irmgard Keun, a German novelist, author of a best-seller in the days of the Republic, Das Kunstseidene Maedchen—The Artsilk Girl—had also committed suicide when the Germans took Paris; that Walter Hasenclever, the German playwright, had killed himself with an overdose of veronal in the concentration camp at Les Milles, not far from Marseille; that Karl Einstein, the art critic and specialist on Negro sculpture, had hanged himself at the Spanish frontier when he found he couldn't get across; and that the partly decomposed body of Willi Muenzenberg, once a German communist deputy, and later a violent opponent of the communists, had been found hanging from a tree near Grenoble several weeks after the defeat. One by one I crossed these men off my lists. What had happened to a lot of the others nobody knew, but I often wondered how many more of them I would have to cross off in the weeks to come.

In the course of time we learned that some of the refugees on my lists had already escaped from France without our help. But the great majority were stuck, and wouldn't have been able to get out at all if it hadn't been for us. With the help of the American affidavits and the Czech passports, we were able to get quite a lot of them out of France in those first weeks. Besides Paul's underground-worker friends, they included, among many others, Hans Natonek, a Czech humorist; Hertha Pauli, an Austrian journalist; Professor E. S. Gumbel, a German refugee scholar on the faculty of the University of Lyon; Leonard Frank, German novelist and poet; Heinrich Ehrmann, a young German economist; Friedrich Stampfer, a German trade-union leader and the former editor of the Berlin Vorwaerts; Dr. Otto Meyerhoff, Czech physicist and Nobel Prize winner; Alfred Polgar, German novelist; and Konrad Heiden, the biographer of Hitler.

Of them all, probably none was in greater danger than Heiden. What he had written about Adolf Hitler and the origins of the Nazi party the Fuehrer would neither forgive nor forget. Heiden had been interned in a French concentration camp at the beginning of the war, released a few weeks later, reinterned in May. Just before France surrendered, the captain in charge of the camp decided to evacuate the internees to Southern France. They set out on foot, under guard, but when German planes appeared overhead and began machine-gunning them, they all escaped, the guards first.

Heiden made his way to Montauban, and from there he came to Marseille. At the Marseille Consulate he got an American visa and "affidavit in lieu of passport," under his own name. He wanted to use the affidavit to go to Lisbon, but I felt I couldn't take the responsibility of letting him travel through Spain under his own name. So I got him a Czech passport under the name of David Silbermann, and, after a good deal of hesitation, he used the Czech passport as far as Lisbon, changing back to his rightful personality there.

Most of the others had no choice. If they had American visas, they used them for travel documents. If they didn't have them, I got them Czech passports, often under their own names, and sent them through that way. In those first days not one of them was arrested, either in France or in Spain.

It was obviously too good to last.

It didn't.

-7-

By the end of the second week, the crowds waiting outside my door were so large that the management complained, and I had to ask everybody to wait downstairs in the lobby and summon them up by telephone, one at a time. A few days later the police came along with the Black Maria and picked up the whole lot of them. They took them to the police station (called the Evêché because it was housed in a fine old eighteenth-century mansion which used to be the bishop's residence) and questioned them about me and my activities. Then they released them.

After that I decided I'd have to go to the Prefecture myself and explain what I was doing. But before I could get an appointment we had an unexpected visitor at the Splendide.

It was early in the morning. My telephone rang while I was eating breakfast in my room. When I answered it I heard Bohn's voice at the other end of the line. He was speaking in a hoarse stage whisper.

"It's the police, old man," he said. "Don't worry. We had to expect this. The Consulate will take care of us if anything serious happens. I'm going down now. You'd better look around your room and destroy your papers before they come for you. I'll see you downstairs."

I didn't share Bohn's faith in the militancy of the Consulate or the inviolability of telephone conversations, but I hid my lists behind the mirror where I kept the map of the frontier and tore up some other papers and put them down the toilet. Then I waited. In a few minutes the phone rang again. This time it was the hotel clerk.

"On vous demande en bas," he said dryly.

I went down. In the writing room an embarrassed inspector

was waiting for me. He asked me to sit down, and when I had done so, he questioned me about my work and my credentials. I showed him my passport and my various letters of introduction and told him I was making a study of the refugees' needs and giving some of them relief. I didn't say anything about sending them over the frontier, and he didn't ask me about that. When he had finished, he apologized again for bothering me and we shook hands and he went away.

After that Bohn and I decided we'd have to take steps to square ourselves with the authorities or the jig would be up before the job was half finished. We had been doing our "underground" work almost literally in the open. The term is always a misnomer, because "underground" work is almost never really carried on under ground. Instead, it is carried on behind a screen, the screen of some "cover" activity or other which is entirely innocent in itself but serves to explain the part of the work which can't be hidden and to conceal the rest. In our case the obvious cover activity was relief work.

When I got my appointment at the Prefecture, I took Bohn with me, and the Consulate lent us an interpreter, because Bohn didn't speak French. We asked the Consul-General to come along, but he refused. At the Prefecture we were received by a high official, the Secretary-General. We told him we had come to France to help refugees in distress and asked for permission to found a small committee for the purpose.

The Secretary-General was very correct, but very frigid. He said the French authorities would welcome the committee provided it did nothing illegal. We pretended to be amazed and hurt by the suggestion that we would even think of doing anything illegal, and the Secretary-General gave us the permission we had asked for. But we felt we'd have to be very careful after that if we weren't to land in the jug, or be expelled.

-8-

Meanwhile my work had grown so that I had to get more help. Besides callers, I had begun to get letters from all over the unoccupied zone appealing for help, many of them from the concentration camps. An American relief worker whom I asked to recommend a secretary sent me Lena Fishman. Before the occupation, Lena had worked in the Paris office of the Joint Distribution Committee—the great agency which distributes the funds of the various American Jewish charities to the functional organizations which spend it. Lena was vivacious and ebullient, like her Polish ancestors. She could take shorthand with equal ease in English, French and German, and she spoke and wrote Russian, Polish and Spanish as well.

By this time Beamish's work was keeping him out most of the day, so Lena took his desk. With great difficulty we managed to buy a typewriter—for an astronomical price—and Lena wrote answers to the letters all day and typed the cables every night. She also took a hand at interviewing and was generally useful, especially in calming the excited.

"*Il ne faut pas exagérer*," she used to say.

It generally worked like magic on a case of hysterics.

Lena had her own way of talking. When I first met her, she asked me who my publisher was. I told her, but the name obviously meant nothing to her.

"*Je n'ai jamais couché avec*," she said.

She was always mixing languages. At the end of the day, when she was about to go, she would take out her compact and say, "*Je fais ma petite beauté*, and I leave you."

She was the best-natured secretary I've ever had. She would work all day and half the night, under the most difficult and trying circumstances, and then bounce in again the next morning, fresh and bright, ready to begin another day.

We had given away so much money without keeping proper records that we hardly knew where we stood. Franzi used to keep the money in a rubber-lined toilet bag. Whenever we took something out of the bag, we would put in a slip of paper. At night Franzi would take the bag home with him, so the police wouldn't find it if they made a surprise visit to my room in the early morning. But we needed someone to set up our books and keep proper records for us.

It was Heinz Ernst Oppenheimer who took over that job,

as an unpaid volunteer. He was a German-Jewish production engineer who had run a relief committee in Holland after Hitler came to power and had been sent on a mission to the United States by the French *Ministère d'Armement* just before the war. For months he worked away on our books, disguising the illegal expenses in various ingenious ways and preparing beautiful statistical charts, all utterly legal and aboveboard. Instead of entering the grants to departing refugees as "travel expenses," which would have implicated us in illegal departures, he put them down as "living expenses." It was also illegal to pay out dollars, but we had to pay travel expenses in dollars, because francs couldn't be changed in Spain. Oppy translated all the dollar payments into francs before entering them in the books. Thanks to him, we were always ready for the police.

-9-

After the frosty little talk at the Prefecture, I went to a Marseille lawyer and had him draw up papers establishing the *Centre Américain de Secours*. It was Oppy who chose the name.

"*Ça fait bien français,*" he said.

"The American flag will cover a multitude of sins," Beamish, approving, cynically added.

About the same time I met a French-Jewish merchant who had seen the writing on the wall and had decided to give up his business in Marseille before he was forced to sell it at a sacrifice price. He dealt in handbags, pocketbooks, billfolds, coin purses and leather novelties. He gave us his office on the front of the second floor of an old building in the rue Grignan, rent free through the end of the year, and we moved in even before he had had time to move out. There, at the end of August, we opened the *Centre*. For several days the refugees got badly mixed up with the pocketbooks, packing cases and moving men, and it was some time before everything had been straightened out and we had gotten rid of the counters and shelves of the pocketbook business and had replaced them with desks and chairs.

One reason for opening the *Centre* was to mix the political refugees with a lot of ordinary relief cases. After the experience at the Splendide, it seemed unwise to go on interviewing only persons in political danger. By mixing them in with ordinary relief cases, we hoped to be able to provide some measure of protection for them.

Of course we had no funds for ordinary relief work ourselves, but we got the Quakers to give us meal tickets. After opening the *Centre* we handed out meal tickets to people for whom we could do nothing else. The *Comité d'Assistance aux Réfugiés*, the local Jewish relief organization, also resumed relief work about that time. So before long we were able to refer people we couldn't help ourselves either to the Quakers or to the C.A.R., depending on their religion. But only for relief—not for emigration. We were still the only organization in France which was helping refugees escape. On the door of the local office of the Hicem, the great Hebrew emigration society, there was a large sign reading FERMÉ. It was not until several months later, when France began giving exit visas to the refugees, that the Hicem was reopened to the public.

The opening of the office made the crowds of frantic refugees who came to us for help larger than ever. We had to get someone to handle the traffic in the waiting room and outside in the hall and stairs. There were several young Americans in Marseille who had served in the American Volunteer Ambulance Corps before the armistice. We picked out one of them as doorman and reception clerk. His name was Charles Fawcett, but everyone in Marseille called him Shar-lee.

Charlie was a youngster from the South—Georgia, I think— who had been doing "art" work in Paris before the war. I put that word in quotation marks because as far as I could see Charlie's conception of art consisted of drawings of pretty girls, preferably nude. He had many feminine admirers, and there was always at least one of them in the office as long as he worked for us. Most of the time it was a young Polish girl named Lili. Charlie was so chivalrous about Lili that he was actually trying to get her husband up from North Africa, where he was stranded, so the two could be together again.

As a doorman, Charlie had one great drawback. He couldn't speak anything but English, and most of the refugees didn't speak any English at all. But his ambulance-driver's uniform awed the over-insistent ones, and his good nature cheered the depressed among them. If few understood what he said, none disliked him. In fact, I think he was probably the most popular member of the staff.

With Beamish devoting most of his time to work outside the office, Lena attending to the correspondence and typing, and Oppy doing the bookkeeping and statistics, we had only one full-time interviewer, Franzi, and Franzi was planning to leave for Lisbon himself very soon. The crowds were now so great that we had to get more interviewers to help him out.

One of them was Miriam Davenport. After graduating from Smith, Miriam went to Paris to study art. On the trek down from Paris she ran into Walter Mehring, the German poet, at Toulouse. After the police picked up the refugees at the hotel, Mehring, not daring to come around to see me himself, sent Miriam with a message. I added her to the staff immediately. She spoke French and German as few Americans do, and her knowledge of art and artists made her very useful when we had to distinguish between the many refugees who claimed to be artists worthy of our help. When she had never heard of them, and they had no specimens of their work to show, she would tell them to go down to the Vieux Port and make a sketch. When they brought the sketch back she would look at it and decide right away whether they were any good or not.

She also handled university professors with tact and skill, and sometimes with considerable ribaldry. I remember once overhearing a conversation between Miriam and the daughter of a professor of urology. The daughter had brought in an enormous *dossier* of letters from urological societies to prove that her father was an intellectual of sufficient eminence to deserve our special attention.

"But who *is* your father?" Miriam asked.

"He's a professor of urology," the daughter answered.

"Yes, I see," Miriam said, doubtfully. "But what is urology?" The daughter explained. Miriam shrieked.

"Why didn't you tell me right away your father was a professor of *pipi*?" she said.

Miriam was always either laughing or coughing, and Bohn worried a good deal about her health.

"I tell you," he would say, "that girl has t.b. I don't like that cough at all. You ought to send her away for a good long rest."

But Miriam only went on laughing when she wasn't coughing.

## III. *Forgery Is a Fine Art*

IN THE early days of the office, when the leather merchant was still packing up his wares, we used to have our conferences in my room at the Hotel Splendide. Those of us for whom there were no chairs sat on the bed or the floor as we talked over the day's cases and decided what, if anything, we could do for each applicant.

One night I came in and found Franzi stretched out, fully clothed, in the bathtub, dictating letters to Lena, who was sitting on the floor of the bathroom, with her typewriter on the *bidet*. Oppy was at one of the desks and Beamish at the other.

That night I decided I'd have to get a larger room right

away. The next morning I took a large double room in the front of the hotel. I had one of the two beds taken out, and we used the writing desk, converted the dressing table to make another, and had a third brought in. In the middle of the room there was a larger table, which we used for our conferences.

Outside the window a narrow balcony extended over the sidewalk of the boulevard d'Athènes and brushed against the tops of the truncated plane trees which line both sides of the street. A little way up the boulevard to the left you could see the monumental staircase of the Gare St. Charles, and across the street and a little way down to the right the café where Breitscheid and Hilferding sat every day. Several blocks further down you could just make out the busy intersection where the boulevard Dugommier crosses the Canebière.

Whenever a train came into the station, or was about to leave, you could hear the patter of a thousand feet on the pavement below as passengers came down from the great staircase or hurried up toward it. In the early morning, heavy *camions* would lumber down the hill to the city's markets or rattle by with a few iron pipes or some empty oil barrels as their only load. Somehow they always seemed to be at least three-quarters empty.

-2-

Beamish had three problems to crack. One was to find new sources of passports; the second was to provide a supply of identity cards; and the third was to discover ways of getting fairly large sums of money into France without having the authorities know we were getting them or where they were coming from.

The Czech passports were working all right, but we felt it was risky to send too many people through Spain with them. If the Gestapo caught on to what was happening, the mere possession of a Czech passport might be enough to cause a refugee's arrest. If too large a number of travelers began going through Spain on Czech passports, the Spanish authorities might become suspicious. Sooner or later, one way or another, the truth would be out. Then if we had no other source for passports our work would be stopped.

The money business was also important. The $3,000 in cash I had brought with me from New York didn't last more than a couple of weeks. If I had asked the committee in New York to cable me additional funds, I might have been called to account at any time. That would have made it difficult to use the money for illegal purposes. Besides, the legal exchange rate was much less favorable than the rate on the black bourse, for France was full of people trying to get their money out of the country and willing to pay very high prices for dollar credits in New York.

For a very short time, one of the refugees helped me out by giving me dollars in Marseille against my promise that he would be paid back when he got to America. But he was planning to leave as soon as he could. When he did, we would have to have some other and more permanent way of transferring money, or close up shop.

It was these three problems that Beamish was working on. He solved them all. He got Polish passports from the Polish Consul in Marseille, and Lithuanian passports from the Lithuanian Consul at Aix-en-Provence. He also found a way of sending men to Casablanca who wouldn't go through Spain under any circumstances.

The French army was being rapidly demobilized, in accordance with the armistice agreement. Men whose homes were in Morocco were being sent by troopship from Marseille across the Mediterranean to Oran or Algiers, and from there by troop train to Casablanca. Each man received a demobilization order from the officer in command of his regiment. The soldier didn't need any ticket or money. His passage would be paid by the French government, and he would be fed by the French army. When he got to Casablanca he would be paid 1,000 francs as his *prime de démobilisation*.

Beamish made an arrangement with one of the army officers to buy some demobilization orders for refugees. The price was reasonable enough—200 francs an order, or about $5.00. With each order, the officer supplied detailed information about the regiment the refugee was supposed to have been a member of, the names of all the officers, the place and date of mobilization, the engagements the regiment had been through, its losses, and so on. Once he had memorized this information, the refugee could pass any sort of superficial examination. All he needed, besides an ability to speak fluent French, was a private's uniform, and you could buy uniforms for practically nothing from the soldiers who had been demobilized in Marseille. We sent several refugees to Casablanca this way. It wasn't until October that the officer who had been selling the demobilization orders was arrested and court-martialed.

Beamish also discovered an Austrian refugee named Reiner who sold everything—demobilization orders, French identity cards, passports and forged exit visas. He seemed to be on good terms with the Czech and Polish Consulates. In fact, he could get Czech and Polish passports à volonté—and also French identity cards, which he either sold at high prices or offered to ladies of his choice. Formerly, Beamish said, they took flowers. . . .

Once we had met Reiner we couldn't get rid of him. At first he used to come around to my room at the hotel. Later, when we opened the office, he was invariably there. One day I came back from an errand and found him in my private office typing out a demobilization order on Lena's typewriter. As I didn't want to run any risk of having the police identify Lena's machine as the one the false demobilization papers had been made out on, I pulled the paper out and burned it in the fireplace. But Reiner seemed genuinely surprised and grieved at losing his fiche, and he protested indignantly when I threw him out of the office and told him never to come back again.

-3-

It was just a few days before the episode of the demobilization paper that Reiner brought Frederic Drach to see me. I was having a conference in my new room at the Splendide when he knocked on the door. Beamish opened it and Reiner came in. Behind him was a fat, roly-poly man with small, twinkling eyes, a button nose and a soft mouth that was always smiling. Beamish looked as though he had just gotten word of the capitulation of England when he saw him.

"This is Monsieur Drach," Reiner said. "Monsieur Drach has an interesting suggestion to make, and I brought him around because I knew you would want to hear it."

"I have heard a great deal about you, Mr. Fry," Drach said, "and I think you have heard something about me. I admire the work you are doing and I'd like to help you. I am an old criminal myself."

He was. In fact, he was typical of those people the French call *louche*. My dictionary says the word means "squint-eyed, dubious, doubtful, ambiguous, suspicious, equivocal, not clear." Frederic Drach was all of these, and more too. After a dubious career in the German socialist movement, where he was suspected of having acted as an *agent provocateur*, he came to France in doubtful circumstances in 1923. Ten years later he was occupying an ambiguous position on the staff of the two French weeklies *Vu* and *Lu*, both of them reputedly financed by Moscow. The outbreak of the war found Drach playing an even more suspicious part, that of close collaborator of Mr. Lemoine, head of the German section of the *Deuxième Bureau*—the intelligence service of the French army. It was Mr. Lemoine who was responsible for gathering information about German military preparations. Drach was his first assistant. To judge from the deplorable lack of preparedness of the French army and air force, Drach's role seems to have been an equivocal one, to say the least. But it wasn't clear exactly what he did or did not do for the

*Deuxième Bureau.* Yet everybody who knew him had warned us against him.

Drach's "interesting suggestion" had to do with Dutch and Danish passports. His story was that he was selling them for a general of the *Deuxième Bureau* who wanted to make a couple of hundred thousand francs before retiring, and was going to tell his superiors he had lost the passports in the retreat. We weren't taken in by the story, and I don't think Drach expected us to be. But the passports looked real enough to fool anybody, and he claimed to have a suitcase full of them. Some were new and some were used and some, though new, had been made to look as though they were old. With the help of a set of rubber stamps Drach carried in the same suitcase, some grease, and a judicious rubbing with fine sandpaper, in half an hour he could make a brand-new passport look as though it had been issued in Páris, the Hague or Copenhagen before the war. He could add rubber stamps which "proved" that the owner of the passport had traveled back and forth between France and Denmark, France and Holland and France and England again and again. His passports were so plausible that it was only natural the price should be high. He wanted 6,000 francs apiece for them— about $150 at the official rate of exchange.

The high price, and the fact that Drach was an intelligence officer who might also be a Gestapo agent, as far as we knew, made it inadvisable for us to use his passports, and I pretended to have no more than an academic interest in them when Reiner brought him in. Later, when the pinch got tighter, Beamish bought a number of them for various of our clients, and they used them with complete success. We also put two or three rich refugees in search of passports in touch with Drach. They bought his passports and got to Lisbon on them without the slightest trouble.

As a provider of false identity cards Beamish turned up a little Viennese cartoonist who called himself Bill Freier. Bill had been one of the most popular cartoonists in France before the war, but after it began he went through the usual experiences: internment in a concentration camp, escape, flight to Marseille. He was a likable little fellow, and he seemed, and I'm sure was, a perfectly honest young man who wanted to help his fellow refugees and at the same time make enough money to keep alive.

Freier had a girl-friend named Mina with whom he was deeply in love. They were hoping to get married and go to America together, and I guess he needed money for Mina's support as well as his own. He was a very skilled draftsman, and he could imitate a rubber stamp so well that only an expert could have told it had been drawn with a brush. He used to buy blank identity cards at the tobacco shops, fill them in, and then imitate the rubber stamp of the Prefecture which made them official. I think he used to charge us only twenty-five francs—fifty cents—for the finished job. We made extensive use of his services, as did many other people. We also added him and his fiancée to the list of our clients, and cabled New York to ask the committee to get them visas.

-4-

The story of how Beamish met Dimitru and solved the money problem for many months to come follows a trail from the American Consulate to the gangsters of Marseille. Beamish liked women—there was no getting away from that. In Paris he had had a mistress, but in Marseille he had none, so he took out the Consulate's bleached blonde with blue eyelids. Through her he met a Corsican businessman named Malandri.

Malandri professed definite pro-British and anti-German views. As almost all Corsicans hate the Italians, Beamish felt he could be pretty sure that Malandri wasn't an Ovra agent, or, by extension of the same logic, a Gestapo agent. At the time, Malandri was absorbed in the problem of getting a friend of his out of France. The friend was a Prussian banker named Frankel. Frankel claimed to have financed von Papen in Germany when von Papen was trying to out-maneuver

Hitler in the winter of 1932-33. Later, in Paris, he said he had
financed Leopold Schwarzschild's anti-Nazi weekly, the *Neue
Tagebuch*. He had some documentary evidence to prove this
as well as the fact that he had been expatriated and expro-
priated by the German government. Malandri had been able
to get him an extraordinary set of papers, including permission to travel all over the unoccupied zone. For a person of
German origin who was not in the good graces of the German
government, this was practically unheard of. It was obvious
that Malandri had powerful connections.

Beamish spoke to Malandri about the money problem, and
Malandri presented him to Jacques. In public life Jacques
was the proprietor of an almost completely respectable restaurant called the Sept Petits Pêcheurs. In private life he was
the head of one of Marseille's leading Corsican gangs. On the
street outside his restaurant, vendors of *clovisses, crevettes,
Portugaises, moules, oursins* and *violettes* had their booths
and noisily sold their wares, while inside, Marseille businessmen, refugees from Paris and American relief workers lunched
or dined, with Jacques presiding somewhat wryly over the
proceedings, drinking bicarbonate of soda, and conducting his
own affairs from his seat behind the cash register. His own
affairs consisted presumably of brothels, the black market and
the traditional *coco*.

According to Malandri, who had a vast acquaintance with
Marseille-Corsican gangster circles, Jacques was one of the
most powerful men in the city and could easily solve our
money-transfer problem for us. But when Beamish first told
him what we wanted to do, Jacques was skeptical. He had
been in the United States two or three times, traveling without benefit of passport or visa on French cargo vessels, direct
from Marseille, and it was evident that he had had some
disillusioning experiences in America. Perhaps he had been
double-crossed by American gangsters smarter or more un-
scrupulous than he. Anyway, he had come back to Marseille
with a strong distrust of all Americans and a marked disin-
clination to do business with any of them.

"*Ils ne sont pas réguliers, ces gars-là,*" he kept repeating.
"*Je vous le dis.*"

Though he was reluctant to have any dealings with Americans directly or indirectly, Jacques was not averse to making a profit where he could. This must have caused him a troublesome conflict. In the end he found a way to make the profit without himself having to deal with Americans at all. He presented Beamish to Dimitru.

If Jacques was an inconspicuous member of the local Marseille fauna, Dimitru was almost excessively cosmopolitan. In Russia, where he was born, he claimed to have been a big landowner. In Paris, where he had lived until the defeat, he said he had been a member of an exclusive club. Before ordering wine he would always ask:

"*Etes-vous né bordelais ou bourguignon?*"

Discreet inquiries revealed that Dimitru had worked in the office of the American Express Company at Paris, that he liked money, which he spent rapidly on women and liquor, but that he was probably reliable in financial matters. Personally he was not attractive. He was less than five feet tall, had manners which were extravagantly polite, and a right hand which felt like an empty glove when you shook it. He could turn his smile on and off like an electric light.

But he knew a lot of people who wanted to get their money out of France, and he was very much interested in Beamish's proposition. Among them, Beamish, Dimitru and Jacques made a deal, agreeing to split the commission three ways. Dimitru would introduce Beamish to his clients and Beamish would arrange to take some of their money and pay dollars for it to their agents in New York. Dimitru usually got fifty per cent in advance and fifty per cent after the clients had received confirmation that the money had been paid. He never seemed to have any difficulty finding clients, and his rates were very good. They began at ninety francs to the dollar and rose to 180 or 190 francs to the dollar as the value of the franc dropped. For many months Dimitru was our trusted agent in such financial transactions. During all that time he never failed to give prompt service and complete satisfaction.

I think I need hardly add that Beamish turned his commission over to the committee. Nothing seemed more natural to Dimitru and Jacques, he said, than that he should be taking a cut on every transaction. If he had refused, they would not only have been astonished and incredulous—they would also have split the difference between them.

-5-

Everything went along smoothly until early September, when Walter Mehring set out for the frontier. Mehring is one of the best of the modern German poets, but in appearance he is completely inconsequential looking—so small that we generally called him Baby. In the dirty, unpressed clothes he was wearing when he got to Marseille, after a series of hair-raising adventures on the way, he looked more like a tramp than a poet—or a baby. He had an American visa and "affidavit in lieu of passport," but he refused to travel through Spain on it, for fear of being arrested there. When I got him a Czech passport under another name, he set out for the frontier.

At Perpignan he had to change trains. To his surprise and delight there was no police control at the station. He walked out of the Perpignan station without being asked for anything more than his ticket, and sat down in a café to celebrate his approaching deliverance.

Within five minutes he was picked up by a plainclothesman. I suppose the poor *flic* thought he had found the explanation of all the purse-snatchings and petty thefts of the previous six months of Perpignan's criminal history. But when the Perpignan police discovered that Mehring was a foreigner traveling without a safe conduct, they ordered him sent to the nearby concentration camp of St. Cyprien, the pest hole of France.

Mehring had a double set of papers on him, his American

visa and his Czech passport, but he wasn't searched at the police station. On his way to the camp he asked permission to go to the toilet. He got rid of the false papers there—his beautiful Czech passport and all the lovely visas on it were scattered in small pieces on the railway ties between Perpignan and the camp.

When we got his telegram telling us what had happened, we hired a lawyer to take up his case with the authorities. Maître Murzi was a typical Corsican, short, squat, dynamic, voluble, and full of promises. He wore the nails of his little fingers long—a mark of elegance in Corsican circles—and he had a habit of jumping up from his chair and buttonholing you as he talked, which was always. I don't know whether he was able to do anything for Mehring or not. He telegraphed a colleague at Perpignan, and a few days later the commandant of the camp called Mehring into his office and gave him a release order, unsigned. He told him he was sorry he couldn't sign it without getting an authorization from Vichy, but Mehring took the hint. The order worked just as well without the signature as with it.

When Mehring got back to Marseille his permis de séjour, or residence permit, required of all foreigners, had expired. If the Corsican lawyer hadn't had anything to do with Mehring's release, he was undoubtedly useful in the next stage of the proceedings. He took me to see the chef du service des étrangers at the Prefecture, a Monsieur Barellet, and Barellet told me what to do. All he needed, he said, was a doctor's certificate stating that Mehring had been too ill to go and apply for the renewal of his permis de séjour at the time it expired. He even told me which doctor to see.

It worked beautifully. We put Mehring to bed in a room at the Splendide. The doctor came and looked at him out of one eye and then signed a very impressive certificate. It not only said that Monsieur Mehring had been souffrant, and so had been unable to call at the Prefecture for an extension of his permis de séjour; it also said that he would continue to be unable to leave his room until mid-November.

I took the certificate back to Barellet, and he gave Mehring a two-month *permis* immediately. This was unheard of for a non-French refugee; usually they got only two weeks at a time.

I happened to hit Barellet at a good moment, I guess. He had just had a visit from two Gestapo agents, and he was properly indignant. He seemed to have a good deal of sympathy for the refugees, but he explained that France was powerless to resist German pressure, and the pressure was increasing daily.

"Yesterday," he said, "there were two Gestapo agents in my office all afternoon. They went hither and yon, looking into the files and questioning my subordinates about my politics and the way I run my office. Then they came back here and gave me the names of three foreigners they want me to arrest."

He picked up a small piece of paper from the blotter on his desk and waved it angrily. When I asked if I could see it, he handed it to me at once. Written in pencil in a German hand were the names of Prince Ernst Rüdiger von Starhemberg, Georg Bernhard and Max Braun.

Starhemberg was the Austrian Prince who led the Heimwehr against the Vienna socialists in 1934. Later he opposed the Nazis. Georg Bernhard had been editor of the *Pariser Tageszeitung*, the émigré German anti-Nazi newspaper published in Paris. Max Braun was leader of the opposition to Hitler in the Saarland before the plebiscite gave it back to Germany.

I made a careful mental note of the three names and then handed the list back to Barellet.

"If you know where these men are," he said, "get word to them to beat it [*filer*]. We French will hold off arresting them as long as we can, but we can't hold off forever."

He paused a moment.

"Happily we don't know where these men are," he went on. "But suppose they should ask us to arrest Breitscheid and Hilferding. How could we possibly avoid it? We couldn't pretend we don't know where they are. All Marseille knows they sit every day in the same café on the boulevard d'Athènes. They are endangering the whole German emigration by their behavior. You can tell them I said so, if you like."

I went straight back to the Splendide and told Bohn what Barellet had said, and Bohn and I both went across the street and told Breitscheid and Hilferding. But Breitscheid refused to move, and Hilferding, as usual, followed Breitscheid's lead.

"Pish and nonsense," Breitscheid said. "Hitler wouldn't dare ask for our extradition."

And both men continued to sit in the same café every day. But soon afterward they began carrying vials of poison in their vest pockets, just in case. . . .

The fact that we knew that Starhemberg was in London and that Max Braun was probably there too, while the Gestapo apparently believed they were still in France, almost made up for the shock of realizing that we had been working under the very noses of Hitler's dread secret police all along. If it was alarming to have definite confirmation that the Gestapo was at work in Marseille, there was some consolation in knowing it wasn't as well informed as it was generally cracked up to be.

The conversation with Barellet also made us realize, if we hadn't realized it already, that we couldn't rely on the French authorities. They were being pushed. They had nothing against the refugees, but they would do nothing for them either. Most of them couldn't see that the honor of their country would be involved if they arrested their former guests and turned them over to the Germans to be executed.

If they did realize the question was one of honor, as Barellet evidently did, they preferred dishonor to the risks of defiance. Consequently you could never count on them. They would make all kinds of protestations of good will one day, and forget them the next. They persisted in the delusion that by doing the Nazis' dirty work they could somehow improve the situation of France. They forgot that Hitler's contempt for a vanquished foe grows in proportion to the foe's subservience.

Yet, so far as anyone knew, there had been only one extradition under Article 19 up to that time. That was the extradition of Herschel Grynszpan. Grynszpan was the young Polish Jew who shot and killed the Councillor of the German Embassy at Paris in the autumn of 1938—with such terrible consequences to the Jews of Germany. He was in a Paris prison, awaiting trial, when the German army broke through the French lines at Sedan. The French authorities transferred him to Orléans, and then to Limoges.

On the way to Limoges the train he was traveling in was bombed by German planes. Grynszpan escaped, but instead of going into hiding he went on to Limoges on foot and presented himself to the district attorney. The district attorney made out papers for him in another name and sent him to Toulouse, in the company of two gendarmes. They arrived in Toulouse on a Sunday and, finding no one at the Prefecture, they told Grynszpan to take a room for the night and come back the next morning. He came back, was arrested, and placed in prison. A month later the Toulouse Prefecture received an order to transfer him to Vichy. From Vichy he was taken to Moulins, on the German side of the demarcation line, and there he was turned over to the Nazis.

Grynszpan's case was typical of the attitude of the French authorities: they would give a man a chance to escape before they arrested him, but if he didn't take it, they would arrest him and turn him over, in obedient fulfillment of the terms of the armistice. And now that the Gestapo was roaming the unoccupied zone in search of the refugees, the chance to escape was likely to be a pretty slim one.

-6-

A few days after Mehring's arrest, we got another piece of bad news—several of our protégés were arrested in Spain. Like so many before them, they had crossed the frontier from Cerbère to Port-Bou. What had happened to them afterward, and why they were arrested, we didn't know. We only got postcards from them—read and stamped by the Spanish mil-

itary censor, as is all mail in Franco Spain—saying that they
were in the prison at Figueras, a town near the border, and
asking us to get them out. Had they been arrested because
their names were on a Gestapo list? Or was it only because
they had gone deep into Spain without reporting at a frontier
post, as we had warned them to? We didn't know, and we
had no way of finding out.

We decided, though, to reduce the chances as much as we
could. Instead of letting the refugees go down to the frontier
alone, we would take them down in convoys, with an experienced underground worker or a *débrouillard* American in
charge. This would increase the risk for us, because if we were
caught we could no longer claim that the refugees were acting
on their own responsibility and that we had nothing to do
with helping them get out of France. On the other hand, it
would reduce the chances that they would be caught, and our
first duty was to them, and not to ourselves. Refugees who
seemed likely to be in special danger would have to be conducted all the way to Lisbon.

Whenever we had an experienced underground worker who
was ready to leave, we made up a party to go with him. When
there wasn't an experienced underground worker ready to go,
we sent the refugees down to the frontier in the company of
an American named Richard Ball.

Dick Ball had been one of Charlie Fawcett's pals in the
Ambulance Corps. He was born in Montana. In 1932 or there-
abouts, he went to France and somehow or other he got to
be the owner of a lard factory in Paris. He traveled all over
the country, from Alsace to the Pyrenees and from Menton
to Dunkirk, selling his lard. He spoke a vulgar French such
as I have never heard on the lips of anyone but an *apache*
from the dives of Paris, and he also knew a good many local
*patois*. He was a rough diamond, a knight in overalls, eager
to help wherever he could and whomever he could, and fond
of boasting of the things he had done to help refugees and
the remnants of the B.E.F. on the way down from Paris. He
and Charlie claimed to have gotten quite a lot of English

soldiers out before the Germans occupied the whole of the
Atlantic coast of France.

Ball certainly knew France inside out, and for a long time
he was one of the most valuable members of our little band
of conspirators. He made trips from Marseille to the frontier
every other day or so, taking two or three refugees with him
each time he went, and seeing that they got safely over the
frontier into Spain before he started back to Marseille to get
the next lot.

-7-

Early one morning toward the end of the first week of
September, I was having breakfast when someone knocked
on my door. The knock was so loud I thought it was certainly
the police. I made a quick dive for some compromising papers,
but the door opened before I could get my hands on them.

It was Bohn. He was more excited than I had ever seen
him before. He talked so loud I was afraid the people in the
next room would hear him, and I tried to quiet him down
even before I had grasped what he was talking about.

"They've got it, old man," he said.

"Got what?" I asked.

"The boat," he said. "The Italian armistice commission put
a guard on it this morning. The Captain began taking on food
and water yesterday, and they must have noticed what he was
doing. He had to have supplies for thirty people for a week.
It was pretty hard to get all that stuff on without anybody's
noticing it. Anyway, they put a guard on the boat this morning and confiscated the food."

He was pacing around the room like a lion in a cage. I tried
to calm him down. I'd never had much confidence in his boat
plan anyway. Half the refugees in Marseille had known about
it days before the Italian armistice commission woke up to it.

But now that the commission had got wind of the thing,
there was likely to be an official inquiry, and an official inquiry
might lead anywhere. Bohn had good reason to be nervous,

and so had I. Only there was no use letting the neighbors know about it too.

But there was no calming Bohn down that morning. I guess he thought the police would be coming for him any minute, and that this time it wouldn't just be to ask questions.

I hadn't had anything to do with Bohn's boat, except to reserve a few places on it. But I knew the police would think I had, and, if he was arrested, I would probably be arrested too. Only my nervousness took a different form. Instead of talking unnaturally loud, as Bohn was doing, I talked so low that half the time he couldn't make out what I was saying. I think this added to his irritation and jumpiness, because he left almost as suddenly as he had arrived, and we never did decide what we were going to do about it.

The collapse of the boat scheme made no difference for most of the refugees, but it left men like Breitscheid, Hilferding and Modigliani stranded. They had refused to go through Spain, and now neither Bohn nor I had any idea what they could do.

There were also Werfel and Feuchtwanger and Heinrich Mann and a lot of others like them to think of. Breitscheid, Hilferding and Modigliani were Bohn's problem, but Feuchtwanger, Werfel and Heinrich Mann were mine. I had been planning to put them on Bohn's boat. Now I had to find some other way to get them out of France.

# IV. I Become a British Agent

HARRY BINGHAM lived in a villa on the rue du Commandant Rollin, a street which wraps itself around the back of the Corniche, far out from the center of town. I called him on the phone when I learned that Bohn's boat plan had failed, and he invited us both to dinner.

It was already dusk when we took the rue Paradis car on the Canebière, and growing dark when we pushed open the garden gate and walked up the long path to the house. We found Feuchtwanger sitting at a small iron table on the gravel terrace, and Harry just finishing a swim in the shallow fish pond below. Feuchtwanger sat immobile at his table as we told him what had happened.

Feuchtwanger took the news very well. He had waited for weeks for the boat to take him to safety, and now his hopes of rescue were gone. All through dinner he talked and joked as if nothing more serious had happened than the last-minute postponement of a long-planned vacation. A short, wizened little man, he was a dynamo of energy and ideas, and he did far more to keep up our spirits that evening than we did to keep up his. More than anything else he seemed to regret the good French wines he had had to abandon in the cellar of his house at Sanary when he was taken off to the concentration camp in May, and he found at least one consolation in not being able to leave France now: he could arrange to have some of the best of the wines brought up to Marseille.

After dinner we sat in the drawing room, drinking cognac and coffee and trying to find a way out of our dilemma. I said that many people had gone through Spain without French exit visas, and asked Feuchtwanger very tentatively if he would be willing to try that way too. He hesitated a moment, and then he said, "If you will come with me, of course I will."

We agreed right there to go to Lisbon together, as soon as we could get our visas. He had an American "affidavit in lieu of passport" in one of his pen names, James Wetchek, and his wife, who was still at Sanary, had one in her own name. Feuchtwanger said he would write her at once to come to Marseille. Meanwhile, I'd make my plans, and get all the necessary visas for everybody. By the end of the evening we had agreed to leave together around the middle of September.

I had seen the Werfels every day—sometimes two or three times a day—ever since I first had dinner with them at Basso's. At one time Werfel, despairing of ever getting an exit visa, had decided to have himself demobilized in Casablanca. But he was too fat and too soft to pass himself off as a soldier, and there was real danger that he would be detected and arrested if he tried. When I persuaded him to drop that plan, he began to think of going through Spain. He got a letter from the Czech Consul saying that Cordell Hull had invited him to go to the United States to lecture, and letters from French Catholic dignitaries to Spanish Church and lay officials asking them to give all help and protection to one of the leading Catholic writers of our times. (Actually Werfel is a Jew.) With these he felt he could afford to take his chances in Spain. But the big question was how to get out of France. He and his wife never went around the block without taking a taxi, if they could help it. In Marseille, where taxis were scarce, they occasionally had to walk a little, but always on the level, never uphill. For them climbing over the Pyrenees, even at Cerbère, seemed out of the question.

This consideration brought Werfel back to trying to get an exit visa again. He was making a second attempt when I made my agreement with Feuchtwanger. I didn't see any reason for believing Werfel would succeed any better this time than he had the first, so the next day I told him I was going to

Lisbon with the Feuchtwangers and invited him and his wife
to come with me. There was a very good chance, I said,
that I could get them all through Cerbère on the train, even
without exit visas. When they heard this, the Werfels accepted
immediately.

While I was about it, I felt I might as well take Heinrich
Mann along too. What would work for Feuchtwanger and
Werfel would work for him. If I succeeded with one, I'd succeed with all. Of course, I would be putting all my most
valuable eggs in one basket. But time was getting desperately
short. I couldn't be sure of ever having another chance to take
people through to Lisbon myself, and I wouldn't want to trust
any one of those three to anyone else. So I decided to turn the
trip into an all-or-nothing dash.

Mann and his wife had come to Marseille a few days before
and had taken a room in the Hotel Normandie, where Breitscheid and Hilferding were staying. When I told them about
my plan, they accepted right away. Heinrich Mann asked
me to include his nephew Golo, Thomas Mann's son, in the
company, and I agreed. It was arranged that we would leave
for the frontier together as soon as we all had our transit visas.
Dick Ball would go with us as far as Cerbère, and I would take
them on to Lisbon from there. I wrote to Golo Mann at Le
Levandou, where he was staying, and he came up to Marseille
the next day.

I had other reasons for wanting to go to Lisbon besides
a desire to get the Feuchtwangers, the Werfels and the Manns
out before it was too late. For one thing, I was supposed to
go back to New York myself. I felt I couldn't do that until
someone had come over to take my place, but from France
I couldn't very well explain why that was necessary. In Lisbon,
on the other hand, I could write a long and frank report on the
situation. Then, if the New York committee agreed to send
a new man over, I could go back to Marseille and wait for him
there.

There was still another reason why I wanted to make the
trip. I wanted to find out why our clients had been arrested

in Spain, so I could see that it didn't happen again. I also wanted to try and get them out of prison.

Finally, now that Bohn's boat had gone bust, I wanted to see whether I couldn't get the British to help us with Breitscheid and Hilferding, Modigliani and the other Italians, as well as with some of the most prominent Spanish republicans, like Largo Caballero and Rodolfo Llopis. France had just made an agreement with Mexico to let the Spanish republican refugees out, and Mexico was going to give them asylum and provide the boats to transport them. But there was still a lot of red tape to be gone through before any of them could leave, and there was no absolute guarantee that the really prominent refugees among them would be allowed to go even after the red tape had all been cut. Certainly none could ever go through Spain. For them the only way out was by sea.

-2-

It was Emilio Lussu who suggested that I get in touch with the British. Lussu was an Italian political refugee with a small gray goatee at which he was forever tugging. He was living with his wife in a nearby suburb, under the absurd name of M. Dupont. In Paris he had been a member of the group which had published *Giustizia e Libertà*. He was an expert on escaping. When Mussolini came to power, Lussu had been imprisoned on the island of Lipari. By careful planning, and after several failures, he had finally succeeded in making his escape. It was his belief that escape from France was possible for the Italians and the Spaniards only by boat, and that the boat would have to come from some port outside of France to get them. He pointed to the failure of Bohn's project to prove that such preparations can never be made on the spot: they attract too much attention. But if the British should send a small cargo ship, preferably Portuguese or Spanish, to a given spot off the coast at an appointed day and hour, after dark, it would be possible to get the refugees aboard and away before the French police and the Gestapo and the Ovra and the

Seguridad had had time to learn what was happening. The
ship could take them to Gibraltar. From there they could go
to London or New York, as they wished—and their visas
permitted.

Lussu worked out his plan with the same minute care he
must have devoted to his escape from Lipari. He bought
nautical charts and studied the French Mediterranean coast
from Menton to Cerbère. He got information on the French
mine fields from a friend in the French navy. After weeks of
study, he selected as the secret meeting place a spot to the
south of Marseille, on a point of land known as the Cap
Croisette. He gave me a chart of the area with the exact spot
he had picked marked with a big penciled X, and the areas
which the French were supposed to have mined shown with
cross-hatching.

He also arranged a code for messages. It was a passage from
Thomas Carlyle. You began by numbering each letter in
turn, beginning with 7. Then you wrote the whole alphabet
in a vertical row at the left hand side of a long sheet of paper.
Opposite each letter you wrote all the numbers which corre-
spond to that letter in the passage from Carlyle. To cipher
your message you used all the numbers for each letter, never
the same one twice in succession. You put a dash after each
number and took care not to show where one word ended
and the next began. To decode a message you simply ran your
eye down the passage from Carlyle until you came to the
number you were looking for. Then you wrote the correspond-
ing letter down on a sheet of paper, and looked for the next
number.

It was slow and laborious, but Lussu said it was an extremely
hard code to crack. Of course it could be broken down eventually, like every other code, but by that time you would be
using another passage from another author, and the sleuths
would have to begin all over again. The chief difficulty was to
find passages which used all the letters of the alphabet several
times over. But it could be done. Because of his enormous
vocabulary, Carlyle was especially useful.

-3-

When we all had our visas and were ready to go, I wrote the passage from Carlyle in the back of my notebook and put the nautical chart under the lining of my suitcase and pasted the cloth down neatly over it. With a chart of the mine fields in my baggage and a secret code in my pocket, I didn't feel any too comfortable about making that trip. If I were caught I would certainly be taken for a spy. But I told myself that I had undertaken to do a job, and that this was one of the risks.

At the last minute we got word from the frontier that the Spaniards were no longer letting *apatrides*—people without nationality—through. The Werfels were Czechs by birth, and the Manns, though born German, had been made honorary Czech citizens shortly after Hitler's Reich denationalized them. But the Feuchtwangers were ex-Germans, and nothing else. Rather than run the risk of having to send them back from Cerbère, I decided not to take them with me. Instead, I'd go through with the Manns and the Werfels and find out exactly what the Spanish regulations were. Then, if the Feuchtwangers could go through Spain after all, I'd telegraph back.

The rest of us met at the Gare St. Charles early the next morning, Mr. and Mrs. Werfel, Mr. and Mrs. Mann, Golo, Ball and I. Our train left at half-past five. We were all excited and nervous, I perhaps more than anyone else. I was suddenly appalled at the responsibility I was undertaking, and wished I had left the plans of the mine fields and the secret code behind. Besides, the Werfels, I discovered, had brought along twelve suitcases.

We arrived at Cerbère after dark, gave up our tickets at the door of the station and went inside, thinking that we could go right through and out onto the street. But when we got inside, we found that all the passengers were being made to line up before the office of the frontier police and show their travel documents. Panic seized us then, for I was the only one in the group who had an exit visa, and therefore the right to be traveling.

But Ball remained supremely confident. He took all our passports and went into the police office with them, while we stood around talking in low voices and trying to comfort and reassure one another.

After what seemed like an eternity, Ball came out again. We could see from the expression on his face that things hadn't gone quite as he had thought they would. When we asked him what had happened, he said that everything was all right; we could go out into the town and take rooms at the hotel, and then the next morning we'd come back and see whether the police would let us go through on the train or not.

On the way to the hotel, he and I dropped behind the others, and he told me he didn't like the looks of things at all. The commissaire had been very polite, but had explained that he had rigid orders not to let anyone through who didn't have an exit visa. After much arguing, Ball had persuaded him to keep the passports and think it over. As the train to Port-Bou didn't leave until 2:30 the next afternoon, he would have plenty of time to think. But Ball was already afraid from the tone of the conversation that the decision would go against us.

-4-

The next day dawned clear and hot. We had an early breakfast at the station and sat over our coffee while Ball went to get the commissaire's answer. He came back with the look of a man who has failed. He had all the passports but mine in his hand.

"Ça ne va pas," he said. "He says he'd do it if he was alone, but there's another commissaire on duty with him today and he doesn't dare."

Ball's words startled us. We all began talking at once, and we all had the same thought: what now?

But Ball was reassuring.

"Don't worry," he said. "We'll find a way. You can be sure of that."

Then he beckoned to me to come outside with him. As soon as we were outside, he began talking fast.

"Goddamn it," he said, "that would be our luck. We just hit him on a bad day, that's all. If that son-of-a-bitch supervisor hadn't been there he'd have let you all go through on the train. If we wait around a few days, he may still let you through. But then again he may not. It all depends on that bastard of a supervisor."

"What do you think we ought to do?" I asked.

"Goddamn it, I don't know," Ball said. "The *commissaire* thinks you ought to go over the hill. I told him there was an old man in the party, but he thinks you ought to risk it anyway. Says you can't tell what'll happen. Maybe tomorrow there'll be a new order from Vichy and he'll have to arrest you. He thinks you'd better get out while you can. He even came out on the platform and showed me the best way to go."

I looked up at the hill. It was pretty high, and the sun was pretty hot.

"Gosh, Ball," I said, "I don't think Werfel could ever make it. He's too fat, and Mann's too old. How about your going up to Perpignan and trying to buy exit visas for the whole lot of them?"

"I don't know," Ball said. "I don't like the way that guy talked. He seemed to know something was going to happen. He said we'd better get them out while we could, today, and not wait.

"Besides," he went on, "today is Friday. I can't get to Perpignan until late this afternoon, and I probably couldn't see anyone there until tomorrow morning. It would probably be Monday afternoon before I got the exit visas, and Tuesday before I got back here. God only knows what'll happen by that time. I don't like the idea of their hanging around here so long."

We had walked a good way toward the hotel while we were talking. Now we decided to go back to the station and put it up to the others. After all, it was for them to decide.

We found them still sitting at the table.

"We'd like to talk the situation over with you," I said, in a low voice, "but I don't think we ought to do it here. Would you mind coming outside?"

We started back toward the hotel and I told them what Ball had reported. I asked them what they wanted to do. They in turn asked me what I thought they ought to do.

"Well," I said, measuring my words very carefully, "if you think you can make it, I'd advise you to go over the hill today. We know it can be done today. We don't know what will happen tomorrow or the day after."

Heinrich Mann, Golo Mann and Mrs. Werfel decided immediately to go. But Werfel and Mrs. Mann were hesitant. Werfel looked at the hill and sighed. Suddenly he remembered it was Friday the 13th, and he began to quaver.

"It's an unlucky day," he said. "Don't you think we'd better wait until tomorrow?"

But Mrs. Werfel quickly put a stop to that line.

"*Das ist Unsinn, Franz,*" she said, with emphasis, and Werfel lapsed into silence. But whenever he looked at the hill, he gave a deep sigh.

Mrs. Mann began talking hurriedly to her husband in German.

"Listen, Heinrich," she said, "Mr. Fry is a very nice young man. He says he comes to save us. But how do we know? Maybe he is a spy come to lead us into a trap. I think we ought not to do what he advises."

"*Verzeihung, Frau Mann,*" I said, in my best German, "*aber vielleicht wissen Sie nicht dass ich Deutsch verstehe.*"

Mrs. Mann blushed crimson at this, and we heard no more from her.

When they had all decided to go, we had to get them ready for the trip. It was agreed that I would go through on the train with the luggage. The others would climb over the hill and meet me at the railway station at Port-Bou. Mr. and Mrs. Werfel would use their Czech passports, under their own names, and Golo Mann would use his American affidavit, also in his own name.

The Manns had a choice of documents. They had genuine Czech passports in their own names, given them by the Czech government when they were granted Czech citizenship, but they also had American papers, in which their last names had been omitted: on the American papers they were just Mr. and Mrs. Heinrich Ludwig. We decided that it would be too risky for them to go through Spain as Mr. and Mrs. Heinrich Mann, and they handed their Czech passports to me. While we were walking back to the hotel to pack our overnight bags and check out, I made them go through their pockets and pocketbooks and take out everything which had the name Mann on it—calling cards, letters, and anything else they might have. When I asked Heinrich Mann to give me his hat, and began scratching his initials out of the hatband with my penknife, he looked as solemn as a condemned man about to die.

"We are obliged to act like real criminals!" he said.

After we checked our luggage at the station, we walked down to the waterfront and through the village toward the cemetery on the hill. On the way, I stopped in a *tabac* and bought a dozen packages of Gauloises Bleues and Gitanes Grises and Vertes and distributed them to my mountain-climbing charges.

"If you get into any trouble with the police," I said, "give them these cigarettes. I understand it generally works, especially in Spain."

I left them just beyond the Centre Scolaire de Jean Jaurès. Half an hour later, I could still see them making their way across the rough fields of the hill, following the line of the stone walls, and disappearing now and then behind an isolated olive tree, or resting in its half-shade.

-5-

There was no train till afternoon. When it came time for me to get aboard, I felt a little uneasy about having so much luggage. There were seventeen pieces in all, including three knapsacks, and I thought the French police might quite naturally be suspicious of a man who was crossing into Spain with so many pieces, especially since half of them were filled with women's clothes. But the baggage inspector seemed to take it as a matter of course.

In the train to Port-Bou, I went into the washroom and burned up all the papers I had taken from the Manns, including their Czech passports. The paper burned with an acrid, choky smoke, and, not daring to open the door, I had to get down on the floor for air. Everything had been burned and the ashes washed down the toilet by the time we got to Port-Bou.

I had no difficulties at Port-Bou. The police stamped my passport and the *douanier* examined my luggage with no more curiosity than the French *douanier* had shown. I inquired whether *apatrides* were allowed into Spain and was told they were. The report we had had at Marseille simply wasn't true.

When I had completed the last of the formalities, I had the bags—all seventeen of them—taken down to the hotel where I had spent a night on my way to France, and then went back to the railroad station. I asked the frontier police whether they had seen anything of a fat man and a stout woman, an elderly man with stooping gait and a slight limp, a middle-aged woman with blonde hair, and a young man with jet-black hair. They said that no such people had been through that day.

I was getting more excited and nervous with every minute that passed, and I walked back and forth on the railroad platform wondering what in hell I could do. Suddenly I remembered a friendly little porter I talked to on my way from Lisbon the previous month and who had frankly admitted that he was a republican. I found him in the *douane*, sitting on the counter, swinging his heels against the paneling underneath. When I told him what was on my mind he said he'd find out right away whether my friends had been arrested.

I waited in the station while he went down to the *gendarmerie*. He came back in about ten minutes.

"No," he said, "nobody's been arrested at Port-Bou today. It's quite unusual, but it appears to be so."

I asked him what he thought I ought to do.

"Why don't you go up to the sentry-box on the motor highway and see if they know anything about them there?" he said.

I gave him a tip he must be dreaming about still and set off through the town toward the sentry-box on the hill. It was a long, hot climb: first past the shattered and fire-gutted remains of Port-Bou's humble dwellings, then out onto the barren, sun-parched hillside back of the town. When I finally got to the border post I found two untidy sentries sitting on little stools in the shade of the building, guarding the black-and-white-striped barrier which stretched across the international motor highway.

I passed out cigarettes to them. "Have you seen anything of five travelers?" I asked. "A fat man and a stout woman, an elderly man with stooping gait and a slight limp, a blonde woman of middle age, and a young man with black hair?"

I don't know whether it was my French or their own dull wit, but at first the sentries didn't seem to understand me at all. I gave them more cigarettes.

"Look here," I said. "I'm worried about some people who came over the hill from Cerbère this morning. Are you sure you haven't seen anything of them?"

Still the sentries professed ignorance. Instead of answering my question, they led me into the house and sat me down at a little table beside an open window overlooking the village below.

"Wait here," they said.

I waited, smoking innumerable cigarettes, and not knowing whether I was under arrest or not.

In about ten minutes one of the sentries came back.

"Your friends are at the railroad station," he said. "I've just telephoned down. They've just gone through the *douane*. They're waiting for you there."

I don't think I've ever been so relieved in my life as I was by those few words. I took out all the cigarettes I had left and gave them to the sentry, shook hands with him and started back to the railroad station, half-running in my eagerness to prove him right.

The Werfels and the Manns were at the station when I arrived. They had just come out of the office of the Bank of Spain, and they were nearly as eager to find me as I was to find them. We almost fell into one another's arms, as though we were old friends who had been separated for years and had met by accident in some strange city where none of us had ever expected to be.

-6-

On our way down to the hotel, they told me what had happened. It had been a very difficult climb, especially for Heinrich Mann, who was seventy. Ball and Golo Mann virtually had to carry him most of the way. Not that he wasn't game. He was the gamest of the lot. It was simply that he couldn't make the grade without help.

When they got to the crest of the hill, Ball stopped a minute to take his bearings. Before they were able to cross the frontier into Spain, two French *gardes mobiles* suddenly appeared and started toward them. They were now convinced that they were about to be arrested and sent to a concentration camp. But there was no use trying to escape; if they did, the *gardes mobiles* might fire at them. They just stood there, mopping their brows and awaiting their fate.

When the *gardes mobiles* reached them, they saluted.

"Are you looking for Spain?" one of them asked.

Somebody said yes.

"Well," the guard said, "follow the footpath here to the left. If you take the one to the right, it will lead you to the French border post, and if you haven't got exit visas you may get into trouble. But if you follow the left-hand path it will take you straight to the Spanish border point, and if you report there and don't try to go around it, you'll be all right."

He saluted again, and the two *gardes mobiles* stood watching them as they walked single file down the left-hand path. Ball went on with them a few hundred yards. When they had come within sight of the Spanish sentry house, he shook hands with them and said good-bye.

At the sentry house, they had had another scare. The sentries examined their passports carefully. They showed no interest in Mr. and Mrs. Werfel and Mr. and Mrs. "Ludwig." But one of them was very much interested in Golo Mann. His "affidavit in lieu of passport" said that he was going to the United States to visit his father Thomas Mann at Princeton.

"So you are the son of Thomas Mann?" the sentry asked.

Through Golo's mind flashed visions of Gestapo lists. He felt his doom was imminent, but he decided to play out his role heroically to the end.

"Yes," he said. "Does that displease you?"

"On the contrary," the sentry answered. "I am honored to make the acquaintance of the son of so great a man." And he shook hands warmly with Golo. Then he telephoned down to the station and had a car come up to get them.

It was all so *opéra bouffe* that I think it must have gone to our heads. We had a late lunch at the hotel, and with it we drank a good deal of Spanish wine and Spanish brandy. We had all agreed never, under any circumstances, to address Mr. and Mrs. Mann by their right name in Spain. But in the excitement of the approaching delivery from danger, some of us forgot. It was Herr Mann this and Herr Mann that, Frau Mann this and Frau Mann that—until all caution had been abandoned.

There were several other people in the small dining room, including the British Consul, whom I had met on my way through to France in August. We were just about to have another round of brandy when he came up to me and put his hand on my shoulder.

"May I speak to you a moment, old man?" he said.

We went out into the corridor.

"That old chap you have with you is Heinrich Mann, isn't he?" he asked.

I said he was.

"Well," he said, "I'd be a little careful if I were you. You don't know who that bloke in the uniform is, do you?"

I had noticed a man in uniform sitting in a corner of the dining room, but I hadn't paid much attention to him.

"No," I said, "I have no idea who he is."

"Well," the British Consul said, "he happens to be the head of the Spanish secret police of this region. He's not a very pleasant chap, really. I'd be a little careful, if I were you."

I thanked him warmly for the tip. Then I went back to the table.

"May I speak to you a moment, Golo?" I said.

Golo followed me out into the corridor, and I told him what the British Consul had said. We went back to the table together. Golo whispered in German to Mrs. Werfel, and she whispered to her husband. A pall fell over the company immediately. Five minutes later everyone had gone quietly upstairs to sleep until dinner time.

Everyone, that is, except Golo and me. We went out and swam in the harbor, diving off the platform of a shattered pillbox just out of sight of the town. The cool green water made us realize how much too much we had had to drink.

On the way back to the hotel I sent Lena a wire telling her that it would be all right for Harry to send his friends, after all.

-7-

In Barcelona we discovered there wasn't a seat to be had on any of the planes until Monday, when there were just two places to Lisbon on the Spanish plane. Everything else had been requisitioned by the authorities. After a brief discussion, we decided to take those two places and give them to Mr. and Mrs. Heinrich Mann, since there could be no doubt they were in greater danger in Spain than any of the rest of us. We would go on to Madrid by train and see what accommodations we could get to Lisbon from there.

On Monday morning Golo and I took Heinrich Mann and his wife to the office of the Spanish air line to check their baggage and wait for the bus to the air field. When Heinrich Mann saw a portrait of Adolf Hitler on the wall, I was afraid for a moment he was going to lose his nerve.

"We are in the hands of the enemy," he said solemnly.

We took him to a café and got him a brandy to revive his courage. At the air field the Manns checked through the *douane* and got into the plane, and Golo and I stood in the little park and waved our handkerchiefs as it took off and banked and turned to the west.

In Madrid we were able to get two more places on the plane to Lisbon, and we sent the Werfels off the same day. They hesitated to go without me, saying the plane might turn off its course and take them to Hendaye, in the occupied part of France, if there was no American aboard. But I had important business in Madrid, and there wasn't a place for me on the plane anyway. But I went out to the airport with them to see that they got safely through the final formalities.

-8-

Back in Madrid, after the long bus ride from the airport, I took the nautical chart out of the lining of my suitcase, put it in my briefcase and went to call at the British Embassy. The lackey at the gate made me fill in and sign a visitor's slip before he would let me into the building. I wrote that I was a representative of the Emergency Rescue Committee of New York, just arrived from France, and asked to see the Military Attaché.

A few minutes later, I was shown to the office of Major Torr. He got up and came forward as I entered.

"Well, and what can I do for you?" he asked affably.

When I began to tell him what I had in mind, he made me sit down beside his desk. Then he leaned down and pulled the telephone wire out of a plug in the floor beside his chair.

"You can never be too careful," he said. "They can use

these things as listening instruments even when the receiver is down, you know."

We talked about the refugees and the remnants of the B.E.F. in France, and of Lussu's plan to have the British send a boat up to Cap Croisette to get them.

"You've come at just the right moment," Torr said. "We've just received urgent instructions from London to get those chaps out. I was talking to H. E. about it only this morning."

"H. E.," I realized, was Major Torr's way of referring to His Excellency, the British Ambassador to Spain, Sir Samuel Hoare.

"I'm afraid there's nothing doing so far as the Admiralty is concerned," Torr went on. "We've already asked them several times to let us have a ship to get our men out of France, but the commander at Gibraltar refuses to detach a unit from the fleet. It seems it's a cardinal principle of naval strategy never to detach a unit from the fleet. I'm afraid we'll have to work out our own scheme."

Just then the telephone rang. Major Torr plugged in and picked up the receiver. While he was talking I wandered around the room, looking at the maps on the walls and staring out the windows at the Embassy gardens. When he had finished, I went back to my chair beside his desk and sat down again.

"When our chaps cross the border into Spain," he said, "they're all arrested. We've been working for some time trying to get the Spanish authorities to let us send them on to Gib. That was the head of the Seguridad I was talking to just now."

At this point he remembered the telephone plug and bent down and pulled it out.

"I think it's going to work," he said. "I think we'll be able to send the first lot of them to Gib in a few days. If we can do that, we won't have any need for ships. They can all come over the mountains and let themselves be arrested, and after a few weeks we shall get them out and send them on to Gib."

"But suppose it doesn't work?" I asked.

"Oh, in that case, we'll have to find something else," Major

Torr said. "That is, if it's still possible for them to get out of France at all. The Jerries have fifteen armored divisions on the Spanish border now. We don't know whether they're planning to come down here or go east into unoccupied France, but we're rather inclined to think they're planning to go east.

"I say," he said, "I wonder if you could come back in a week or ten days? We ought to know by that time, one way or the other. Then we can talk more intelligently about what we are going to do."

Although I was alarmed to hear about those fifteen German divisions on the frontier, Major Torr's suggestion suited me perfectly. Whatever answer I got from New York, I had already decided I'd have to go back to Marseille, if only for a few days. On the way back I would call at the British Embassy again and see whether I couldn't work out some plan of co-operation with Major Torr. I left him the chart Lussu had given me and went away agreeing to be back in a week. It was a weight off my mind to be rid of that chart. Torr seemed glad to get it, but he was no more glad to get it than I was to get rid of it.

Golo Mann, who had spent the day in the Prado, took the train to Lisbon that night, and I stayed on another day to see what I could do in Madrid about my prisoners. I went to the Seguridad the next morning to inquire about them, but got nothing more than a promise of a report on their cases when I came back to Madrid on my way to Marseille. That afternoon I took the plane to Lisbon.

-9-

I reached Lisbon in the late afternoon, and went straight to the Hotel Metropole. Dr. Charles Joy, of the Unitarian Service Committee of Boston, had established an office there. Working with him was Franzi von Hildebrand. He and his family had come through from Marseille a week or so before.

Franzi was expecting me.

"I have a telegram for you from Marseille," he said, handing me an envelope.

I tore it open and we read the brief message together.

BABY PASSED CRISIS BETTER NOW BUT OTHER CHILDREN QUAR-
ANTINED DOING OUR BEST LENA.

"What the hell is all that about?" Franzi asked.

"It means that all the refugees have been arrested and sent to concentration camps, except Mehring," I said. "He must have got out of it because he's supposed to be too sick to leave his room. Or maybe it means they've all been confined to their hotels. Tell you the truth, I don't know what it means. But I know one thing; I've got to go right back to Marseille."

I had dinner with the Manns that night and spent the next day getting a new Spanish transit visa and a Portuguese exit visa, seeing the refugees I had sent through from France, and writing a long report to New York. Everybody had arrived safely at Lisbon, except the people I already knew had been arrested in Spain. But not all of them had come through without adventures.

Reports on the trip through Spain were as numerous and varied as the people who made them. Some of the refugees had had difficulty with the Spanish authorities at the frontier. Some reported that the examination of their baggage had been very thorough. Some had had to go into a little room in the railway station at Port-Bou or Puigcerda and undress to convince the Spanish authorities that they weren't trying to smuggle money into the country. Others had had no difficulties of any sort. Nearly all agreed that the examination of passports which took place on the trains between the border and Barcelona, between Barcelona and Madrid, and once again between Madrid and the Portuguese frontier was very searching. Those who had traveled on false passports had been frightened almost out of their wits by it. One or two said they had had to pay large bribes to avoid arrest. But none had been arrested. To most, the worst thing about the trip through Spain seemed to have been the fleas in the third-class railway carriages.

Experiences at the French frontier were equally varied. Many had been allowed to go through on the trains, though they had no exit visas; others, like the Werfels and the Manns, had been obliged to walk over the hills. Some had been stopped by *gardes mobiles* and sent back; others, like the Werfels and the Manns, had been directed to the Spanish posts by them. A German political refugee who had been traveling on a false Polish passport said he had been refused permission to leave France until he gave his word of honor that his passport was false. Then he was allowed to go through on the train without any question. Another German political refugee, who crossed after I did, and passed me in Spain, said he had found German agents at Cerbère the day after the Werfels and the Manns climbed over the hill. He and his wife had had to go by a much more circuitous and difficult route, obliging them to spend a night in the mountains.

It was all very confusing, and very difficult to generalize about. Much, obviously, depended on luck. Except for the five who had been arrested in Spain, there seemed no reason to believe we had been wrong in thinking that for most of the refugees the route through Spain was the best one. I turned back to Marseille more determined than ever to persuade the refugees to take that route before it was too late.

One of the last things I did in Lisbon was to go out and buy a couple of dozen cakes of soap. The soap shortage was the worst inconvenience we had had to suffer in France, and Lena had tucked little notes in every part of my baggage to remind me to bring some back with me when I came. Polylingual, she had written them in all the languages she knew. When I opened my toilet kit at Cerbère, I found no soap in it, but a piece of paper with the word *savon* written on it. When I put on a clean shirt, a piece of paper fluttered to the floor, and bending down to pick it up I read the word *sapone*. In between my handkerchiefs, I found a message reminding me of *Seife*. In the toes of a pair of fresh socks was a slip of paper calling my attention to the need for *jabón*. The same reminder was repeated in English, Polish and Russian. It was obviously a compelling need.

-10-

In Madrid I dropped my bags at the Hotel Nacional and went straight to the British Embassy. Torr received me immediately.

"I didn't expect you quite so soon," he said.

I explained what had happened.

"Well," he said, "it's just as well. I expect our time is getting short. Jerry is still holding those fifteen divisions on the border."

He plugged in his telephone and asked to be connected with the Ambassador. When he had finished talking, he pulled the plug out again.

"H. E. will see us in a few minutes," he said.

We talked as we waited. After a few minutes the telephone rang. Torr plugged in and answered it. Then he plugged out again.

"H. E. is ready for us now," he said.

We went downstairs to the Ambassador's room. We found him finishing his tea. He was a man of medium height, gray-haired, and a good deal older than I had expected to find him.

"Major Torr tells me you are willing to help us get our men out of France," he said.

I said I was.

"I am afraid there isn't any possibility of our sending a ship up from Gibraltar to get them," the Ambassador said. "I think Major Torr has already told you that the Admiralty refuses to do that. But Major Torr has made an arrangement with the Spanish authorities to release any of our men who come across the frontier into Spain, on the grounds that they are escaping prisoners of war. Under international law, you know, escaping prisoners of war are not interned. Do you think you can send our men across the frontier?"

I said I thought it would be possible, but explained that I was interested primarily in political refugees, and that some of them couldn't enter Spain because of their activities during the Spanish Civil War.

"I see," Sir Samuel said. "You must have ships for your refugees, is that it?"

I said it was.

"Well," he said, "I am willing to place $10,000 at your disposal. Are you willing to undertake to send our men across the frontier into Spain and at the same time try to organize escapes by boat? If you succeed in finding boats, you can send your refugees and our men on them. There is just one condition I must make. You must never put British on the same vessel with Spaniards or Italians. It might cause us very serious embarrassment here if it should become known that British soldiers and Spanish or Italian political refugees were traveling together."

I hadn't anticipated anything like this. I had come to the Embassy to try to get the British to send ships from Barcelona to pick up men and take them to Gibraltar. I hadn't anticipated becoming a British agent myself, and I didn't particularly like the idea. It was no part of the job I had undertaken to do for the Emergency Rescue Committee, and it might prove very dangerous. France had already broken diplomatic relations with Britain and might any day be at war with her. Even if the worst didn't happen, the Gestapo and the French police would probably be even more interested in my activities as a British agent than they were in my activities as a kind of modern Scarlet Pimpernel rescuing political refugees.

On the other hand I needed the help of the British if I were to get any of the Italian or Spanish refugees out. So I decided to make a bargain. I explained why I was reluctant to accept Sir Samuel's proposal in the form he had made it, but said I would accept it if he would undertake to hire Spanish ships to go up from Barcelona to the French coast and pick up the refugees and the British soldiers there.

Sir Samuel turned to Major Torr.

"What do you think, Torr?" he said.

Torr said he had already done a little work on the idea of employing Spanish fishing boats for the purpose and thought it could be done.

"Very well, then," the Ambassador said. "It is agreed. We will go about finding means to send Spanish fishing boats up to the French coast to take our men directly to Gibraltar. I shall leave you to work out the details with Major Torr. I only wish to add that if you succeed in your task, my government will certainly remember and reward the service you will have rendered it."

We shook hands on it, and Torr and I went back to his office to work out the details. He offered to give me the $10,000 in pound notes then and there, but I said I'd rather have it paid to the committee in New York, so I could pick the money up in France as I needed it, and not have to smuggle currency across the frontier, or travel with it in Spain. We agreed to keep in touch with one another by Lussu's code, which I wrote out on a piece of paper and left on Torr's desk.

The next morning I went back to the Seguridad to try to find out about the prisoners, but I could get no information about them at all. Either the Seguridad was reluctant to talk about the cases, or its slow Spanish ways had prevented it from getting reports in time for my return visit. One way or the other, there was obviously nothing further to be done in Madrid, so I went on to Barcelona by plane that afternoon.

I had called at the American Consulate in Barcelona on my way to Lisbon with the Werfels and the Manns, and had told them about the prisoners. They had agreed to make inquiries, and had given me the names and addresses of several lawyers they thought might be helpful. When I got back to Barcelona I went to the Consulate again, and there I got the information I had sought in vain at Madrid. All the prisoners had been charged with clandestine entry and smuggling. Evidently they had failed to present themselves at the first border post on entering Spain and had gone deep into the country without getting *entrada* stamps on their passports or American affidavits. The Consulate didn't think they had been arrested because of their past political activities in Germany, but simply on border technicalities. When I reported this to the lawyer, he seemed quite optimistic about the possibility of getting

them out, and I left for the frontier, feeling I had done everything I could to help them.

## V. *The Door Swings Shut*

THERE was an ominous gray sky over Marseille when I came
out of the station, and the mistral was blowing the first dried
leaves of the plane trees across the square where the trolley
line ends and a rare taxi waits for a fare.

Lena and Beamish met me at the head of the boulevard
d'Athènes and we all went to the Hotel Splendide and had
breakfast together in my room. Instead of sugar, the waiter
brought us saccharine tablets for our coffee, and instead of the
cherries and syrup of a month before, we now had a brown,
sticky gelatinous mass of *confiture de sucre de raisin*—jelly
sweetened with sugar made from grapes after the wine has
been pressed out of them—in consistency viscid, in taste bitter.
There was no butter for the bread, which was stale (the eating
of fresh bread had been forbidden), and the "coffee" consisted
mostly of burned grain. It was the so-called *café national*.

After breakfast I unpacked my suitcase and distributed the
cakes of soap I had brought from Lisbon. I gave Lena three
or four of them, because it was she who had reminded me to
bring them back with me.

"Oh, Mr. Fry," she said, her eyes big with joy, "*il ne faut
pas exagérer.*"

From her and Beamish I learned what had happened while
I was away. Lena had received the telegram I sent her from

Port-Bou and had dispatched the Feuchtwangers to Lisbon in the company of a representative of the Unitarian Service Committee a few days before my return. But I had misunderstood the telegram Lena had sent me. It wasn't true, as I had thought, that all the refugees in France had been arrested and interned. A few days after I left, the *Sûreté Nationale* had come to get Breitscheid, Hilferding, Walter Mehring, and a fourth refugee named Arthur Wolff. They had orders to put them all in *résidence forcée* at Arles. Breitscheid, Hilferding and Wolff had gone, and Mrs. Breitscheid and Mrs. Wolff had gone with them. Mehring had been saved by his putative illness, but only after a battle with the police in which Lena had played the star role.

Nobody seemed to know why the police had acted, whether it was to prevent the men from "compromising the whole German emigration," as Barellet had said Breitscheid and Hilferding were doing, or whether it was for other and more ominous reasons. But there had been a very alarming hint in the explanation given by the two *Sûreté* agents who came to the Hotel Splendide for Mehring. They had told him that they were very sorry, but their orders came from Vichy and "your compatriots"—meaning, presumably, the Nazis.

But this was not all. The Prefecture had also called in the American Consul and told him it was *inquiet*—uneasy— about the "activities of Dr. Bohn and Mr. Fry." It had also complained about Lowrie's activities in behalf of the Czech soldiers, and had warned Vochoč not to use any more false passports. Lowrie had given up his illegal activities, and Vochoč had decided to issue no more passports.

Despite all this, both Lena and Beamish felt I ought to stay. Without an American there to protect them, they said, they would soon be arrested and sent to a concentration camp, and everything would come to an end. Our work was by no means finished. We had not succeeded in sending out everyone we had located, even weeks before, and we were locating more of the refugees on the lists every day. Somehow, we had to find a way to get them out of France.

The events of the next few days were so close-packed that, in retrospect, they all seem to have happened at once.

One of the first things I did was to have the office telephone changed. We told the post office we wanted to be able to move it around from room to room, and they came and put an outlet in each room and installed a plug on the instrument cord. But we really wanted to be able to unplug between conversations, like the British at Madrid. When the change had been made, we were careful to pull the plug out as soon as we had finished talking, plug it in again only when the phone rang. At the Splendide, where we could scarcely ask to have changes made, we put a hat over the phone, which hung on a little wooden box on the wall, whenever we wanted to talk about matters we weren't eager to share with the police. Periodically we inspected both the office and the hotel room for signs of microphones.

Then I went to the American Consulate and saw the Consul-General. He advised me to leave France at once, before I was arrested or expelled. He wouldn't tell me what the Prefecture had said, or show me the text of the report he had cabled the State Department while I was in Spain. But he did give me the text of the Department's reply, which contained the definite statement that "THIS GOVERNMENT CANNOT COUNTENANCE THE ACTIVITIES AS REPORTED OF DR. BOHN AND MR. FRY AND OTHER PERSONS IN THEIR EFFORTS IN EVADING THE LAWS OF COUNTRIES WITH WHICH THE UNITED STATES MAINTAINS FRIENDLY RELATIONS."

I telegraphed the Embassy at Vichy, asking them to suspend judgment until I had had a chance to see them, but all I got for an answer was a message from the Chargé d'Affaires, by telephone to the Consulate, acknowledging my wire and saying there was no use in my going to Vichy "as a report had been sent to the State Department over a week ago conveying the information the Prefecture had asked the Consul to communicate, and no other action was contemplated."

I decided to go anyway, but I found I couldn't get a safe conduct unless the Consulate or the Embassy asked for it, and neither of them would. When I asked the Consul to cable the Department my side of the story, he refused, on the grounds that my case had already been judged, and nothing I could add now would make any difference.

-3-

While I was vainly seeking to find out what my situation really was, I was also trying to make every minute count for the refugees. But luck was against me. We got a lot of people away in those last days of September, but we also had a lot of disappointments and disasters.

As I have already said, Beamish had discovered that the honorary Lithuanian Consul at Aix-en-Provence, a Frenchman, would sell Lithuanian passports, had, in fact, been selling quite a number of them to Frenchmen who wanted to join de Gaulle. For a few days we thought these would replace the Czech passports. They were very good papers to have, because Lithuania was a neutral country, and so there would be no difficulty with them in Spain, even for men of military age. We bought a number of them for our clients, but before they could get the necessary visas on them Portugal stopped giving transit visas on Chinese, Siamese and Belgian Congo visas, and we were stumped again. Portugal's action also destroyed the value of the Czech passports Vochoč had issued before I left for Lisbon—unless the Spanish and Portuguese transit visas were already on them, and still valid, which was seldom the case.

It was then that we turned to Drach and his Danish and Dutch passports. The urgency of the situation overcame our reluctance to deal with him, and we bought several of his handsome little cloth-bound booklets. On them we had the honorary Consul of Panama at Marseille place Panamanian visas—with the solemn understanding that they would never be used for the purpose of entering Panama. We even agreed with the Panama Consul to instruct every refugee who got one of his visas to report to a certain person in Lisbon for help. By arrangement beforehand, we said, that person, instead of giving help, would take a rubber stamp and bang the word *cancelado* on the visa. Then he would hand the passport back to the bewildered refugee. The arrangement hugely amused the Panama Consul, a French shipping agent by the name of Figuière. Actually, of course, we trusted our refugees and had no need of any such ruse to prevent them from using the visas to enter Panama. They would have been quite satisfied to get as far as Lisbon with them.

For a few days it was still possible to get Portuguese transit visas on the strength of the Panama visas. But only for a few days. After that the rules changed again, and Panama visas were of no more use than Siamese or Chinese visas.

I hadn't been back in Marseille more than a few days before someone brought us word that Georg Bernhard and his wife were at Narbonne. Bernhard was one of the three men Barrelet had told me the Gestapo was looking for. We sent Ball down to Narbonne to get the Bernhards and bring them back to Marseille, with the idea of sending them through Spain as fast as we could. We hid them in one of those hotels called *maisons de passe* which serve, in France, one of the principal functions of tourist camps in the United States. The proprietor, thinking them just another amorous— if somewhat over-age—couple enjoying a clandestine romance, obligingly overlooked the formality of reporting their presence to the police. Their American visas were waiting for them at the Consulate, and we were planning to buy them some kind of false passport on which they could safely travel to Lisbon, when all the rules changed again and false passports became of little use as travel documents.

We also tried to get Mehring out. He still had his American affidavit, but after what had happened we were inclined to agree with him that he couldn't risk the trip through Spain under his own name, or travel again in France without a permit. So we decided to buy him a Lithuanian passport under an assumed name and try to get him a safe conduct to some town near the Spanish border.

For the passport we needed photographs, and the problem was how to have them taken. Anyone else could have gone into the photomaton shop on the rue St. Ferréol and had them taken in a few minutes, for ten francs. But Mehring was supposed to be too ill to get out of bed. As a matter of fact he got dressed every day, and frequently came up to my room, where we consulted with him about German refugees who were applying to us for help. (Later he became a member of our *comité de criblage*, or sifting committee, which considered and recommended the appropriate action to take on each applicant.) But he would go back to his room and get into bed for meals. When he was surprised in his chair by a knock on the door, he would jump hastily into bed, pulling the covers over his head so vigorously that they often came untucked at the bottom and revealed his shoes to the startled and puzzled maid or waiter.

Once when some members of one of the German armistice commissions lost their lives in an airplane accident over the Mediterranean, and Vichy held a state funeral for the dead men at Marseille, a German officer who had come to the city for the occasion took the room next to Mehring's, and a German sentry paced up and down the corridor night and day, his rifle on his shoulder. Then Mehring stayed in his bed, and for a while we thought he was really going to die.

Ordinarily, though, he spent a good deal of time in my room. But we were afraid that if he went out of doors, the fraud which had kept him from being sent to Arles would be discovered. On the other hand, having a photographer come to the hotel and photograph him there would be conspicuous and highly suspicious. We finally found a trustworthy refugee photographer to do the job. But before we could get his transit visas, Spain closed its frontier.

-4-

I remember very well that terrible day. I went down to the office in the morning as usual, but I could tell from the hum

of excited conversation in the tiny waiting room that something was wrong. At first I thought it was another râfle.
As I tried to work my way through the crowd to get inside,
the refugees seized me by the sleeves and asked me if I had
heard the news.

With the Spanish frontier closed, and no ships leaving
Marseille, except French ships bound for Oran and Algiers,
it really did look like the end. You couldn't even get across
the Mediterranean to Africa without special permission,
almost never granted a foreigner and seldom granted a Frenchman other than a Vichy official. Now, it seemed, the refugees
were really trapped. They were to be kept in France as cattle
are kept in the pens of a slaughterhouse, and the Gestapo
had only to come and get them. There would be no more
escapes.

But it was not quite as bad as it seemed that first day,
though there was panic among the refugees for several weeks.
During that time the Spaniards opened and closed their
frontier again and again. Sometimes it would be open for
only a few hours a day, and sometimes for a whole day. You
could never tell in advance, and you never knew when it
closed whether it would ever open again or not. It would be
hard to imagine a crueler way of torturing human beings.
Every opening meant hope renewed, every closing hope abandoned.

Then, on October 1st, the Portuguese Consul received new
instructions. Henceforth he couldn't grant any transit visas
himself, but had to telegraph all requests to Lisbon, and,
before he could do that, he had to see a genuine overseas
visa and documentary proof that the applicant had a fully
paid passage on a ship sailing from Lisbon on a fixed date.
All this information was carefully checked at Lisbon by the
Portuguese "international" police, with the usual leisure of
Latin, and more particularly Iberian, bureaucracy. If they
found that the information was true, the Portuguese police
would telegraph the Consul a few days before the ship sailed
from Lisbon giving him authority to grant the visa.

Shortly after the change in the Portuguese regulations, the Spanish Consul got similar instructions from Madrid. Now he too had to cable his government and await the reply before he could grant a transit visa. For men of military age of the nations at war with Germany, he would not even cable.

The result of all these new rules was to make it almost impossible to have all the visas valid at the same time. You couldn't even apply for a Spanish transit visa until you had already received the Portuguese visa, and by the time you got the Spanish visa the Portuguese visa had generally expired. That meant that your ship had sailed without you. Then you had to get a new reservation on another sailing and begin all over again. For some time to come, the only people who were able to leave France were those who had already had both transit visas in their passports before the end of September— and Americans, for whom the rules were eased.

The situation was given a touch of bitter irony by the fact that almost at the same time that Spain and Portugal changed their rules the French announced a new exit-visa policy. Previously, all requests for exit visas had had to be referred to Vichy, which was said to refer them to the German armistice commission at Wiesbaden. That was the last you ever heard of them. Now the local Prefectures could grant visas to nationals of neutral countries like Russia and Rumania without going through Vichy and Wiesbaden. They could even give them to Poles born in the part of Poland not occupied by Germany. But the new regulations did almost no one any practical good, because a French exit visa wasn't any use without Portuguese and Spanish transit visas, and for a long time Portuguese and Spanish transit visas were practically unobtainable.

-5-

The Consul-General kept telling me I'd be expelled any day if I were lucky enough not to be arrested and held on charges. But there were four friends of Paul Hagen's in the camp at Vernet he had asked me particularly to help, and I didn't want to go until I had gotten them out of France.

The first step, obviously, was to get them out of Vernet. We had sent letters to the *commandant* in the name of the committee, and Bingham had sent him letters and telegrams in the name of the Consulate—all to no avail. There were only two things left to try: escape, and feminine wiles.

Escape from Vernet was extremely difficult. Because it was the camp of the "undesirables," Vernet was more closely guarded than any other concentration camp in France. It was surrounded by a high, barbed-wire fence, and the section where Paul's friends were interned had a second barbed-wire fence inside the first. The sentries were old soldiers, armed with rifles. They were held personally responsible for all escapes, and their instructions were to shoot to kill.

Feminine wiles were safer, and we had a made-to-order charmer in the person of Mary Jayne Gold. The gregarious Miriam had met Mary Jayne at Toulouse. Young, blonde and beautiful, she was one of those fabulous Americans who used to live in France in the good old days. In Paris she had had a large apartment and a Vega Gull low-wing monoplane, in which she used to toot around Europe, flying to Switzerland for the skiing and to the Italian Riviera for the sun. At the outbreak of the war, she had presented the plane to the French government. It would have been hard to find a better person for the job we had in mind.

Miriam spoke to Mary Jayne and Mary Jayne said she was willing. A few days after my return from Lisbon, she went to Vernet, saw the *commandant*, and succeeded where everybody else had failed. Accompanied by two soldier guards, the four men were allowed to come to Marseille and take their American visas. When they had them, they were supposed to go back to the camp, still under guard.

But Beamish and I had other plans for them. We were planning to send them through Spain. We hoped that by the time their guards realized what had happened and had given the alarm, they would already be in Lisbon.

Everything worked all right up to a point. The four men came to Marseille, went to the American Consulate, and got

their American visas the same day, thanks to Harry Bingham.
But before we could get them Portuguese and Spanish transit
visas, the Spanish frontier was closed, and we had to find
some other way of smuggling them out of France at once—or
resign ourselves to seeing them go back to Vernet, to what
fate we couldn't know.

By great good luck, Beamish's researches in the port had
turned up a boat. The boat was a yacht called the *Bouline*.
Some French de Gaullists had just bought her and were planning to sail to Gibraltar on her, taking with them two Polish
officers, two Belgian officers, and the former owner, who was
to act as skipper. The skipper was an old Marseille sea captain
with the sentiments of qualified patriotism appropriate to his
kind. When asked why he had decided to sell his boat and sail
her to Gibraltar, in defiance of all Vichy's prohibitions, he
said simply, *"Je fais ça pour l'honneur de la patrie et pour
assurer ma vieillesse.* I am doing it for the honor of my country,
and to provide for my old age."

Though his boat would hold only fifteen passengers comfortably, and he already had seventeen scheduled to go, not
counting himself, the skipper was willing to add our four
refugees—at a price which, though hardly serving to enhance
the honor of his country, would undeniably contribute ma-
terially to the security of his old age.

The four men from Vernet got rid of their guards for an
evening by giving them some money and telling them to go
off and have a good time, and Beamish and I met them in a
brothel on the rue Dumarsais to tell them about the *Bouline*
and find out whether they were willing to risk the trip. We
chose a brothel as our meeting place because it was too dangerous to have them come to the office or the hotel, or be
seen with us in a bar or restaurant. It was a cheap, plebeian
house, with a large room on the second floor where men sat
at small tables against the walls, had drinks, stared at the
obscene murals, got acquainted with the girls, and, if they
felt inclined, took them upstairs to the bedrooms.

In that room, with its lugubrious atmosphere of sordid

pleasures, surrounded by soldiers and prostitutes, we sat with four German anti-Nazis and discussed soberly and in low voices the means at our disposal for saving their lives. But we couldn't sit alone for long without arousing suspicion. The girls kept trying to get on our laps and rumple our hair. They were surprised at our almost total lack of interest in them. None of the four refugees had had a woman—or even seen one until they got on the train at Vernet—for more than a year, but they were too anxious about their fate to take advantage of the opportunities the girls were offering them. One of them hesitated a long time.

"It's very tempting, but I don't think I could," he said in the end. "I'm too nervous."

Finally, to make it seem a little more normal, Beamish decided to take one of the girls upstairs.

"*Je vais me sacrifier,*" he said, leaving the room with a readiness which belied his words.

While Beamish was upstairs, the rest of us sat, each with a girl on his lap, drinking cheap cognac and discussing, in English and German, neither of which the girls understood, the prospects and the risks of the *Bouline* adventure.

Realizing that we were speaking German, one of the girls asked us if we were Boches.

"No," I said, "we're Americans. Why did you think we were Boches? Are there many Boches in Marseille?"

"Oh, yes," she said, "many. In the armistice commissions. But they usually come in the daytime, when there aren't so many customers."

By the time Beamish had come downstairs again, the four refugees had decided to trust their lives to the sea rather than linger any longer in Pétain's France.

-6-

Just before the *Bouline* left, Harry Bingham invited me to dinner at his villa, to meet Captain Dubois. Captain Dubois was a member of the Marseille staff of the *Sûreté Nationale*.

Though a Vichy policeman, he was friendly to England and America, and Harry thought it would be useful for me to know him.

It was. Dubois was the first French official I had met who was familiar with my case and willing to talk about it. When I asked him what the police had against me, he said, with a sly smile I couldn't quite fathom, "Smuggling people out of the country."

"Anything else?" I asked.

"Yes, trading in foreign exchange."

"Is that all?"

"Yes, that's all."

"Is it serious?"

"What do you mean, serious?" he asked.

I told him what the Consul-General had said.

"C'est de la blague," Dubois said.

Dubois also knew the port very well. He knew all about Bohn's boat, for instance, and said that if he had known Bohn he would have warned him to drop the project long before the Italian armistice commission got wind of what was going on. The control of the port and the coast was so strict that it was getting pretty difficult to escape by boat now.

"Take a yacht called the *Bouline*, for instance," Dubois said, in his thick Marseille accent. "It's been sold and resold half a dozen times. Yet it's never been able to leave the spot where it's tied up, and probably never will be as long as the war lasts."

When I told Beamish this, he reported it to the skipper, the Belgian officers and the four refugees. The skipper denied that the boat had ever been sold before, said he knew the port was closely watched, and promised to get away anyhow. The Belgian officers made an inquiry of their own and came back with much the same report. The refugees accepted the opinion of the Belgian officers. The port was watched so closely that we couldn't examine the boat ourselves, but had to accept the word of the others that she was seaworthy and would be able to get away when the time came.

Fortunately the time came soon, for the soldier guards were growing impatient, and it was becoming more and more difficult to find excuses for prolonging the stay at Marseille. Luckily, the guards were very fond of women and liquor, and could easily be persuaded to spend a night in a brothel —if given the money for it. They were too drunk to know much of anything on the night the *Bouline* sailed.

When Beamish came back to the Splendide, about two o'clock in the morning, and reported that the boat had actually left, with the four refugees on it, I had the same sensation of mingled satisfaction and dismay a man must have who has just murdered a hated rival. Paul's friends had gotten away at last. But how could we hope to escape retribution? When the guards sobered up in the morning, and discovered that their prisoners had disappeared, they would certainly go to the police. The police would make an investigation, and the investigation would point directly to us.

-7-

I think it must have been four or five days later that Ball brought us the news. He had just come up from Narbonne, and he said that on getting off the train he had seen the four refugees, chained together and heavily guarded, waiting on another platform. We wouldn't believe him at first, though he kept on insisting that there couldn't be any mistake about it. But we got our Corsican lawyer to make inquiries, and we soon learned that Ball was right.

The *Bouline* had slipped out of the port without any difficulties, in spite of the watch and Dubois' warning. She had sailed all that night and all the next day. Toward evening she had run into a storm. The wind tore the sails; the waves lashed the deck. By nightfall, the little boat was out of control and leaking badly. Half the passengers were so seasick they didn't care whether they lived or died. The others worked the pump till it broke. Then they bailed out with pails.

Toward morning the storm subsided, and day dawned calm

and clear. Paul's friends wanted to continue the trip at all costs, if not to Gibraltar, then to Spain or Corsica. But everyone else on board had had enough of it, and, in that devastating indifference to all claims of honor and decency which is born of seasickness, they ignored the pleas of the political refugees and the consequences to them of the decision they were taking. At about half-past eight in the morning, the skipper brought his boat about and started back toward Marseille.

Toward noon a French coast-guard vessel overhauled them and took them into the little harbor of Port de Bouc, somewhat to the west of the city. There they were arrested and sent to Aix-en-Provence, to await trial on a charge of attempting to leave France without authorization. It was while they were being transferred from the train to the Aix trolley that Ball had seen them.

We hired a battery of lawyers to defend them, and expected to have to hire another battery to defend ourselves at any moment. But after three months in jail, awaiting trial, the four men were sentenced to one month in prison, and, because they had already served three times as long, were immediately set at liberty by the court. But not so by the Vichy administration; it returned them all to Vernet, under considerably heavier and more reliable guard than had accompanied them to Marseille. Of our connection with their attempted escape nothing was said at all. If the police had their suspicions, they did not reveal them.

-8-

During all this time Bohn and I had been summoned to the Consulate almost every day to be asked when we were planning to leave France. We had also been receiving cables from our relatives, friends and employers in the United States urging us to come back. Bohn succumbed to the pressure and left Marseille at the end of the first week of October. I stayed. With Mehring in bed, the Bernhards in a *maison de passe*, and Paul's friends in prison, I felt I couldn't leave no matter what pressure was brought to bear on me.

There was another reason for my decision to stay. Charlie had a friend, also in the American Ambulance Service, who had a cousin in the German army. Charlie's friend's cousin was stationed in Paris. He had a German officer friend of his call on Charlie's friend in Marseille. Among other things they talked about me.

"Sure, we know all about Fry," the German officer told him. "We know he's trying to get our political enemies out of France. We aren't worrying. We're confident he won't succeed."

It was a challenge difficult to ignore, and I determined to show them they were wrong. But I applied for new Portuguese and Spanish transit visas and cabled the New York office urging them once again to send someone over to replace me before it was too late. I wouldn't have been at all disappointed to see him show up the next day.

The night before he left, Bohn asked me to take over his work in France, and I agreed. Lena went down to Cerbère with him. She had a Polish passport and had gotten her Portuguese and Spanish transit visas just before the change in regulations. Bohn went through on the train, taking Lena's luggage with him, and Lena went over the hill. But the Spaniards sent her back. Since the new regulations went into effect, they weren't admitting any Poles—man, woman or child—they said.

A few days after Bohn had left, his chief assistant, Bedrich Heine, the young German socialist, began coming to our little office in the rue Grignan to consult us about his people and advise us about ours. Now, in addition to the intellectuals, the Catholics, the younger socialists, and the British, I also had the responsibility for Breitscheid, Hilferding, Modigliani and all the other older leaders of the various labor and socialist movements of Europe.

# VI. *The Ship That Didn't Sail*

THERE were Gestapo agents at Cerbère when Lena crossed the frontier, and Heinrich Himmler, Gestapo chief, was being feted at Madrid when she got back to Marseille.

We didn't know what Himmler's visit to Madrid meant, but we could guess. The presence of Gestapo agents on the French side of the frontier, the closing of the Spanish border, the new regulations obliging the Spanish Consul to telegraph the names of all visa applicants to Madrid before granting the visas—all these could only mean that Berlin was at last giving serious attention to the refugees in France.

For some reason which we couldn't understand, the Gestapo had given us more than six weeks to get the refugees out. We had never been able to explain the delay, but we had been grateful for it, and we had profited by it. Now we knew that our days of grace were over.

The new Spanish visa regulations were especially alarming. It was easy enough to believe that the Portuguese were really concerned to see that no one with a transit visa stayed in Portugal, either because his overseas visa wasn't genuine or because of lack of room on the few ships which were sailing from Lisbon to the Western Hemisphere. There was no need to look for a political explanation of what the Portuguese were doing. Their country was already jammed to the gunwales with stranded refugees, and they didn't want any more. That was all.

But the behavior of the Spaniards was entirely different. They knew as well as we did that no refugee was going to stay in Spain if he could help it. For most of the refugees Spain was even more terrifying than France, and they hurried through as fast as they could.

The only adequate explanation of Spain's new regulations was a political one, and Himmler's visit to Madrid seemed to confirm it. We were convinced that every name telegraphed to Madrid was submitted to a Gestapo agent, and that no authorization for a visa would be granted until the Gestapo agent had given his consent.

The worst of it was that we didn't know whether the consent, if granted, would be a favorable sign or not. Had the Gestapo despaired of being able to keep the refugees it wanted in France, and decided instead to lure them into Spain, to be arrested there? In France, they would be hard to find, unless they were in concentration camps. But if they were encouraged to try their luck in Spain, the Gestapo could simply wait for them to come over the border. It could tell the Spanish government to telegraph a favorable decision to its Consul at Marseille, secure in the knowledge that the refugee would be crossing the frontier within a week. Perhaps the Gestapo had even "persuaded" the Spanish authorities to telegraph the Spanish border police an order for the man's arrest at the same time it telegraphed the Consul the permission to give him a visa. It would be just the sort of trick the Gestapo delighted in.

For this reason we felt we couldn't encourage the refugees who were in danger in France to go through Spain or ask for Spanish transit visas, even if the Consul should begin to get favorable answers to the telegrams he was sending to Madrid—at the refugees' expense. Of course, there must have been many refugees in France the Gestapo wasn't particularly interested in. It probably wasn't interested in Poles born in the part of Poland occupied by Russia, for instance, or it wouldn't have allowed the French to grant them exit visas. But for the rest we couldn't be sure. We knew that Georg Bernhard was a wanted man. But how about the others? We had already sent half a dozen people into Spanish jails, and they were still there. At any moment they might be handed over to Germany. We weren't going to take the chance of having that happen again, if we could help it.

If we could have made use of false passports, we might have sent the endangered refugees through Spain under assumed names, trusting that they wouldn't be recognized by Gestapo agents on the way. But the new regulations made even the best and most plausible false passports as useless as a high-powered car without gasoline as far as travel through Spain and Portugal was concerned.

One of the difficulties we had been having all along was the difficulty of communication. All "underground" methods are immensely slow and complicated. It is bad enough not to be able to use the mails and the telephone in your dealings with people in the same city. It takes time to arrange meetings in cafés and hotel bedrooms. You either have to depend on trusted messengers or go yourself and find the person you want to see. If you make an appointment, and the other person misses it, you may have lost the link with him for days. Then you are reduced to fuming impotence until he turns up again.

Communicating by "underground" means with a committee thousands of miles away, across two international frontiers and a great ocean, often took months. We used to give messages and reports to departing refugees and ask them to mail them at Lisbon. Generally we typed the reports on long strips of thin paper, pasted them end to end; wound them into a tight roll, inserted the roll in a rubber finger, and tied the finger securely with a piece of silk thread. Then we would open the bottom end of a tube of toothpaste, take out some of the paste, and push the rubber finger well up into the tube, closing the bottom again carefully after it was in place. The result was a loaded toothpaste tube which looked exactly like any other. But sometimes the refugees took fright and threw the tubes away before they left France. Even when they succeeded in taking them safely through to Portugal, it was very doubtful whether we would ever get an answer; the traffic was all in one direction. We had plenty of people going to New

York, but the committee in New York almost never found anyone who was going to Marseille. So we had to do the best we could with what poor facilities we had. Whenever we dared, we cabled openly, or wrote letters which we posted in Marseille. But for all confidential messages, such as lists of endangered refugees needing visas and ship reservations, we depended on the refugees who were leaving. And, after October 1st, our departing refugees were fewer every day.

-2-

On the other hand, with every day that passed, it became more and more urgent to get the refugees out of France. Though obviously against her will, France was steadily and ineluctably accommodating herself to the exigencies of Hitler's "New Order." Early in September it was decreed that the Prefects should have the right to intern without trial anyone, French or otherwise, who was deemed "dangerous to public safety." In mid-September, Léon Blum, leader of the French socialists, and former Prime Minister, fell victim to this decree: he was interned "administratively" (i.e., without right of *habeas corpus*) in the fourteenth-century château at Chazeron, near Riom.

At the beginning of October it was announced that foreigners between the ages of eighteen and fifty-five might be formed into forced-labor gangs, to be placed at the disposition of employers in need of help. The men would receive no wages for their work, but their families would have the right to draw relief. A few days before Himmler's visit to Madrid, the French adopted their first anti-Jewish law. Besides barring French Jews from all public offices, including commissions in the army, navy and air force, and forbidding them employment in the teaching profession, journalism, motion pictures, and the radio, the new law gave the Prefects the right to arrest all foreign Jews and intern them in concentration camps, or send them into *résidence assignée* in small towns, without explanation or the right of appeal. Late in October Vichy adopted a law forbidding people to listen to English and de Gaullist broadcasts in public places. And there were repeated rumors that the Nazis were going to occupy the so-called "free zone."

While Himmler was still in Madrid, Marshal Pétain went to Montoire, met the Fuehrer and announced the policy of collaboration with Germany. Was closer co-operation between the French police and the Gestapo part of that policy?

The French police certainly became more active late in October. There was a new series of râfles, and many refugees were picked up and sent off to concentration camps—including a good many of our own protégés. Even refugees who had volunteered in the Foreign Legion at the outbreak of the war were sometimes interned. They were demobilized one week, arrested the next, and, if found to be Jews, or without a job or means of livelihood, shipped off to a concentration camp a few days later.

But more than anything else it was the Kundt Commission which made us feel that we should have to act quickly if we were to save any more of the refugees who were in danger in France. The Kundt Commission was a group of German army officers and Gestapo agents which was visiting the French concentration camps, looking over the names of all those interned, and selecting the ones to be sent back to Germany under Article 19 of the armistice. We had heard vague rumors about this commission before, but it wasn't until mid-October that we got definite documentary proof of its existence.

I think it was Klaus Dohrn who first told us about it. Klaus Dohrn was a young German-Catholic friend of the Werfels. Mrs. Werfel had recommended him to me just before we went to Lisbon. I met him in the restaurant of the Gare St. Charles, where he was waiting for a train connection. He had been a *prestataire* during the war—one of the many thousands of young refugees the French had rounded up into forced-labor gangs and put to work building fortifications, roads, barracks and railroads behind the lines. After the armistice he was transferred to a *prestataire* camp at Albi. He was on his way to still another *prestataire* camp, on the Riviera, when I met him.

He was sitting in the restaurant with a friend, also a *prestataire*, when I went across to the station, in response to a mysterious phone call, to look for him. Both men were dressed in the khaki *prestataire's* uniform, and both looked as though their last hour had come. They said that while they were at Albi a German commission had visited the camp and demanded to see the list of the men interned there. The *commandant* of the camp had been an honorable Frenchman not at all in sympathy with the Vichy idea of selling the political refugees to the Nazis as small coin in a shameful bargain. He had hidden Klaus and his friend in the infirmary and had left their names off the list. Both men believed that he had thus saved their lives.

Yet somehow I only half-believed their story about the German commission. So many of the refugees tended to exaggerate the danger they were in, in an attempt to persuade us to do something for them, that we had gotten into the habit of discounting everything they told us.

But to make sure I wasn't letting Klaus and his friend walk into a trap, I persuaded them to forget their *prestataire* career and desert. I showed them how to get out of the Gare St. Charles without passing through the police control at the gate. They took rooms at a Marseille hotel, changed into civilian clothes, and began to look around for ways to get out of France. Neither had any kind of overseas visa, so we got Klaus a Czech passport and a Siamese visa, and we sent his friend to Casablanca on a false demobilization order. When the Siamese visas and the Czech passports were no longer of any use, we had someone take Klaus's name to Lisbon and cable it to New York from there, and we advised him to wait in Marseille until his American visa was ready.

-3-

The events on the political horizon, the new Portuguese and Spanish visa policies, the presence of Gestapo agents on the frontier, the existence of the Kundt Commission—all these developments had two consequences for us. They meant that we would have to reorganize our work, abandon once and for all the idea that it could be finished in a few weeks, and plan for a long haul. They also meant that we would have to support many of the refugees and try to keep them out of jail or concentration camp.

Reorganizing the work involved constricting as much as possible the band of conspirators and turning the office, previously a half-transparent cover for illegal operations, into a genuine relief office, staffed by professional relief workers, most of whom would have no idea that we were doing any underground work at all. So, as the original workers left, I resolved to replace them with new recruits who would not know anything about the real purpose of my mission to France and could therefore easily deny, if questioned, that we had any illegal activities or ever had had. Eventually I hoped to be able in this way to divorce the "underground" work from the office altogether.

Thus, when Lena left for the frontier, I replaced her with a new secretary named Mrs. Anna Gruss, a queer little gnome about four and a half feet tall, with a good heart, a sharp tongue, an immense capacity for work, and the virtue of genuine innocence of our undercover work. If Mrs. Gruss realized what we were doing, she never let on to it. When Lena came back from Cerbère, I took her back on the staff, and she stayed until she left France for good, the following Spring.

With Mrs. Gruss came several other workers, all as ignorant as she, at first, of what we were trying to do to get refugees out of France without exit visas. One of them was Daniel Bénédite, a young Frenchman of the Left who had worked in the office of the Prefect of Police in Paris before the war, dictating many of the Prefect's letters and helping to write many of his speeches. He was slight and dark and wore a small mustache, but his most conspicuous characteristic was his extreme cocksureness which his mother attributed to the Alsatian blood in her son's veins.

In Paris Danny Bénédite had had much to do with refugees,

winning their friendship by his kindness and his readiness to renew their *permis de séjour*.

Danny became my *chef de cabinet*, taking my place whenever I was too busy to see someone myself, and performing a hundred other tasks ably and cheerfully. When I hired him I warned him that it would only be for two or three weeks. Believing the Consul-General, I didn't expect the police to let us operate any longer than that. Actually, his job lasted four years. In the course of that time he advanced from private secretary to leader of the underground network which rescued many of the refugees and kept many others safe in hiding after the Germans had occupied the whole of France.

With Danny came his English-born wife, Theodora. They had both been friends of Mary Jayne Gold's in Paris, and Theo had worked in the office of International Business Machines there. She was a little severe, perhaps, and perhaps a little too inclined to keep a watchful eye on her young husband: she was always terrified that he would get into some sort of political trouble. But she had all the strength of character he had and many qualities which—like tolerance—he lacked.

Still another new recruit to the staff was Danny's war comrade, Jean Gemahling, a blue-eyed, flaxen-haired youth from Strasbourg who would have been extremely handsome if it hadn't been for the fact that his nose was a trifle too long for his face. Whereas Danny was a Protestant, or had been brought up as one, Jean was a Catholic—at least, he had been born a Catholic. His father had been professor of history at the University of Strasbourg, and Jean had been educated at an English boarding school. He spoke English extremely well, though with a slight French accent, discernible under the English public schoolboy's intonation. In Paris he had been a research chemist. Why, I could never find out, for he seemed to have very little interest in chemistry, and a great deal in the arts. In our office in Marseille he started as an interviewer but quickly graduated to other and more dangerous tasks. He was very quiet, and strongly inclined to blush

furiously when spoken to, but in the course of time he
displayed a courage and a devotion to duty as he saw it
which many far rougher men would have had difficulty
matching.

At Mehring's suggestion, I also hired Marcel Chaminade
about this time. Born in Berlin, he was the son of the mu-
sician Moskowski. In a sense, Chaminade replaced Franzi.
After the First World War he had held the rank of *Consul
de France* at the Quai d'Orsay, where he was attached to the
press division; but he had had to resign from the French
foreign service when a pamphlet he wrote attacking Poincaré's
policies created a furor in the ministry. His views were Catholic and conservative, but not fascist, Mehring said. He was
as much opposed to the anti-Semitism and the vague totalitar-
ianism of Vichy as he was to the socialism and equalitarianism
of the Republic. Mehring recommended him to me because
of his wide connections. He was undoubtedly acquainted with
large numbers of the aristocracy and upper bourgeoisie, and
could get through doors which might have been closed to
Frenchmen with more liberal records.

Chaminade was certainly not very prepossessing in appearance. Short, bald, and with big protruding ears, he looked
and acted like something left over from the court of Napo-
leon III. I remember that when I first met him he bowed so
low in shaking my hand I thought for one horrible instant he
was going to kiss it. Obsequious, luxury-loving, lazy, he gave
the impression of a man who has learned to seep through life
with a minimum of effort. But he seemed to be genuinely
concerned about the refugees, among whom were some of his
old friends from Berlin and Paris, and I felt that in the
France of 1940 he might be able to do more for them than
many more sympathetic Frenchmen. He became our *Secrétaire d'Etat aux Affaires Etrangères*—in other words, our
ambassador to the French authorities—and performed his
duties faithfully, if somewhat ostentatiously, for many months
to come. We never took him into the inner circle, and I don't
think he ever knew more about our clandestine activities than

he could pick up from wisps of conversation. But Beamish distrusted and hated him, and Danny Bénédite became very suspicious of him later.

So many of our intellectual customers were having nervous breakdowns, or threatening to have them, that we also put a doctor on the staff to treat them. He was a young Rumanian, just out of the Paris medical faculty, named Marcel Verzeanu. Not wanting to compromise himself too deeply, he preferred to go by the name of Maurice, and most of the refugees never knew him by any other name. Perhaps it was just as well, for later he engaged in distinctly non-medical work.

With our new recruits, most of whom were French, and all of whom were professionally qualified in one way or another, our relief office took on a much more normal appearance than it had had before, and we were able for the first time to present a really respectable face to the authorities.

In the office we received an ever-increasing number of refugees every day, and most of them were flat broke. There were writers who could no longer collect their royalties or get their manuscripts to their publishers, and painters who could find no market for their pictures. There were professors who had had to leave their posts at the French universities and were no longer drawing their salaries. There were scientists who had been driven from their laboratories by the Nazi invaders or their Vichy accomplices. If some had money in banks in Paris, London or New York, their accounts were blocked. Others had no funds anywhere. Almost all were without means, and many would have gone hungry, or been interned, if we hadn't helped them. Most of them considered internment the worse alternative. By giving them small weekly living allowances (really for living now), we could keep at least some of them out of the camps. To those who were in the camps we could and did send small weekly food parcels. Our relief program was no longer an excuse for being; it was now and for a long time remained the principal part of our work.

-4-

During most of the month of October Beamish and I investigated sea routes. I think we must have examined at least twenty different boat schemes in that time. In New York it had been easy to talk about sending the refugees to Casablanca or Gibraltar. All one had to do there was to open an atlas and trace a line on a map. But in Marseille it was a different thing altogether. There were only yachts and fishing boats, and the yachts were all forbidden to leave their moorings and the fishing boats all belonged to Marseille types who were either gangsters or had missed their true calling.

Again and again we were told enticing stories about fully equipped vessels of the latest design all ready to slip away to Gibraltar in the dead of night, and capable of making the trip inside forty-eight hours—only to find on closer examination that the boat which was being offered us for a high price to take our protégés to safety was a gaunt hulk whose bare ribs were being held upright only by the support of the sand in which she had been firmly embedded for twenty years, or a phantom ship which didn't exist at all, and never had.

Nor were we alone in these discoveries. The Poles, with whom I got in touch as soon as I returned from Lisbon, were having similar experiences. I used to go to General Kleber's hotel in the shadow of the Prefecture and talk it over with him. He was in charge of evacuating the Polish army from France, under the general direction of Count Lubienski, who had his headquarters in Vichy. Both men were actually secret agents of the Polish government-in-exile in London, but I had the impression that the French were pretty well aware of what they were doing and were closing their eyes to it and even helping whenever they could.

Kleber had sent the bulk of his men through Spain on false passports which represented them as either under eighteen or over forty, or to Casablanca on false demobilization orders—until Spain stopped letting any Poles through, and the French officer supplying the demobilization orders was arrested. Then Kleber began looking for boats. He had exactly the same experience we had. One day he would be optimistic, tell me he was on the track of something really solid, promise to let me put a few of my most endangered refugees on it, advise me to return at the end of the week. When I went back he would be gloomy as only a Pole can be, say the French of Marseille were all cheats and blackguards without exception, curse the whole French nation for its cupidity, its deceitfulness, its willingness to sell out even its most courageous allies if only there were a profit to be made in the transaction. For, like us, he found that the boats which were offered to him were either nonexistent or good only for firewood.

I had also gotten in touch with the British as soon as I got back from Lisbon. There were two young Englishmen named Graham and Lloyd living at the Hotel Nautique. I had run into them at the American Consulate some time before. They introduced me to an English officer, a young, blond and pink-cheeked captain of a Northumberland Regiment named Fitch. Despite his youth, Fitch was the highest-ranking British officer available, and, as such, had assumed charge of evacuating the men of the B.E.F. The men, more than three hundred of them in all, were interned in Fort St. Jean, one of the two old forts which guard the entrance to Marseille's Vieux Port. Actually their internment was more formal than real, for they were allowed to go out into the town during the day. Thus it was an easy matter to send them down to the frontier by twos and threes.

I told Fitch all I knew about routes over the border and gave him money from time to time—the money that had been entrusted to me by Sir Samuel Hoare. To fill the gaps in the thinning ranks of the men at the fort, he substituted civilians from the British Seamen's Institute. The French officer in charge of the fort merely counted noses every morning; if there were always the same number of men in the fort, he was satisfied. Thus Fitch was able to get away many highly skilled men, pilots and specialists. He wasn't much interested in boats as long as his men could enter Spain. As there was no question of visas for them, they were able to enter Spain even after the refugees were barred.

-5-

Toward the end of October Dr. Charles Joy came through from Lisbon. He had traveled from Narbonne to Marseille standing up in the toilet with four women and a potted chrysanthemum, and he was tired by the trip and exhausted emotionally by the unaccustomed experience—very upsetting for a New England clergyman, even of so modernist a sect as the Unitarian. He hadn't seen anybody in Madrid, but a man named Darling, newly arrived in Lisbon from London to take charge of evacuating the B.E.F. from France, had asked him to tell me not to send any more men into Spain. Evidently Torr's plan for getting them released from prison or concentration camps wasn't working. In the future I was to send the British direct to Gibraltar, by sea, Joy said.

I saw Fitch later that same evening and told him, and he began to turn his attention to boats the next day. We put Ball to work on the project, too. His ability to speak the tough French of the port made him an obvious candidate for the job.

For the first time since my arrival in France I was able to take an occasional Sunday off. I still began work at eight o'clock in the morning, and still worked until eleven at night, and sometimes until one. I still saw dozens of people every day, and was witness to displays of every possible quality of character, from heroic to despicable. I still had poor, driven refugees stalking me in the morning when I went out, and in the evening when I came in. I still had from six to twelve phone calls an hour, and got twenty-five letters a day. But the pressure slackened just the same—not because the situation was improving, but because more and more of our charges were being arrested and interned, and there was little or nothing we could do about it.

I profited by the decline in activity to see something of Provence and get a little rest. One Monday afternoon, after my return from a weekend excursion to Arles, the telephone rang. It was Mrs. Gruss.

"Wait there," she said. "I'll be right over. Don't come to the office till I've seen you. It's important."

She came in a few minutes later, as gnomelike as ever.

"The police have been looking for you all morning," she said. "They have an order to search the office and your room, but they couldn't do it without you."

"What are they looking for?" I asked.

"It's funny," she said. "They're looking for false passports. They've already searched the Hicem and the Joint Distribution Committee."

"What'll I do?" I asked.

"I guess you'd better go to the *Evêché* and tell them you're here," she said.

"All right," I said. "But I want to see Beamish first. Can you find him and send him right over?"

"Okay," she said.

"Send Chaminade over too, if he's there," I said.

"Okay," she said.

As soon as she had gone I took my maps of the frontier from behind the mirror and burned them. I went through all my other papers and burned many of them too.

Beamish arrived a half hour later.

"Where the hell were you?" I asked.

"What do you mean?" he said.

"*Toujours dans la lune,*" I said. "Don't you remember those maps of the frontier?"

"Yes," he said.

"Suppose the police had found them?"

He shrugged.

"Everything's okay. It was a break your being late. Gave me time to clean things up," he said.

"Are you sure everything's okay?" I asked.

"Absolutely," he said.

"What do you think I'd better do?"

"I think you'd better go to the *Evêché* and say you're back. There's no use trying to get away. Let them search. They won't find anything. After that maybe they won't be so suspicious."

Chaminade came in a few minutes later, and we went to the *Evêché* together. Chaminade was magnificent there. He introduced himself as *ancien consul de France*, made a little speech about the American who had "risked so much" to come to France and "help her in her darkest hour," said I had an appointment with the Bishop at five o'clock (a complete lie) and asked them to hurry up with their search if they had to make it.

I don't know whether it was Chaminade's speech or the natural sympathy of the French for Americans, but they made the most superficial search you could ask for. We went around to the office in a police car, and they looked in a few drawers and cupboards, and then made out a *procès verbal* which said that they had searched the premises thoroughly and had found *rien de suspect*. They signed it and I signed it. Then we shook hands and they went away. That was all.

After the police had gone Beamish and I made a little search of our own. In the stove in the waiting room we found several false identity cards. Were they a plant, or had someone unloaded them there when the police came in to look for me in the morning? We didn't know, but I gave Charlie instructions to burn all the papers in the stove every day after that. It became one of his daily rituals.

-6-

It was the following week, I think, that Ball found the solution to all our difficulties. The solution was a *chalutier*, or trawler, with an auxiliary motor, large enough to take seventy-five persons to Gibraltar. Ball found it through a Frenchman he met in Snappy's Bar, back of the Opera. Snappy's Bar was a favorite hangout of the British officers in Marseille. The Frenchman, who went by the name of the

"Baron," professed to be an ardent de Gaullist. He put Ball in touch with the captain and crew of the boat, and it wasn't until he was convinced the whole thing was absolutely straight that Ball came to me about it.

The price was 225,000 francs. I was incredulous at first; the thing seemed just a little too good to be true: a large, seaworthy fishing boat, with good, strong sails, a motor in working order, enough oil already on board to make the long trip, and the right to go out of the harbor at any time, to fish. Lussu was also incredulous—so incredulous that he refused to have anything to do with the business. But when we discovered that Colonel Randolfo Pacciardi had faith in it, we decided to try it.

Pacciardi was leader of the Italian republicans in exile. He had been Commander of the Garibaldi Brigade in the victorious battle of Guadalajara, in which Mussolini's "volunteers" were put to rout during the Spanish Civil War. To me he seemed somewhat naive and even a trifle swashbuckling, but I knew that the people back in New York had great confidence in him. He too had been negotiating with the "Baron," and was persuaded he was honest. Fitch also looked it over and brought back the same report. Both he and Pacciardi were enthusiastic.

As for Ball, he was not merely hopeful—he was boastful. When Beamish (who, like me, was inclined to be skeptical) asked him for details, the name of the ship, its owner, its captain, and so on, Ball would say, "Take it or leave it. Either you have confidence in me or you don't have."

There was one thing about the plan which especially troubled me. As seventy-five people could scarcely board a fishing boat in the harbor without attracting attention, the plan was to have the *chalutier* come down from where she was anchored through the various basins to the outer harbor shortly after midnight. Meanwhile the passengers would gather in a boat-house on the Anse des Catalans, back of the lighthouse. After passing through the outer harbor, the *chalutier* would pick up the passengers. Then she would sail straight out to sea.

But in coming down from her station in the farthest

basin to the outer harbor, the boat would have to pass under six drawbridges, and her masts were too high to enable her to pass under them unless they were raised. Whereas if she went out to sea to the north, she would not have to go under any drawbridges at all.

But when I put that question to Ball, I found him scornful of my unbelief.

"I tell you," he said, "these guys are okay. They know everybody in the port. They're going to fix it up with the men who run the drawbridges. Give 'em a thousand francs apiece to keep their mouths shut. Don't worry about that."

"And the armistice commissions?" I asked.

"Hell," Ball said, "you don't think the armistice commissions are around the port at that time of night? They're all in bed with their little French friends."

"But wouldn't it be better for the boat to go directly out to sea from where she is, instead of coming all the way down to the lighthouse?" I insisted.

"Don't you see, she's got to come down there to pick up the passengers," Ball said, growing exasperated.

Fitch was of the same opinion. As for Pacciardi, he was convinced that the captain was honest. Twice already, he told us, he had paid him money to get away, and, when something had gone wrong, the man had given the money back unhesitatingly.

In the end, moved by Pacciardi's insistence, I agreed to take a chance on it, but only on one condition: that no money should be paid over until all the passengers were on board and the ship was clear of the harbor. Fitch and Ball readily agreed to this condition, and I gave the English money to Fitch and the money for the refugees to Ball: 225,000 francs, or nearly $3,000 at the current black-market rate: forty-five beautiful, big, 5,000-franc notes.

I told Fitch about Sir Samuel Hoare's objection to mixing the British with the refugees, but he waved it aside. Hoare couldn't have realized how rare these chances were, he said. We arranged to put sixty British soldiers and fifteen refugees on the ship, including the Bernhards, Walter Mehring, Klaus Dohrn and Pacciardi's Italians. Each man was to bring his own food and water sufficient for four days. Everybody was to meet in the boat-house at ten o'clock Sunday night.

-7-

Just in case something should go wrong, I went out of town again that weekend. If the police questioned me later, I wanted to be able to say I had not only not had anything to do with the boat but had been off on a casual holiday the day the escape occurred. This was in accordance with the principle of decentralization of responsibility Beamish and I had agreed upon. I knew that if I stayed in Marseille, I would inevitably be the center of the conspiracy, with someone or other coming to me every five or ten minutes, and there was no use inviting arrest, at least until my successor arrived. But that was one occasion when I would much rather have stayed in Marseille than gone away. It was Beamish who insisted on my going. So I took the train to Tarascon on Sunday morning.

On the way back to Marseille the next afternoon, I half expected to be met at the station by a delegation of the *Sûreté Nationale*, waiting to arrest me for the crime of helping British soldiers escape from France. But there was no police delegation there, nor was there anyone from the office at the Splendide. Had they all been arrested? I couldn't telephone to find out, and I couldn't go down to the office dressed as I was. It would look too much as though I knew that something special was afoot.

I was hastily changing my clothes when somebody tapped very gently on my door. I opened it and found Mehring outside, looking as if his last hour had come. I knew then that something had gone wrong.

They had all met in the boat-house after dark, he said. It was a terrible night, cold, and with a high wind. They had waited there in the wind and the dark, the sixty British soldiers, the Bernhards, little Mehring, big Klaus Dohrn, the Italians—

until two o'clock in the morning. Then Beamish had come and told them it was all off, and they had gone back to town, one or two at a time, to avoid attracting the attention of the police.

Beamish told me more of the story an hour later, at the office. There had been long conferences in Snappy's Bar, with the captain claiming he couldn't get the boat from the owner until the money had been paid, and Fitch refusing to pay a franc until everybody was safely on board. Even at that, Fitch had taken the precaution of dividing the British money in small parcels among his men, so no one man could be hit on the head and the money seized. But Ball had persuaded Fitch to get the money back from his men and give it all to him. Then Pacciardi and Ball had fallen for the captain's story that he couldn't get the boat from the owner until the money had been paid (though this was in contradiction to everything the captain had previously said), and had paid the whole sum over to the captain in advance. Once he had the money in his pocket the captain had gone out "to buy the boat"—and had never come back.

-8-

For several days Ball insisted the boat would still sail. When it was obvious even to him that it never would, and that he had been outwitted and cheated, he insisted that he'd pay the money back out of his own pocket.

"This'll never cost you one damned cent, I can tell you that," he swore. "I'll sell my lard factory in Paris if I have to. I'll sell my villa at St. Paul de Vence. It'll cost me pretty damned near everything I've got. But it won't cost you one damned cent, you can be sure of that."

Meanwhile the British had taken more direct methods to get the money back. They had kidnapped two or three members of the "captain's" gang and had taken them to Fort St. Jean as hostages. There they gave them the third degree. But the poor little gangsters were no better able than anyone else to say where the captain had gone with the money.

In the end, in desperation, preferring arrest to any more of the fists and boots of the burly English and Scotch, one of them dropped a note out of a window, and the police came and took them all away.

Perhaps because they were regarded as prisoners of war already, Fitch and the British soldiers weren't arrested. Fitch testified at the trial of the gangsters that he had got the money by taking up a collection among all the men in the fort, and the judge accepted his word for it. The gangsters were convicted of being parties to fraud and were given short terms. Though the police looked for him, or pretended to, nothing was heard of the captain or the money.

The Sunday after the failure of Ball's great escape plan I went to Nîmes. All afternoon I sat in the lovely eighteenth-century Jardin de la Fontaine, listening to the water running through the colonnades of the central basin, watching the yellow leaves drift slowly down from the plane trees in the thin, late-autumn sun, and feeling for all the world like the last act of *Cyrano de Bergerac*.

## VII. *The Villa Air-Bel*

THE first time I saw the Villa Air-Bel it was closed as tight as a fortress, the walks and garden were overrun with weeds, and the hedges hadn't been trimmed for years. But the view across the valley to the Mediterranean was enchanting and I was impressed by the terrace with its enormous plane trees and the double flight of steps which led down, right and left, to a formal garden and a fish pond.

The owner showed me through. He came up the drive, a

little old man in a dirty bowler hat, stooped with age, and weighted down still further by the enormous key he was carrying in his rheumatic hand.

He showed me everything, from the parlor on the ground floor to the linen room under the roof. Disappearing into the darkness of one room after another, he would struggle with the bolts of the windows and blinds while I waited at the door, forbidden to cross the threshold until there was light to guide me.

"Permit me, Dr. Thumin. I can do it better than you," I said.

"*Mais non, mais non,*" his thin, cracked, little-old-man voice would come back out of the blackness. "Stay there! Don't move! Wait! *Ça y est!*"

And light would burst into the room and almost blind me, and Dr. Thumin would hobble back to the door and say, "*Maintenant,* you may enter," and I would go in and look at the furniture and marvel.

I was enchanted with the house. It was solid nineteenth-century bourgeois from top to bottom. The parlor had an elaborate inlaid-wood floor, stiff gilt furniture, hideous landscape paintings in heavy gilt frames, an upright piano with brass candlesticks on either side of the music rack, a marble mantel with a gilt-framed mirror, a brass clock above and much elaborate brass hardware below. The dining room, on the other side of the entrance hall, was dark and gloomy, with brown wallpaper embossed to look like leather, and heavy carved chestnut furniture. On the ground floor there was a bathroom with a zinc tub, like the one Marat died in, and taps in the shape of swans' heads, and a kitchen, with a coal stove twenty feet long, a soapstone sink with running cold water (when the spring hadn't gone dry), and no trace of any modern conveniences. The library, on the second floor, was the best room in the house, furnished with Louis XVI and Empire furniture, papered in black-and-white picture wallpaper depicting scenes from classical mythology, and equipped with leather-bound sets of Lamartine, Musset, Vigny and Victor Hugo ("*Notre plus grand poète,*" as Dr. Thumin

Varian Fry on the job in Marseille, fall 1940. *(Varian Fry Papers, Rare Book and Manuscript Library, Columbia University/Friends of Le Chambon)*

Photo Essay by Marvin Liberman with Susan W. Morgenstein, from the exhibition *ASSIGNMENT: RESCUE, The Story of Varian Fry and the Emergency Rescue Committee*, United States Holocaust Memorial Museum.

Vichy French police on patrol in Marseille, 1940. *(Hiram Bingham Collection, United States Holocaust Memorial Museum)*

View along the harbor, Marseille, fall 1940. *(Varian Fry Papers, Rare Book and Manuscript Library, Columbia University/Friends of Le Chambon)*

Refugees seeking United States visas wait outside the American Consulate, Marseille, 1940. *(Hans Cahnmann Collection, United States Holocaust Memorial Museum)*

Members of Fry's staff (left to right), Charles Wolff, Theodora Bénédite, Danny Bénédite, Lotte Feibel, Louis Cooperman, Marcel Verzeanu, Jean Gemähling, Marseille, 1941. Photograph by Varian Fry. *(Varian Fry Papers, Rare Book and Manuscript Library, Columbia University/Friends of Le Chambon)*

Miriam Davenport (center left) and Mary Jayne Gold with their friends, "Beaver," "Killer," and "Sarge" in the Vieux-Port, Marseille, fall 1940. *(Miriam Davenport Ebel Collection, United States Holocaust Memorial Museum)*

Justus Rosenberg, a.k.a. "Gussie," (at desk in center) and Danny Bénédite (standing) in the office of the *Centre Américain de Secours* (American Relief Center) on the Boulevard Garibaldi, Marseille, 1941. *(Varian Fry Papers, Rare Book and Manuscript Library, Columbia University/Friends of Le Chambon)*

Staff and refugee "clients" outside the office of the *Centre Américain de Secours*
(American Relief Center) on the rue Grignan, Marseille, fall 1940. *(Varian Fry Papers,
Rare Book and Manuscript Library, Columbia University/Friends of Le Chambon)*

Members of Fry's staff, including Danny Bénédite, Hans Sahl, and Marcel Verzeanu, meet secretly in the office at night to review "client" files and plan rescue operations, Marseille, 1940. Photograph by Varian Fry. *(Varian Fry Papers, Rare Book and Manuscript Library, Columbia University/Friends of Le Chambon)*

Varian Fry and Miriam Davenport in the office on the rue Grignan, Marseille, fall 1940. Photograph by Lipnitski. *(Varian Fry Papers, Rare Book and Manuscript Library, Columbia University/Friends of Le Chambon)*

Bill Freier (Willi Spira), artist and forger for Fry's secret operation, in a French internment camp, 1940–1941. *(Donald Carroll Collection, United States Holocaust Memorial Museum)*

Lion Feuchtwanger, a novelist, in the French internment camp, St. Nicolas, near Nîmes, France, 1940. *(Donald Carroll Collection, United States Holocaust Memorial Museum)*

Max Ernst, André Masson, and André Breton, standing behind Jacqueline Lamba Breton and Varian Fry, in the office of the *Centre Américain de Secours* (American Relief Center) on the boulevard Garibaldi, Marseille, April 1941. Photograph by Ylla. *(Photo Archives, Museum of Modern Art, New York)*

Varian Fry and the Surrealists at the Villa Air-Bel, winter 1940–41. *(Varian Fry Papers, Rare Book and Manuscript Library, Columbia University/Friends of Le Chambon)*

Jacques Hérold (standing), Max Ernst, and Danny Bénédite hang paintings by Max Ernst and Leonora Carrington, Villa Air-Bel, 1941. *(Mme. Daniel Ungemach-Bénédite Collection, United States Holocaust Memorial Museum)*

Hans and Lisa Fittko on a street in Marseille, c. 1940–41. *(Lisa Fittko Collection, United States Holocaust Memorial Museum)*

Danny Bénédite with French vineyard workers at the foot of the Pyrenees near the French-Spanish border, c. 1941. *(Mme. Daniel Ungemach-Bénédite Collection, United States Holocaust Memorial Museum)*

Varian Fry with Marc and Bella Chagall and Hiram Bingham, American vice-consul, outside Chagall's studio, Gordes, France, 1941. *(Cynthia Jaffee McCabe Papers, United States Holocaust Museum)*

Refugees, including Victor Serge (far left) and Wifredo Lam, aboard the *Paul LeMerle* en route to Martinique, Western Atlantic, spring 1941. *(Dyno Lowenstein Collection, United States Holocaust Memorial Museum)*

Varian Fry's colleagues await his expulsion from France at the train station at Cerbère, August, 1941. Photograph by Varian Fry. *(Varian Fry Papers, Rare Book and Manuscript Library, Columbia University/Friends of Le Chambon)*

Varian Fry, escorted by an agent of the Vichy French police, on the train leaving France, Southeastern France, August 1941. (*Varian Fry Papers, Rare Book and Manuscript Library, Columbia University/Friends of Le Chambon*)

always called him). And finally there were the bedrooms, each with its heavy mahogany bed, its marble-top washstand, and its white-marble fireplace.

-2-

Beamish was opposed to the whole idea of the Villa Air-Bel. It was half an hour from town, and there was no telephone. He thought I ought to be more easily available, in case of emergency. Of course he was right. But I was fed up with being available day and night, weekdays and Sundays, and utterly exhausted by it. I had to have a little rest, at least a few hours a day, if I was to be of any use at all. Otherwise I risked becoming so nervous and depressed that I would no longer be able to go on working.

It would have been hard to find a better place to rest and relax. During the *été de la St. Martin*, the French equivalent of our Indian summer, the days were fair, the sky was blue, and the sun was so warm that, on Sundays, we often had lunch out-of-doors. But there was not only the house, the view and the garden: there was also the company we assembled.

Victor Serge was a dyspeptic but keen-minded old Bolshevik who had once been a member of the Comintern but had been thrown out at about the time Stalin broke with Trotsky. During his long career he had evolved from an extreme revolutionary to a moderate democrat. At the house he talked for hours about his experiences in Russian prisons, recalled conversations with Trotsky, or discussed the ramifications and inter-relations of the European secret police, a subject on which he had a vast store of knowledge. Listening to him was like reading a Russian novel.

André Breton, the dean of Surrealism, and once the incorrigible bad boy of Dadaism, had been a doctor in the French army during the war, but at Air-Bel he made collections of insects, pieces of broken china polished by the sea, and old magazines; he talked magnificently and always entertainingly about everything and everybody, and held Surrealist reunions on Sunday afternoons, attended by the entire Deux

Magots crowd, as mad as ever. On his first day in the house Breton caught a scorpion in the bathtub and placed a bottle of live praying mantises on the dining-room table, in lieu of flowers.

Danny Bénédite laid down the law about wine, women and politics, three subjects on which he had very decided opinions.

He was an ardent advocate of Burgundy wine, and had the utmost contempt for anyone who preferred claret. I think he suspected the claret drinkers of reactionary political views.

"Burgundy is the king of wines," he used to say. "Bordeaux is only a poor substitute. *N'en parlons pas.*"

In politics he was a revolutionary socialist and a dogmatic Marxist, with a strong tendency to pity anyone who was not. "The only war that makes any sense is a civil war," he would say.

His attitude toward women was what the psychoanalysts call ambivalent. He was always very tender with his wife, and by no means blind to the charms of other women. He had been particularly impressed by his experiences during the fighting around Dunkirk.

"It was strange," he said one night at dinner. "During the whole time fighting was going on I never gave a thought to women. But the minute I set foot on Folkestone quay, oh, *là là!*"

But perhaps because he was the only son and the youngest child of a widowed mother with two daughters, he could not abide women in groups. Often, when he sensed some little conspiracy or other among the women at the house or had trouble managing the stenographers at the office, he would unburden himself of his true feelings about the female sex.

"Ah, *les femmes!*" he would say, in disgust. "*Quelle sale espèce!*"

An hour later, I would catch him with his hands on Theo's shoulders, kissing the back of her neck.

Danny's friend and army comrade, Jean Gemahling, the blond and taciturn Alsatian, gave most of his attention to the women who shared the house with us and blushed scarlet whenever anyone spoke to him at dinner. The rest of us listened to Serge and Breton and Bénédite laying down the law or played games in the dining room after dinner. Jacqueline Breton, André's Surrealist wife, was blonde and beautiful and savage, with painted toenails, necklaces of tiger's teeth, and bits of mirror glass in her hair. Aube, their five-year-old daughter, was already hailed by the Surrealists as a promising artist.

Laurette Séjourné, Victor Serge's friend, was a woman as unlike Jacqueline as Jacqueline was unlike everybody else. She was dark and quiet and very reserved. She generally stayed in her room during meals, professing not to be interested in food; but the servants reported a large consumption of leftovers between meals. Vladi, Serge's twenty-year-old son, was a passionate Marxist and an excellent draftsman.

The company was completed by Theodora Bénédite, Danny's English-born wife, their charming three-year-old son, Pierre, Mary Jayne Gold, who was obviously enjoying everything, and not least the danger we were all in, and Miriam Davenport, who laughed and coughed and shrieked until she left for Yugoslavia to marry a young Slovene art student she had met in Paris before the war.

On Sunday afternoons the other Surrealists came: Oscar Dominguez, a large Spaniard who was living in a nearby villa with his fat and elderly but rich French mistress; Benjamin Péret, the French poet whose verses sometimes read as though they had been copied down from the walls of public toilets; Wilfredo Lam, the tragic-masked Cuban Negro who was one of the very few pupils Picasso ever took; Victor Brauner, the one-eyed Rumanian painter whose women and cats all have one eye; and many others. Then Breton would get out his collection of old magazines, colored paper, pastel chalks, scissors and pastepots, and everybody would make montages, draw, or cut out paper dolls. At the end of the evening André would decide who had done the best work, crying, "*Formidable!*" "*Sensationel!*" or "*Invraisemblable!*" at each drawing.

montage or cutout in turn, chuckling with merriment all the while.

-3-

One Sunday we went down to Dr. Thumin's house to view his collection of stuffed birds, "the largest in Provence," as he had repeatedly told us. Dr. Thumin met us, all excitement and anticipation, at the door. He was not wearing his bowler hat, and his frayed coat was covered with dust and grease spots.

He led us into a room which was lined with glass-topped museum cases. The cases were filled with stuffed birds, butterflies, shells and other curios, including a wooden doll, a polished section of a stalactite, a piece of coral, and several large pine cones. On one of the walls, hanging by the neck, was the skin of a white albatross.

Dr. Thumin began on the birds.

"You see here," he said, "the largest, the most complete collection of the birds of Provence in existence—over 300 species! I have been offered unbelievable sums for this collection, but I have always refused to sell. It has been my lifelong hobby."

Most of the birds were small and olive green, and one looked surprisingly like another, the effect of uniformity being further enhanced by the fact that all the birds had faded.

But Dr. Thumin was rapturous.

"Voyez vous," he was saying, "are they not extraordinarily natural?"

We went from case to case, proceeding from the smaller birds to the larger, and with each progression Dr. Thumin became more excited. He had eaten every one of them, and delighted to recall the fact. When we reached the owls and eagles, his rapture overflowed.

"Now that one there," he said, pointing to a particularly large and fierce-looking owl, "that one there is *Bubo ignavus*, the eagle owl. I acquired it in 1883. Or was it 1884? 1883, I think. Or 1884? No matter. A hunter sold it to me, and it was so fresh that I was able to sample the flesh. You would scarcely believe that an owl would be edible, but that bird was delicious. I shall not soon forget the flavor of the liver."

He stopped before a kind of heron.

"Now the flesh of the heron," he said, "is less agreeable. It is inclined to be fishy. I acquired this specimen in 1897, and, after I had trimmed the meat from the bones, I boiled it. It was scarcely edible, but I managed to get it down."

When he had finished the rounds of the room, describing the taste and fixing the date of each bird, he stopped, and, assuming an air of mystery, announced that he would now show us something really extraordinary. Then, mounting on a chair with André's help, he took a flashlight from his pocket and called to someone to switch off the light at the door. When the room had been plunged into darkness he turned on the flashlight and flashed its feeble beam at the cases on the walls.

"You see," he said, excitedly, "how instantly they come to life? The effect is extraordinary, *n'est-ce pas?*"

The birds remained utterly dead, and in that thin light their glass eyes seemed even more obviously vitreous than ever.

"*Stupéfiant,*" André said, but I thought his voice lacked its usual conviction.

"I find the effect really extraordinary," Dr. Thumin went on. "They become so *vivants* that one almost waits for them to take wing, is it not?"

He was flashing the beam of the flashlight rapidly over the cases now, but the more rapidly he flashed the deader the birds seemed. They remained what they were to Dr. Thumin: dusty reminders of distant dinners.

When he had climbed down from the chair again, helped by André, and the ceiling light had been turned on, he began to tell us about the man who made the glass eyes.

"He was an extraordinary artist," he said. "He had his shop in the rue Paradis. Or was it the rue Breteuil? *Tenez!* I believe it was the rue Paradis. Number 107, rue Paradis. Yes, number 107. *Voyons.* I think it must have been number 109. But 107 or 109, no matter. His name was Muret. Or was it Miret? *En tout cas,* he was a master of his craft. There was none better in all France.

"Poor man, he died in '98," he continued thoughtfully. "*Enfin,* it was just as well, perhaps: he was spared many painful experiences which we whom God has blessed with longer lives have had to endure. Still, it was a great loss to me to have him go. I have never been able to find satisfactory eyes since."

And he led us sadly toward the door.

In the parlor Dr. Thumin's aged sister was preparing tea. There was very little of it, and it was more than usually stale, even for Armistice France, but we drank it eagerly all the same.

"And now," he said, "for a special treat. My liqueur!"

His sister brought some small glasses, and Dr. Thumin poured out the thin, colorless liquid.

"I made it myself," he said. "Before the other war. It is a rarity, I can assure you."

The liqueur was utterly tasteless. Whatever flavor it may once have had had left it years before.

"Is that not a delicacy?" Dr. Thumin asked. "It is my own secret formula."

We agreed that it was indeed a delicacy.

"Ah," he said reflectively, "it will be long, I fear, before France will again bask in the riches of her former life. What a favored nation we have been, indeed! And now to have to live under the boot of the Boches! It is very hard. But I remember '70," he went on. "We came through that, and we shall come through this, too. Above all, with the Marshal at our head, we can have confidence."

Danny began to bristle at this, but I gave him a look that made him subside without launching into an attack on Marshal Pétain, as I was afraid he was going to.

When it came time to go, we thanked Dr. Thumin for his hospitality and told him he must promise to visit us the following Sunday.

"Oh, you are too kind," Dr. Thumin said. "But I shall come with pleasure. And then you must come and visit me again. The birds always repay a second visit. And even a third and fourth.

"Feel free to come and regard them at any time," he said. "I know how much they mean to you. Bird lovers understand one another."

-4-

Serge called the villa "Château Espère-Visa" because half its inhabitants were waiting for visas, and we put up a sign with that name at the gate. At any other time, life within its walls would have been idyllic. In the winter of 1940-41, it was far from that. We slept under our overcoats, and foraged in the *pinède* for wood on Sunday mornings. There was no central heating, and there wouldn't have been any coal for it if there had been; wood was our only fuel. The cooking was also done with wood.

For the bedrooms we bought *poêles*, small, round, iron stoves, and into them we stuffed paper and wood before going to bed, to be ready for lighting in the morning.

Finding food was almost as much of a problem as keeping warm, and if any of us had realized how difficult it was going to be I doubt whether he would have traded the relative security of hotel and restaurant life for Air-Bel, no matter what its charms and virtues. Rationing had been introduced by that time, but there wasn't enough food in the shops to meet even the very modest requirements of the rationing program. Our housekeeper, a middle-aged Marseillaise named Madame Nouguet, seemed to spend all her time in the market, and would often come home with a tired and worried look on her face and very little in her market basket. But there was a clandestine cow on the grounds (that is, one not declared to the authorities) and so we had milk for our "coffee," and sometimes even butter for our bread.

What helped a lot was wine. As food grew scarcer we drank more and more of it. Occasionally, especially on Saturday evenings, we would buy ten or twelve bottles of Châteauneuf-du-Pape, Hermitage, Mercurey, Moulin-ò-Vent, Juliénas, Chambertin, Bonnes Mares or Musigny and have an evening of drinking and singing. Danny Bénédite knew the words and music of many old French songs, some of them unbelievably rollicking and bawdy, others very tender, or melancholy, or haunting, and we passed many hours singing them. Among their favorites were "*Les femmes de France*," "*Nous étions trois jeunes héros*" and "*Sur les bords de la Loire*." But it is "*Passant par Paris*" which I identify particularly with Air-Bel: I can never whistle it, even today, without having before my eyes a vivid picture of the dingy dining room, with bottles and glasses on the table, and Danny and Jean leaning back in their chairs and singing that beautiful refrain.

## VIII. *Journey Into the Night*

THE visa situation began to show improvement after the first of November, when both Spain and Portugal eased up somewhat on their requirements. Only now it was necessary to take extreme precautions in crossing the French frontier. There everything was changed. The good old days of August and early September were gone forever. There were no longer any accommodating *commissaires* at the railway station at Cerbère, and the border was patroled now by *gardes mobiles* who were more inclined to use their rifles than courteously to indicate the path to Spain.

It was in this period that Beamish and I organized and perfected the "F" route. Johannes F—— was a German social democrat who had smuggled underground workers in and out of Germany across the Dutch border before and during the war. At our request, he and his wife went down to Banyuls, near Cerbère, and took rooms in a house on the outskirts of the town. They could do this because they had beautiful French identity cards, made for them by the little Austrian cartoonist, Bill Freier. The cards made F—— and his wife French citizens from the forbidden zone, where no Frenchman could go to check up on their credentials.

In Banyuls, in the center of the district where the sweet wine of that name is grown, F—— and his wife established themselves as French refugees who could not return to their homes. They applied for and received the small weekly allowances the Pétain government granted such persons. They became friendly with their neighbors. They worked in the vineyards. Often they took jobs in fields near the frontier. On weekends they walked in the hills, studied the trails and observed the habits of the frontier guards. When they knew every footpath intimately, they gave us a prearranged signal, and we began sending the clients down to them.

So that the clients might not risk arrest on the way, we usually provided them with Freier identity cards. So that no police agent could present himself to F—— as a client and discover our system, we also gave each of our departing protégés half of a torn strip of colored paper. On the end of each strip there was a number. F—— had the other half, with the same number on it. If the numbers agreed, and the two pieces of paper fitted each other perfectly, he knew that the person was what he represented himself to be.

F—— had already explained to his neighbors in Banyuls that he had many French friends he intended to invite when he got settled. They were, he said, like him, refugees from the forbidden zone, and, like him, unable to *rejoindre leurs foyers* —rejoin their hearths—as the official phrase had it. They would enjoy a reunion with old friends from the same district or town. The neighbors were sympathetic and welcomed the refugees as they would have welcomed any French citizens driven from their homes by the Germans. They readily offered them work in their fields.

Dressed as farm laborers, or country people on a holiday, F—— and the clients would go out in the early morning, carrying their few possessions in colored handkerchiefs or string bags, as though they were loaves of bread and bottles of wine for lunch. Sometimes they would work in the fields all day. At other times they would go straight to the hills for a picnic. After dark, F—— would come back to Banyuls alone. If asked, he would explain that his friends had had to return unexpectedly to their temporary homes in other towns. Generally he wasn't even asked; he did his work so skillfully that no one was suspicious of him.

In the course of about six months F—— passed more than 100 people over the frontier this way. Not a single one of them was ever arrested, or even questioned by the police.

-2-

To obtain the release of our protégés in the concentration camps, we decided on a campaign of pressure on the Vichy government. We sent Danny Bénédite on a trip around Southwest France, visiting the camps and writing long reports on the conditions he found. At the same time we prepared lists of the most distinguished of our clients who were interned in them.

The conditions in French concentration camps could, with difficulty, have been worse. There was no deliberate torture, as in Nazi concentration camps, but there was everything else: cold, hunger, parasites and disease. In some of the camps, like Argelès, the men slept on damp sand. In others, there were no windows except those donated by American relief organizations. Everywhere the food was terribly inadequate. One man wrote that rat meat had become a much-sought delicacy in his camp. There was the usual French indifference to sanitary precautions, with the result that dysentery was endemic and typhoid epidemic. And everywhere there were lice, fleas and bedbugs.

In these camps we found, on checking over our records, that we had many of our most distinguished people, men like Peter Pringsheim, one of Europe's leading physicists, and, incidentally, Thomas Mann's brother-in-law; Erich Itor-Kahn, the pianist; Paul Westheim, the art critic and historian; and Wolf Leslau, one of the very few European scholars who know Amharic, the language of Ethiopia.

Armed with Danny's reports and our lists of prominent internees, Chaminade and I set out for Vichy in mid-November to see whether we couldn't shame the French government into releasing them. Since literally no one was leaving France legally, we couldn't very well ask for more. Ostensibly, we wanted only to settle them in more comfortable circumstances. Of course, Beamish and I had other plans. But not even Chaminade knew that.

I had still another reason for going to Vichy. I wanted to find out what my own situation was. The American Consul had warned me not to go without police permission, and, though I had applied for that permission a long time before, it had never been granted. In the end I decided to go without it. The Consul called it "putting your head in the lion's mouth," but I wasn't as sure as he was that the Sûreté would arrest me when I got off the train at the Vichy station. I still believed in the prestige of America. He apparently didn't.

-3-

Going to Vichy, even from Marseille, was like making a journey into the night. Vichy was a compound of fear, rumor and intrigue. The town itself is one of the dullest watering-spots imaginable. It must be bad enough in the "season" in normal times; in winter, in conquered France, it was horrible. It is symbolized in my mind by groups of iron chairs standing in the rain, and old men moving slowly from spring to spring in wheel-chairs.

At the end of a day of trudging wearily from hotel to hotel, when we had begun to despair of finding a room and were beginning to think of sleeping in Riom and commuting from there, we walked into the Hotel Albert Premier just as somebody was unexpectedly checking out, and grabbed the room he was vacating. There was no heat in our room except the little we could get from a small electric heater, and there was never any hot water in the taps in the mornings. It was about as cozy as a butcher's refrigerator, for Vichy can be cold as Marseille never is.

But we were not much worse off than the government officials. They too were living and working in summer hotels, and keeping warm, or trying to, with electric heaters or small iron stoves, often with the stovepipes leading through round holes cut in the windows. Some of the hotels were strange sights from outside, with scores of long stovepipes sprouting through the windows and shooting up to the eaves, like giraffes straining to see over the roofs.

Inside, they were equally odd. Each bedroom was occupied by a government official, who sat at a small boudoir table from which the mirror had been removed, or at a larger table brought up from the dining room. On the beds there would often be collections of file baskets marked *Intérieur, Affaires Etrangères, Vice-Présidence,* and *A classer.* Or else the bed would be stacked up in the bathroom between the *lavabo* and the *bidet.* And on the tops of the bureaus, in the *armoires,* and on the floor there were piles of letters and documents and copies of the *Journal Officiel.* Often the government's filing was done in large paper boxes, for lack of anything better.

The atmosphere was a little more orderly in the Hotel du Parc, where Marshal Pétain and Pierre Laval had their offices, along with their respective "cabinets" and most of the Ministry of Foreign Affairs. But it was a far cry from the Elysée Palace or the Quai d'Orsay. You announced yourself to a *gendarme* in the entrance lobby and then waited in a narrow hall, between jewelers' display cabinets, until your name was called. Often the official you wanted to see would come downstairs and talk to you, explaining that his little bedroom upstairs was so crowded that he couldn't receive anybody there. Important diplomatic conferences were sometimes held in the hotel's waiting room.

If you were asked to go upstairs, a *garde mobile* would lead you down the long hotel corridors, past bedroom doors marked with hand-printed slips of paper reading *Vice-Présidence du Conseil, Chef de Cabinet, Entrez sans frapper,* or other doors more permanently marked *Hommes, Dames,* or *Bains.* On the way you would pass the familiar lackeys of the Quai d'Orsay, with the silver chains of their office around their necks, risking, in this hotel atmosphere, to be taken for wine stewards, and looking as though they knew it; or force your way among ambassadors called back to report and waiting patiently in a hallway until they were summoned; or bump into Monsieur Laval in the elevator or in the restaurant downstairs.

-4-

We set about our work methodically. We tried to get a typewriter to copy Danny's reports on the concentration camps, but as the only machine we could find in Vichy had a Hungarian alphabet we sent for Lena and a typewriter from the office, and had the reports mimeographed while we were waiting for her to arrive. We left copies of the reports with every official we called on, and gave them to all the ministers and ambassadors of the Latin American countries for transmission to their governments.

At the Ministry of the Interior we were refused an audience with the Minister, Marcel Peyrouton, but saw instead a Dr. Limousin, a pasty-faced young fascist in charge of concentration camps. When we began our speech, which was based on the assumption that of course a concentration camp was not a desirable place to live in, he bristled.

"What is wrong with our concentration camps?" he asked. "The occupying authorities have felicitated us on them. May I ask what you find wrong with them?"

At the end of nearly two weeks we had to admit that we had been given the run-around everywhere. There seemed to be no possibility of getting anyone out of a concentration camp legally unless he already had an exit visa, and the government was mysterious and obviously embarrassed about exit visas. Furthermore, with the exception of Mexico and Cuba, none of the Latin American countries seemed likely to give any more entry visas. Sousa Dentas, the Ambassador from Brazil, who had given many diplomatic visas in the weeks during and after the fall of France, explained now that his government had reprimanded him for his generosity and had refused to recognize any more of his visas unless specifically authorized from Rio. The Ambassador from Chile showed us a list of Frenchmen to whom he had been instructed to grant visas, but as they were almost without exception Frenchmen who had been closely identified with the Communist Party they didn't interest us very much. Everybody was very polite and very sympathetic about the refugees, but nobody seemed able to do anything for them.

At the American Embassy they were neither very polite nor particularly sympathetic. As the *Chargé d'Affaires* was always too busy to see me, I finally saw the Third Secretary.

"We can't do anything for you, Mr. Fry," he said. "You don't seem to realize that the *Sûreté* has a dossier on you."

When I said that the *Sûreté* had a dossier on everybody and asked if he knew what was in mine, he answered that I was suspected of helping refugees escape from France.

"You must understand," he said, "that we maintain friendly relations with the French government. Naturally, in the circumstances, we can't support an American citizen who is helping people evade French law."

"How about helping me get some exit visas then?" I asked.

To my surprise, he agreed, and when I got back to Marseille I had a list made and sent it to him. But when the list, which contained a few dozen names, reached the *Chargé d'Affaires*, he wrote me a letter saying that I must have misunderstood the Third Secretary. "For obvious reasons," the Embassy "could not . . . obtain individual exit visas for the many thousand refugees who wish to leave France, much as we sympathize with the desire of these poor unfortunates to find a haven overseas," he wrote.

As my own French visa had just expired, I made inquiries about having it renewed while I was in Vichy, but was told to go back to Marseille and make the application at the Prefecture there. As all the other American relief workers had provided themselves with Swiss visas and French exit visas, so as to be able to leave France for Switzerland at a moment's notice in case of trouble, I also called on the Swiss Minister and asked him to put a visa on my passport, as he had on the others. The Swiss Minister seemed friendly enough, and said he would be glad to give me a visa if I would bring him a letter from the American Embassy asking him to do so.

"It is a pure formality," he said, "but my instructions require me to have it."

But at the American Embassy they refused to give me the letter.

"How many times do we have to tell you," they asked, "that we can't do anything for you?"

Two weeks of hard work had accomplished nothing. We decided to go back to Marseille.

The train back was so crowded that we had to stretch out on the floor of the corridor, separated from one another by the bodies of other sleeping passengers, and chilled by the drafts and the total absence of heat.

In the morning Lena reported that she had been bothered half the night by a Frenchman who wanted to make love to her right there in the corridor and couldn't understand why she refused. "Be nice to me," he kept saying. "You won't spoil your pretty fur coat."

Somehow, after our immersion in the atmosphere of Vichy, it was good to have this reminder that we were still in France.

# IX. *The Marshal Comes to Town*

WE GOT back to Marseille in time for the bombing. It wasn't much, as bombings go. I was having dinner with the Chagalls when it happened. Marc Chagall had been living in an ancient stone house in the half-abandoned town of Gordes, to the northwest of Marseille. He hadn't wanted to leave France when I first wrote him, because he had been naturalized French some years before, and he didn't see any reason why he should go. As it is a serious responsibility to uproot and transplant a great artist, I didn't press him. But after the adoption of the anti-Jewish laws, he was so disgusted that he changed his mind. Almost the first anxious question he put to me was, "Are there cows in America?" When I said yes, there were, I could see from the look of relief on his face that he had already decided to go.

He and his family had come to Marseille to talk it over, and we were just finishing a late dinner when the sirens sounded. The manager drew the blackout curtains, put the lights out and set a candle under one of the central tables. For a while we sat in the semi-darkness, listening to the air-raid wardens blowing their whistles on the street. Then we paid the bill and went outside.

The streets were completely dark, and we could already hear the drone of the planes. People were hurrying toward the buildings marked ABRI, and we followed the crowd. Somehow we got into the Gare Noailles, and we stood there in the darkness while the wardens went about outside blowing their

130

whistles and shouting, *"Lumière, eh, lumière là-bas!"* From time to time we could hear the dull thud of bombs in the distance and the bark of anti-aircraft fire. When we peeked out the door of the station, we could see the sky criss-crossed with searchlights. But the wardens shooed us back in again, and we had to stay in the station until the raid was over.

-2-

Charlie Fawcett had left while we were in Vichy, and when I got back to the office I learned that he had been arrested in Spain. He had been having a good deal of trouble with Lili ever since she learned that he was planning to leave, but he had finally managed to get away without a major scene. Lena thought he had been arrested because he was wearing his ambulance-driver's uniform. He had promised her to have it dyed before he set out, but she thought he probably hadn't. The news produced panic in Beamish and me, because we knew what Lena didn't know: Charlie had been loaded down with secret papers and reports, including some for the British. Beamish and Lussu had fixed him up. Since he was a sculptor they had simply put some of the reports in the heads he had modeled, and Charlie had poured in wet plaster to seal them up. One of the most secret of the reports, listing the principal Spanish Republican refugees in hiding in France, and urging visas for them, had gone into the third valve of Charlie's trumpet. Charlie had tightened all the valves with a wrench covered with a cloth and had learned a couple of tunes he could play without ever having to use the third valve, in case any questions were asked. Still other reports had been pasted into the rim of his suitcase. Less compromising but fairly numerous papers he carried openly. Altogether, it would have been quite a haul for the secret police of any country, and the thought that it might already be in the hands of the Gestapo was no sedative to our badly frayed nerves.

The Honorary Consul of Lithuania at Aix was also arrested about this time, and a few days later it was little Freier's turn.

The police surprised him with all his identity-card-forging paraphernalia around him. Though we hired a lawyer to defend him, we had little hope of being able to get him off, and every reason to believe that the finger of suspicion would point to us.

It was during the same week, I think, that Beamish and I ran across Captain Dubois, our police friend. He was having a drink with some pals in the rear of a café on the Canebière when we came in to get a late supper. After a few minutes he got up and came over to our table.

"*Bon soir,*" he said. "*Comment ça va?*" And then, looking at me, "May I speak to you a minute?"

I excused myself and walked slowly toward the front of the café with him.

"What do you know about the Consul of Siam?" he asked.

"Nothing much," I answered. "Why?"

"Ever had any dealings with him?"

"No," I said honestly, "none at all. I've met him, and heard him talk about his 'possibilities'; but I haven't tried them. Why do you ask?"

"Well, since it's you who tell me, I believe you," he said. "We're going to raid him tomorrow, and I wouldn't want you to have an *histoire.*"

"I don't see how I could have an *histoire,*" I said.

"Well," he said, "if you haven't had any dealings with him, you won't have this time. But I don't mind telling you they expect to find the evidence they've been looking for to get you with."

"Thanks for the tip," I said.

"*Pas de quoi.*"

We shook hands.

"*Alors, bon soir, et bonne chance,*" he said.

"*Bon soir,*" I said.

When he had gone I went back to the table and told Beamish what I had just learned. We decided we'd have to hurry.

Because we were certain our days were now definitely numbered, we redoubled our efforts to get people out. All those with the necessary visas and the willingness to go we sent down to F—— at Banyuls. On Fitch's insistence, we also sent the British into Spain. Fitch himself was among the first to go. He left another officer, an Irishman, Captain Treacy, of the R.A.F., in charge of evacuating the remaining men.

Treacy had made a forced landing in the occupied zone a few weeks before, and had got as far as Marseille, where he was hiding until the time came for him to go on to Spain himself. We used to see him in his room at night, talk over his plans, and, if we approved them, give him the money to carry them out. He generally sent his men down to the frontier in threes and fours, and, miraculously, never had an arrest that had serious consequences. But it was dangerous work, especially for us. Treacy and his men enjoyed the immunity of prisoners of war; we did not.

-3-

When it was announced that the Marshal would visit Marseille, Beamish decided to leave town.

"I always make it a practice to clear out when the head of a fascist state comes to town," he said. "I know from long experience what happens."

He went down to the frontier to look over some new routes, in case the "F" route should be discovered and closed. I stayed in Marseille.

The Marshal was due on a Tuesday. He was to spend the day in Marseille and then go on to Toulon to inspect the fleet, returning to Marseille the next day, on his way back to Vichy. I had arranged to work at Air-Bel that Monday morning, and Lena had agreed to come out and take dictation.

It was a crisp December day, and there was a heavy mist in our valley. The roofs of the houses and the tops of the umbrella pines emerged out of the feathery whiteness in receding planes of lighter and lighter gray, like the peaks of mountains in a Japanese print. You couldn't see the cemetery or the sea at all.

After breakfast Danny and Jean left for the office, and I went up to my room to work. By ten o'clock there was still no sign of Lena, and I was just about ready to give her up and go down to the office myself when she arrived.

"*Mille pardons*," she said, "but I have been arrested this morning, and that is why I am *tellement en retard*."

"Arrested?" I asked. "What do you mean?"

"*Oui*, arrested," she said. "There are enormous *râfles* going on in town. They came to the hotel early this morning and made us all go downstairs *en chemises de nuit*, and then they kept us there for hours while they looked over our papers. *Finalement* they let me go. But many they took away."

"What's the idea?" I asked.

"*C'est la visite du Maréchal*," she said.

"Oh," I said. "Well, it's bad for our protégés. We'll have to try and get them out this afternoon. Meanwhile, let's get to work."

I had finished the first letter and was beginning the second when someone tapped on the door.

Lena got up and opened the door. It was one of the maids.

"Excuse me, monsieur, but the police are downstairs," she said.

"*Mon dieu!* Have I got to go through that again?" Lena said. "*Il ne faut pas exagérer, quand même.*"

"Let's finish this letter before we go down," I said.

"*A votre service*," Lena said, picking up her notebook and pencil again.

We were just finishing the letter when Serge appeared in the door.

"The police insist that everyone in the house assemble in the grand hall at once," he said.

I gave a quick glance around the room. On the table was my address book, with the names and addresses of almost everyone I had met in France, and detailed records of all my illegal financial transactions. I knew that address books often interest the police more than anything else, so, with real pain, I threw it into the fire, and we stood there watching it burn. When it was burned to ashes we went downstairs together.

We found everybody else in the house already assembled in the entrance hall. Standing at the door, as though to bar our exit, was an enormous *commissaire*. Near him were three plainclothesmen. Everybody, including the *commissaire* and the plainclothesmen, looked very nervous.

"Well, is that all?" the *commissaire* asked, in a loud, bullying voice, addressing the housekeeper.

"Yes, sir, that's all," she answered, in her soft, superior-servant tone.

"*Alors, procédez*," the *commissaire* shouted, as though drunk.

"Proceed to what?" I asked.

"To search the house, of course," he yelled.

"May I ask," I said, "by what authority you expect to search this house?"

"We have the authority," he bellowed. "Don't you worry yourself about that."

"I should nevertheless like to see it," I said.

"Oh, so you want to make trouble, do you?" the *commissaire* sneered.

"Not at all," I said, growing extremely excited, and speaking the French words with exaggerated precision and very slowly. "But I wish to insist upon my rights, and the rights of my friends. We have nothing to hide, but we will not submit to a search unless you have written orders to conduct one."

Producing from an inner pocket a soiled and folded paper, the *commissaire* handed it to me with a flourish.

"*Voilà, monsieur*," he said, with mock courtesy.

I took the paper and unfolded it, and Serge and Lena looked over my shoulders as I read it.

It was a carbon copy of an order from the Prefect to the Chief of Police, authorizing him to search all premises "suspected of communist activity."

"This order does not apply to us," I said. "These premises are not suspected of communist activity. You have no right to search these premises. I refuse to permit you to do so."

"That's where you're wrong," the *commissaire* bawled.

"These premises are suspected of communist activity, and I intend to search the house from top to bottom."

"We protest and reserve all rights," I said, remembering the formula I had learned from one of our lawyers on a previous occasion.

"Tell it to the judge," the *commissaire* barked. "Proceed." He began diligently to pick his nose. From the corner where Breton was sitting I distinctly heard the word "*Formidable!*"

One of the plainclothesmen sat down at the small round table in the center of the room and produced a sheaf of *procès verbaux*, on which he began to write our names, using a separate paper for each individual or family group. While this was going on another plainclothesman took Serge upstairs to search his room. The rest of us waited. The *commissaire* and the third plainclothesman looked about the room, staring at the pictures on the walls, opening the drawer of the console table and pawing over the contents, or inspecting the meager supply of linen in the cupboard.

When the man who had gone upstairs with Serge came back again he was carrying a portable typewriter and a pearl-handled revolver. He showed them to the *commissaire*.

"*Eh ben!* Here's something already," the *commissaire* said, with evident pleasure. "Continue."

Breton was the next victim. He was led off to his room on the top floor.

Suddenly I remembered that among the books on the dresser in my room there was a false passport. Somehow I had to get up there again, alone, and get rid of it.

I decided to try the old trick. The nearest toilet was at the end of the corridor next to the door of my room. I asked to be allowed to use it. The *commissaire* hesitated. Then he assigned the unoccupied plainclothesman to accompany me upstairs.

On the way up I sounded out my guardian.

"Your boss seems a little rough," I said. "I wish he'd take it easy. He's got the women and children frightened almost out of their wits."

"I know," the man said. "He's always like that. A natural bully."

We had come to the door of the toilet. I went inside and closed the door. He waited outside.

How was I to get into my room without him? It would take only a few seconds to get rid of the passport once I was there, but I had to be alone. I decided to make a try at it. I pulled the chain, and when the water had stopped running I unlocked the door and came out again.

"I just have to get a handkerchief," I said. "I'll be right back."

Miraculously, he stayed where he was.

"All right," he said. "Take your time."

I went into the room. He did not follow me, and from where he was standing in the hall he couldn't see me.

I took the passport and threw it up onto the top of the wardrobe. There wasn't any time for anything else. Then I opened the bureau drawer and took out a clean handkerchief. I was blowing my nose with it when I came out of the room.

"All right now?" the man asked.

"Yes," I said. "Thanks."

When we got downstairs again Breton and his plainclothesman were already there, and there was a large service revolver on the table beside Serge's pearl-handled one.

The next to go was Mary Jayne. While she was upstairs Madame Nouguet, the housekeeper, asked and obtained permission to return to the kitchen with the maid to prepare bowls of hot "coffee" for everybody. The *commissaire* was in the dining room, with Serge and Breton, inspecting the china. The only person watching us was the detective at the center table.

I sat down next to Lena.

"Engage that guy in conversation," I whispered. "I want a chance to go through my pockets."

"*Entendu*," she said. "But when you finish, I want a chance to go through my pocketbook."

"All right," I said. "I'll do what I can."

She got up and walked over to the table in the center of the room.

"That's a nice suit you're wearing," she said. "In these days it's so hard to find anything to wear. Do you mind telling me where you bought it?"

The plainclothesman was obviously flattered. He beamed.

"You like it?" he asked.

"Oh, yes," she said, "it's beautiful. Such nice material, such good taste."

I was emptying my pockets into the fire in the tile stove.

"I have my own tailor," the plainclothesman confessed.

"You must be rich," Lena said.

He blushed. He was very blond, and his face was now very red.

"Oh, no," he said. "He's not really expensive at all."

"Won't you write out his name and address for me?" Lena said.

She was doing fine. I was almost through emptying my pockets.

The plainclothesman bent down over the table and began writing on a slip of paper.

I picked up a log and pushed it into the stove after the last of my papers.

"*Voilà, mademoiselle*," he said, handing Lena the address.

"Oh, thank you," Lena said. "You are so kind."

"*Pas du tout, mademoiselle, pas du tout*," the plainclothesman said, smiling from ear to ear.

Lena came back to her chair next to mine.

"Did you get enough time?" she whispered.

"Yes," I said. "Thanks a million. You did fine."

"*Maintenant*, it's your turn," she said.

I went up to the plainclothesman.

"How long do you think this will last?" I asked.

"I don't know," he said.

"What's he going to do?"

"I think he's going to take you all down to the *Evêché*."

"What for?"

"For control of your situations."

Out of the corner of my eye I could see Lena bending down to poke the fire.

"What does that mean?" I asked.

"Just an inquiry, an examination of your papers, and then if you are *en règle* you will be released."

"I hope so," I said. "I haven't got much time to waste. How will we get down?"

He got up from his chair and led me toward the window.

"Look," he said.

I looked. Parked in front of the house were a large police van and a smaller police car. Standing between them was a fifth detective.

"All that for us?" I asked.

"Yes," he said, "all that for you."

"We must be pretty important," I said.

Behind me, I could hear the door of the stove close.

"*Qu'est-ce qu'il y a?*" Lena asked, coming up behind us.

"We're just looking at the view," I said. "Have a look."

Lena looked.

"*Mon dieu!*" she said. "I hadn't seen those before. Are they for us?"

"Yes," I said. "They're for us."

Just then the *commissaire* came back from the dining room with a Surrealist drawing in his hand.

"What's going on here?" he yelled.

The plainclothesman hurried back to his place at the table. "Nothing," he said, nervously.

"Enter this," the *commissaire* said, handing him the drawing.

It was one of the things left over from the previous night's contest. It contained, among other things, a gallic cock. Beneath it someone had printed the words: "*Le terrible crétin de Pétain.*"

"Revolutionary propaganda," the *commissaire* snorted.

"But I insist," Breton was saying, "that the word is not Pétain but *putain*. It is a comment by a friend on a friend. It does not concern the Marshal."

"And the cock? The cock is France, isn't it?" the *commissaire* shouted.

"*C'est contestable*," Breton said weakly.

"Revolutionary propaganda, as clear as the nose on your face," the *commissaire* said. "Enter it."

The plainclothesman entered it.

"*Invraisemblable*," Breton said, returning to his chair with a shrug of resignation.

When it came my turn to go upstairs, the *commissaire* himself went up with me. He did not look on the top of the wardrobe, but he gathered up all the papers on my table, stuffed them into my briefcase, and carried them triumphantly downstairs again, along with my portable typewriter.

"Documents in foreign languages," he said to the plainclothesman who was acting as the recording secretary of the expedition. "Probably revolutionary propaganda. Enter them."

The plainclothesman entered them.

Just then there was a stir outside. The *commissaire* rushed out, followed by two of the plainclothesmen. Through the open door we could hear him shouting.

"Arrest them, I tell you, arrest them!" he yelled. "Don't let them get away!"

A moment later the policemen came in again, leading Danny and Jean by the arms. They had come back to the house for lunch and had walked into the trap.

By the time everybody had been taken upstairs to preside over the search of his room, it was nearly one o'clock. Madame Nouguet served "coffee" and dry bread.

"It's all there is," she apologized. Then, addressing the *commissaire*, she added pointedly, "As I was prevented from going to market, there is nothing in the house to eat, *monsieur*."

But the *commissaire* paid little attention. He was gathering up the typewriters, revolvers and documents and getting ready to take us all down to the *Evêché*. We protested that the children, at least, were a little young to be taken to the police station.

"It will only be for a short time," the *commissaire* said, suddenly changing his attitude. "You will all be back before nightfall. A mere formality."

But after some argument, he agreed to allow the children, their mothers and the servants to stay behind.

To me he adopted a tone which was almost pleading.

"There is absolutely nothing against you," he said. "No suspicion of any sort. But you would oblige me by accompanying the others, merely as a witness. You will be able to return to your work within an hour. I give you my word of honor that I will not detain you longer."

Won over by his politeness, and thinking I might be able to help the others if I went with them, I agreed to go.

-4-

As we were all being led out the door the *commissaire* remembered that he had left my briefcase on the table. He sent one of the plainclothesmen back for it. On the way to the van the man handed it to me. I still had it when we got to the *Evêché.*

There we were taken through the motorcycle garage and up a flight of stairs to a low-ceilinged room on the second floor which must once have been the sleeping room of the Bishop's stable boys. We sat at school desks, with many other prisoners, and from time to time more were brought in.

Lena and I used the opportunity to go through my papers again. They were all supremely innocent, except one. That was an autographed manuscript of Breton's he had given me to smuggle to the United States. While far from revolutionary, its comments on the defeat and the new government were not calculated to improve his situation or ours, and although it was not signed, its fine, even calligraphy, in bright-green ink, identified it unmistakably. We extracted it from the other papers, and Lena put it in her blouse. Then she asked to be allowed to go to *le petit endroit.* When she came back she was smiling.

"*Le chef d'oeuvre* exists no more," she said.

A few minutes later the *commissaire* who had arrested us came bounding into the room.

"What are you doing with that briefcase?" he shouted. "You have no right to have it."

"You forgot it at the house, and I thought you might want it," I said, handing it to him. "At your service, sir."

He scowled as he snatched it from me.

Toward the end of the afternoon we were called into the office one by one and asked to sign the freshly typewritten copies of our *procès verbaux*. As they consisted only of lists of what had been found in our rooms, we signed without protest.

At six o'clock a newspaper vendor came in, and we persuaded him to go down to a nearby *bistro* and buy us wine and sandwiches. It was the first time we had had anything to eat or drink since Madame Nouguet's "coffee."

By seven o'clock we had begun to grow restless and to say "*Quand même*" and "*Il ne faut pas exagérer.*" We asked the *gendarme* who was guarding us whether we couldn't see the *commissaire* and find out when he expected to release us, but the *gendarme* said the *commissaire* had gone for the day.

"He won't be back until tomorrow morning," he said.

By eight o'clock still nothing had happened, and we were all saying, "*Formidable!*" and "*Invraisemblable!*" and some of us were saying, "*Merde alors!*"

At nine o'clock we were led downstairs again and around a corner of the building to the small rear court, thence back into the building and upstairs to the large room of the *Brigade des Râfles*, where Chaminade and I had reported some weeks before. It was stuffed full of human beings now, among them some of our clients. Still more people were brought in from time to time. It was obvious that an enormous *râfle* was going on.

-5-

At eleven o'clock that night we were taken downstairs again and back to the small rear court, where we were loaded into an even larger van than the one which had come for us at the house.

I sat next to one of the detectives.

"Where are they taking us now?" I asked.

"I think they're taking you to a boat in the harbor," he said.

I have to admit that I began now to feel that sense of high indignation which Americans sometimes feel when they are not treated as superior beings in foreign lands.

"This is an outrage," I said. "I am an American citizen. I demand to be allowed to communicate with my Consul."

"I'm afraid there isn't a thing I can do about that," the detective said.

"What can I do, then?" I asked weakly.

"Nothing, I'm afraid," he said.

We were driving along the quays of the modern port now. After going what seemed an interminable distance, we turned down one of the docks and drew up alongside a ship, black and forbidding in the semi-darkness. Here we were ordered out of the van and immediately conducted up the ship's ladder to the main deck. Once we were on board, the detectives returned to the quay and drove off in the van.

We found ourselves in a dense and milling crowd of puzzled humanity. By inquiring, we learned that we were on the S. S. *Sinaïa*, along with some six hundred other prisoners, all as baffled as we. The *Sinaïa*, our fellow prisoners explained, was tied up at Mole G, Bassin Président Wilson.

"Tiens, Fry," Danny said, when he heard this, giving me a poke in the ribs, "*vive le Président Veelsson!*"

No one knew why we had been arrested or where we were to be taken. All they knew was that for women there were third-class cabins, and for men bunks in the hold. As there seemed no point in standing on the deck all night, we went to bed. We slept in our clothes, on burlap bags filled with straw, each with a single thin blanket for his only covering. As the hatch was uncovered, we could look up through the square opening at the stars above our bunks. In one corner of the hold a group of Spaniards were singing sad flamencos to the music of an out-of-tune guitar. It was very cold, and the dirt in the straw got under our clothes and made us itch.

In the morning we were told that in order to get food we had to form into groups of ten and elect a leader who would go to the galley for the whole group. We elected Breton our leader and he went off in the direction of the galley, coming back in half an hour with half a loaf of black bread and a large tin pail half-full of a light-brown liquid sweetened with saccharine.

For lunch we were given frozen beef, lentils, bread and wine; for dinner there was also soup. The beef, though hot on the outside, was still frozen in the center.

We devoted the day to trying to persuade someone in authority to let us communicate with the American Consulate, but the only person in authority we could find was the *gendarme* at the head of the ladder, and he told us that he had strict orders not to allow anyone on board to communicate with anyone on shore under any circumstances.

We also made the acquaintance of some of our fellow prisoners. We met three French businessmen who had come up from Nice to see the parade and had been arrested within an hour of taking a room on the front of the Hotel du Louvre et de la Paix, on the Canebière. We talked to two young Syrians who had successfully passed a police examination in a café and had then walked out to find a police van parked on the street.

"There are two places left," a detective had said. "Get in!"

And without any further ceremony of any sort they were driven off to the boat.

We also talked to an Englishman and his Egyptian-born brother who had had their papers examined in a restaurant and found satisfactory. Outside, on the street, they ran into another detective, who also asked to see their papers. They explained that they had just shown their papers to a colleague, but the detective shouted, "None of your lip! Get in the wagon!"—and drove them off without further ado. My two

English civilian friends, Graham and Lloyd, were also on the boat, their only mistake having apparently been to live in a room giving on the Quai des Belges, where the Marshal was scheduled to pass.

A man who said he was the correspondent of the *Basler Neueste Nachrichten* was also among us. He had been in a restaurant having dinner with his French girl friend when a detective came in and asked them to show their papers. His were in order, but she had no *carte d'identité*, so the detective said she would have to go to the police station for an investigation. At the police station, the girl was released, but the journalist was taken to the boat. He said he thought it was because in the excitement he was pushed to the wrong side of the room, where the suspects were. Once with them he was lost.

One of the most indignant of our fellow prisoners was a Paris banker who said he had been dragged from his dinner table in the dining room of the Hotel Noailles, where he had been entertaining friends. There were five French doctors. There had even been a Marseille surgeon on board, we were told, but he had been able to persuade the police that he had an emergency operation to perform and had been taken to his hospital, under guard, to perform it. He was expected back, people said, when the operation was over. There were Dutch and Danish businessmen well known in the city. Nor were Mary Jayne and I the only Americans on the *Sinaïa*; there were four others, as surprised and indignant as we.

In the afternoon of the second day, we were all ordered below, and, when we went down, we found that the cover had been put over the hatch and all the portholes closed. We supposed then that we were about to set sail for Africa and a Saharan concentration camp, but though we heard many whistles blowing in the harbor our boat didn't move. When after several hours we were allowed to go up on deck again we learned from a member of the crew that the Marshal had gone by in a coast-guard cutter while we were below.

Toward evening some boys from the town came to the ship's side to take orders for food. We wrote out a message to the

American Consul, wrapped it around a ten-franc piece and threw it overboard while the *gendarme* at the head of the ladder had his back turned. We decided that the chances were ten to one that the boy who picked it up would pocket the coin and throw the message away, but a few hours later a large package of sandwiches arrived for us, with the calling card of the American Consul-General inside. We were grateful for the sandwiches, though we would have preferred freedom.

On the third day we were still without any news of what was to become of us. We spent the day speculating on our fate and singing old French songs to while away the time. We had to sing when subjects for conversation were exhausted because we had nothing to read. The only person who had had the foresight to slip a book into his pocket before leaving the house was Serge. He knew from experience what the rest of us didn't—that "an hour or two" at a police station can easily stretch into weeks and months and even years in any dictatorial state. Unfortunately for him, the book was one of his own novels. After thumbing idly through it he presented it to me, with a dedication: "In memory of our common captivity on the *Sinaïa*, and in complete sympathy." It was a story based on his own experiences in the prisons of the Soviet Union. Although it was anything but cheerful I read it with rapt attention, wondering, as I read, whether my life was destined to resemble his.

### -6-

By the afternoon of the third day Mary Jayne and I had managed to send a note up to the captain and get back an invitation to call on him in his cabin. It was already a strange sensation to sit in chairs, after so many hours on wooden benches, the edges of iron bunks, and the rail of the ship. The captain was more than apologetic to his American prisoners, and seemed to be really distressed when I told him I had once crossed the Atlantic on his ship.

"I am sorry you should have had to see it again under such very different circumstances," he said.

After we had talked a little he ordered beer to be brought up.

"I regret that I cannot offer you anything better," he said, in tones of deep regret. "It is all that I have."

He explained that the Administration had hired his ship as a prison, and that he was in no way responsible for the choice of passengers. Nor had he any idea how long we would be held.

"That is out of my power to determine," he said.

As we were talking, a cabin boy came in and announced that Monsieur le Consul des Etats-Unis was waiting below. Much impressed, the captain instructed the boy to bring the Consul up at once.

When Harry Bingham walked through the door and shook hands with us, whatever doubts the captain may previously have had about us were immediately dissipated. His manner became perceptibly more cordial. He took out a key ring from his trousers' pocket and unlocked a cupboard, revealing a large collection of half-filled bottles. He selected a bottle of cognac and took down four small glasses.

"Voilà, messieurs, dame," he said, pouring us glasses of the brandy. "A votre santé."

As we drank, Harry told us that he had called up the Prefecture several times to find out why we were being held and for how long. But all the high officials were out with the Marshal, or busy protecting him, and he hadn't been able to get any information. He hoped to do better tomorrow, when the Marshal would be on his way back to Vichy and things would be returning to normal in Marseille. A great many people had been arrested in honor of the Marshal's visit, he said, at least seven thousand, and most of them would probably be released in a few days. Whether we would be released or not he couldn't say, but he would do his best to see that we were.

We went to bed that night still not knowing whether it would be our last night on the *Sinaïa*, but about ten o'clock the next morning some detectives arrived with fat *dossiers* under their arms, installed themselves in the first-class lounge, and began calling individuals by name from the eager crowd waiting on the third-class deck below.

Our group was called about noon, and by two o'clock in the afternoon we had all been released—all, that is, except Danny Bénédite, who, for some unknown reason, was still on the *Sinaïa* when the rest of us hit terra firma and started walking down the long quay toward the trolley-car line.

When we got to the center of the town, we found the streets still decorated with flags and bunting, and the street cleaners at work cleaning up the litter left behind by the crowds. Here and there members of Peyrouton's *Groupe de Protection*, familiarly known as the *Garde Pétain*, were still swaggering about, wearing on their arms white brassards with the letters G. P. on them.

After lunch Lena went off to see Captain Dubois about Danny, while Jean Gemahling and I dropped into the office and the others returned to the villa.

Jean and I found everything perfectly normal at the office. Contrary to our worst fears, it had not been closed. In fact, the police had never even gone near it, nor had they arrested any members of the staff, except those who lived at Air-Bel. Yet hardly a refugee had shown his face at the office after the word got about that we had been taken away.

Elsewhere there had been police action amounting literally to hysteria. Three more boats, four *casernes*, and three movie houses had been used, in addition to all the regular jails and prisons. At the last minute the police had even locked people into cafés and restaurants until the parade had passed. In all, twenty thousand had been arrested.

Whatever the explanation of our own arrests, it seemed clear that they had had nothing to do with the office. But we were afraid that, in attempting to justify what they had done, the police would turn to the office and its activities, would certainly search it again, and might even close it. We were also afraid that the story of our arrests, when it got about, would make our relations with the other American relief organizations and with French officials even more difficult than they already were. We felt no doubt at all that whatever hope we had previously had of somehow establishing friendly relations with the American Embassy were finished.

The problem was to know how to treat the episode. Should we insist on an official protest, and risk being rebuffed, either by the Embassy or by the Vichy police, or should we just shrug and laugh it off?

Madame Gruss was for laughing it off.

"*Il faut tourner ça à la rigolade,*" she said.

Lena came in with Bénédite while we were still discussing it. She had found Dubois in his office on the promenade de la Plage. He seemed surprised and annoyed to learn that we had been in trouble and asked rather irritably why we hadn't let him know at once, so he could have us released. When Lena explained that we couldn't even get permission to send a message to the Consulate, he swore.

"*Que ces gars là sont bêtes!*" he said. "How stupid those guys are!"

Dubois drove Lena back to the *Sinaïa* in his police car. On the way he asked her about Charlie.

Lena explained that he had left for Lisbon.

"I'm glad to hear that," Dubois said. "I was about to have the painful duty of arresting him for pro-British activities."

Lena denied that Charlie had had any pro-British activities, but Dubois paid no attention.

"I know all about it," he said.

Lena asked him if it was Lili who had told him.

"Maybe it was and maybe it wasn't," Dubois said.

When they got to the boat, Dubois showed his badge and he and Lena went up the ladder together. Bénédite was free a few minutes later.

# X. The Kidnapping at Cannes

FOR two weeks after the *Sinaïa* affair I was followed by a group of eight dicks, working in shifts. I know, because Captain Dubois told me. The *filature* was being done by the *Commissariat Spécial* at the Prefecture, he said, on direct orders of the *Sûreté Nationale* at Vichy.

Thanks to the tipoff, I saw to it that the *flics'* daily reports were wholly innocuous and, after a couple of weeks, the *Sûreté* apparently got tired of learning where I had lunch and dinner every day and called the whole thing off. But as long as it lasted it was uncomfortable enough, and I had to be very careful what I did and whom I saw.

As soon as I learned I was being followed, I warned everybody to be extremely careful.

Mary Jayne was made so apprehensive that she kept looking back over her shoulder all the rest of the day, with the result that by the end of the afternoon three different Frenchmen really had followed her considerable distances.

One day toward the middle of the month, two plainclothesmen came into my office, showing their badges. When I asked them what they wanted, they said they were looking for "*un nommé Hermant.*" Fortunately Beamish was still out of town, so I told them he had resigned his job several weeks before. When I asked them why they were interested in him, they said there were some serious charges against him.

"Probably a dirty de Gaullist," one of the plainclothesmen said. "If you see him again, let us know."

I solemnly promised I would.

When Beamish got back to Marseille, I told him the story, and he decided the time had come for him to leave France. We took a sad leave of one another, and he set off to see F—— at Banyuls. A few days later I learned that he had reached Lisbon safely.

I felt peculiarly lonely after he left. I suddenly realized how completely I had come to rely on him, not only for solutions to the most difficult problems, but also for companionship. For he was the only person in France who knew exactly what I was doing, and why, and was therefore the only one with whom I could always be at ease. With everyone else I had to pretend, sometimes more, sometimes less; with Beamish and Beamish alone I could be perfectly candid and natural. After he left I was completely alone, and I felt my solitude as I had never felt it before.

A few days before he went, I decided to divide his work between Jean Gemahling and Dr. Marcel Verzeanu ("Maurice"). One night after dinner at the Villa Air-Bel I called Jean up to my room and told him what I had been doing for the British. Jean had always seemed more or less listless and indifferent about his work at the office, but I knew that he was strongly pro-British and utterly disgusted with the goings-on at Vichy. But I wasn't prepared for the strength of the reaction I got to my revelation. Jean's face lighted up as though I had just told him he had inherited a million dollars, and he looked at me as though I were a combination of General de Gaulle and his best girl friend. When I asked him whether he was willing to run the risk of working with me for the British, he blushed furiously and gave a kind of gasp.

"Willing!" he said, in his slightly French version of an English public schoolboy's accent. "There's nothing in the *world* I'd rather do!"

He told me then that ever since the armistice he had been looking for a way to get to England and join de Gaulle. But if he could help the British in France, he said, he would stay.

I told him how great the risks were—the maximum penalty was death—but it didn't faze him at all.

"I might as well be hanged for a sheep as a lamb," he said.

The next day I introduced Jean to Treacy, and he continued to work with the British as long as we had anything to do for them. His enthusiasm never lagged, but he took his duties so seriously that whenever he thought he had made a mistake he went into a depression, and I had difficulty restoring his self-confidence. He was my first introduction to the type of young French patriot of whom the underground and the maquis were later formed. In the course of his work for the British he also had a good deal to do with helping refugees escape, and he always performed his work with a conscientiousness that was almost excessive.

Maurice, our Rumanian doctor, had already had something to do with the illegal departure of refugees even before Beamish left, but afterward he took charge of it. He established relations with F—— at the frontier, and later with his successor, S——. He organized a whole network of underground workers—the "invisible staff," as we called it—managed the secret funds, found new hiding places, directed the movement of refugees from one place to another, and provided them with false passports and visas. When everything else failed, he worked closely with Emilio Lussu in building up an underground railroad all the way to Lisbon. He fancied himself as quite a dog with the ladies, and, superficially, he often seemed to take his work rather lightly. But I soon discovered that the impression was a false one.

-2-

Shortly after Beamish left, I received a letter from Charlie. He had finally arrived in Lisbon. In his letter he talked about trying to be admitted to an art school at the Prado.

"I had difficulty getting my work accepted because I had been a pupil of Buster's," he wrote. ("Buster" was one of my innumerable pseudonyms.) "The chief objections to my entering the school seemed to come from those who thought of composition and color in the manner of the German painters. The latter school seemed to be well represented among the students and professors. . . . However, my sculpture stood up under the test quite favorably. . . . Thank goodness, they didn't drop the matter. You know how fragile my background was."

It wasn't until I got back to the States that I found out exactly what he meant. After a good deal of effort, I finally located Charlie in a hospital in Colorado, where he had been sent for a bad case of t.b. He had gone to England and had tried to join the R.A.F., but when he learned he was sick he had to give up the idea of flying and go home. We exchanged a few letters, and he told me what had happened to him in Spain. First he had been questioned at the French side of the border. Among his questioners he had noticed a young man who had twice come to the office at the rue Grignan to apply for a job on the staff. The French police wanted to know all about our activities, where we got our money, and whether we received mail through the diplomatic pouch. As Charlie apparently gave satisfactory answers, they let him go across the border into Spain.

There he was questioned again, and then allowed to proceed to Barcelona. In Barcelona he went to the American Consulate. As he left the building, he was arrested, put on a train and escorted to Biarritz, in the occupied zone of France. There he was questioned at length by Gestapo officials. But as they didn't speak English, and he didn't speak German, the questioning wasn't very fruitful. After several hours of it, the Gestapo men left him sitting in a waiting room, alone. Being Charlie, he simply got up and stepped onto a train bound for Spain. He walked through the cars to the end, and, as the train gathered momentum, hopped off and stayed out of sight until the next train, which took him to Madrid. From there he was able to go on to Lisbon without further trouble. Somehow he managed to bring his suitcase, cornet and sculptured heads through without mishap, and all his messages reached New York safely.

-3-

For some time the committee in New York had been cabling me that my successor was on his way. One day in mid-December, I found a mysterious message at the office, asking me to be at the Splendide on a certain day and hour, to meet a "friend" at the bar. When I walked in, there was Jay Allen, the American journalist, sitting in a chair with a big glass of Scotch and soda in front of him (he must have brought the Scotch from Lisbon, for Marseille's supply had long since run out), talking to an American woman of more than middle years whom he introduced as Margaret Palmer. He had come to France via Casablanca, to avoid passing through Spain, where his newspaper activities during the Civil War would make him unpopular with Franco, he said. On the way he had managed to get an interview with General Weygand, and he was planning to go up to Vichy and have a try at interviewing the Marshal. He explained that he was representing the North American Newspaper Alliance, but expected to be able to do my job in his spare time. He hoped his journalist's credentials would be a sufficient cover to spare him the police attention I had drawn. In order to avoid showing any direct connection with my office, Jay had decided to put Miss Palmer at my desk as his "alter ego," keeping in touch through her with what was going on and issuing his instructions to the staff through her. He didn't want to meet the staff himself, or even have them know he had any interest in the work.

It was an ingenious idea, but I was a little skeptical about Jay's ability to carry my job in his spare time. I also suspected that journalists were likely to be even more closely watched than relief workers, most of whom the police considered ultra-naive and, therefore, presumably harmless. But we agreed to try it. I would stay until Miss Palmer had learned the job, and then, if everything seemed to be working smoothly, I would turn the office over to her and go. But I was very doubtful that the arrangement would ever be satisfactory to Jean and Maurice.

A few days later Miss Palmer moved into my private office

on the rue Grignan. During the day we worked together over the cases. I told her about everything I had done, legally and illegally, introduced her to all my methods and warned her against ill-considered efforts to get large numbers of refugees away by boat. Every night she went back to the Splendide and reported to Jay on what she had learned during the day. I don't know how much he was able to take in in this roundabout way, but it can't have been much; besides the obvious difficulty of absorbing information second-hand, he was often busy with his newspaper work, and often out of town.

But what troubled me most was the extreme difficulty of getting the "invisible staff" to accept the new order. It would have been hard enough to get them to accept the leadership of an elderly woman if she was making all the decisions herself. But when they began to suspect that she was only the transmission belt for decisions taken by somebody they had never seen, it became well-nigh impossible. For a couple of months I tried to make the new arrangement work, and, if I didn't succeed, I can't feel, even today, that it was entirely my fault.

-4-

Laval's arrest in mid-December started a whole new crop of rumors. On Marshal Pétain's order he was seized by the police at the end of a Cabinet meeting and taken to his house, where he was held under guard. The morning the news broke, there were excited groups on the streets of Marseille, and, for the first time since the Vichy government began censoring them, the newspapers actually sold out. People said that the Germans were going to occupy the unoccupied zone, and some even claimed to know that they had already marched over the demarcation line. It was also rumored that the Marshal had taken a plane to Africa, and that Laval had gone to Paris to set up a new government which would declare war on England. These rumors, of course, proved false, but the rumor that Marseille would be occupied by the Germans on the first of January persisted. We sensed lightning in the air and we knew that whatever happened things were not likely to grow better for the refugees and the French who had refused to accept the policy of collaboration.

A few days after Laval's arrest, Largo Caballero, the exiled Prime Minister of Republican Spain, was taken into custody by the French police. Madrid, we learned, had trumped up charges of grand larceny and murder against him and had asked for his extradition. Vichy had obligingly ordered his arrest and was holding him for a hearing on the extradition demand before the *Cour d'Assises* at Aix-en-Provence. Now not only the Germans and the Austrians and the Italians but also the Spaniards were in imminent danger of their lives in France, and our responsibilities increased accordingly.

Then there was the Niemeyer affair. Niemeyer was a young "Aryan" German art student who had won a scholarship at the New School for Social Research and wanted to go to New York to take it. He had an American visa, but, like nearly everybody else, he couldn't get an exit visa. Rather than leave without one, as we advised him to, or wait any longer for the impotent French to act, he thought he would be clever and go to the source of power. He took the trolley car to Aix to ask the Gestapo commission there for permission to leave France. Instead of giving him an exit visa, the commission arrested him for failing to report for military service and sent him back to Germany for trial. His girl came to the office the next day and told us what had happened. It was our first extradition.

All in all, it still seemed a good idea for people to get out if they could, by any way they could. But not everybody shared our views, and among the most stubborn stayers-on were some of the most important people on our lists: André Gide, Henri Matisse, Alfred Neumann, Theodore Wolff, all of them living in or near Nice.

Shortly before Christmas, Maurice, Miss Palmer and I went to Nice. We found the Rumanian historian, Valeriu Marcu, waiting for us at the station, and we all rode to his villa in a taxi which he had somehow managed to corral. There we feasted on unbelievable things: cheese and sausage and real coffee, all saved from the good old days before the defeat, or acquired since by means known to Marcu alone. We talked about the defeat and the Vichy regime and the refugees until two or three in the morning, when the rest of us went to bed, and Marcu began his nocturnal writing.

The next day, on our way to town, we ran into André Malraux on the back of a street car. He said that he had just escaped from a German prison camp and was beginning a book on his experiences in a tank corps during the battle of France. He did not want to leave.

We found Neumann, the German novelist, as determined as ever to wait for his exit visa, which he somehow seemed sure he would get.

Theodore Wolff, who had once been the much-feared editor of the *Berliner Tageblatt*, was unable to make up his mind to abandon his books and pictures and apartment on the promenade des Anglais, even to save his life. Nearly three years later Theodore Wolff was reported to have died in the Jewish Hospital in Berlin, after undergoing ill treatment in the concentration camps at Dachau and Oranienburg. He was seventy-five years old at the time of his death. Matisse, too, rejected out of hand the idea of traveling. He said he was very comfortable in his apartment in the Hotel Regina at Cimiez and saw no reason why, as a Frenchman, he should have to think of going. With all his genius, he was the successful *bourgeois* at heart, happy in the comfort he had surrounded himself with and proud of his collections of African masks and sculpture, plants and tropical birds. We did all we could to persuade him to leave them, arguing that though he might not be in any personal danger, even as the *doyen* of that "degenerate" art the Nazis profess to despise so heartily, he was nevertheless in real danger of starving to death before the war was over. But he refused to be persuaded.

-5-

André Gide was staying in Cabris, above Grasse, a town high in the mountains back of Cannes. To get there we had to take a bus, and in Pétain's France all the buses ran by *gazogène*. *Gazogène* is a method of producing a more or less

explosive mixture by burning wood or charcoal in a huge
cooker attached to the back of the bus or carried as a trailer.
The gas produced by the slow combustion of the fuel is
cooled and purified by passing it through water and is then fed
to the cylinders, where it is supposed to explode. Sometimes
it does and sometimes it doesn't; and even when it does, it
produces far less power than gasoline. But there is one thing
you can almost always be sure of, and that is that somewhere
en route there will be a breakdown.

Ours occurred on the side of a steep hill a few kilometers
before Grasse. The driver and the conductor got out and
raked the cinders out of the cooker and took a quantity of
sticky black tar out of the cooler and then painstakingly
rebuilt the fire, while the passengers stood around and gaped,
or walked idly up and down the road. Even when the fire
was burning again in the cooker, it was quite a while before
the explosive mixture it produced would provide enough
power to start the bus on the hill. When it finally did, the
driver was obviously afraid to stop for fear he would never
get started again, so we passengers had to follow along on
foot until the bus had reached a level stretch where it could
safely stop and wait until we had caught up with it.

But with all its disadvantages, there is one charming thing
about the gazogène system: instead of being filled with the
acrid, eye-smarting and more or less asphyxiating fumes of
incompletely burned gasoline, a bus driven by gazogène smells
like a room heated by a roaring wood fire. You can lie back
and close your eyes and breathe in the sweet perfume of the
wood and imagine yourself hearing it crackle in a hearth
before your feet. For that I am willing to forgive gazogène
much.

We found Gide waiting for us. He took us into his study
and we had tea and dry biscuits and talked for an hour
and a half. He had caught a cold, and was wearing a sweater
and a thick tweed coat and had a heavy wool scarf around his
neck. Dressed so, and wearing his thick tortoiseshell glasses,

he seemed more like a benevolent grandfather than the author of the *Symphonie Pastorale* and the *Faux-Monnayeurs*. But there was a fineness in the quality of his face and hands and a warmth and eagerness in his speech and gestures which stamped him as no ordinary mortal, and one could see in the man of seventy the youth of *Si le Grain ne Meurt* living still.

Partly because of the cold, perhaps, but certainly mostly because of the fate of France, which greatly distressed him, he seemed depressed. Almost apologetically he said he hadn't been able to write anything but his *Journal* since the defeat. Most of the time he spent re-reading Dickens. He told us that the Germans had been making determined efforts to cajole him into becoming a collaborationist, using flattery and soft gloves instead of threats and the mailed fist, but that he had refused and always would refuse. He showed us the list of books which the Germans had obliged French publishers to withdraw from circulation shortly after they entered Paris. Gide pointed out that not one of his books was included, though practically everything of writers like Georges Bernanos and André Malraux was. He interpreted that to mean that the Germans had long realized his position as dean of French letters and had planned all along to win him over if it was at all possible to do so. That fact alone seemed to make Gide the more determined to reject all the Nazis' advances.

But though he refused to consider collaboration, and fully realized the possible consequences of his decision, he also refused to leave France. Like many other non-collaborationist Frenchmen, he felt that his place was in France, and in France he was determined to stay. He thanked us for all we had done and would do for other writers, and readily agreed to become a member of the *comité de patronage* we had decided to set up as a further protection against the police; but he flatly refused to let us persuade him to become one of our "clients." The best we could do was to get him to agree to report to us immediately if he had any serious trouble with the authorities, French or German.

-6-

On the way back to Nice it began to snow, and when we got to Marcu's there was a light fall under the orange trees and rose bushes.

Marcu greeted us with the news that something had happened to Fritz Thyssen, the German industrialist who had long backed Hitler, only to turn against him at the outbreak of the war. The *Petit Niçois* had printed a little piece from Vichy saying that a spokesman at the Ministry of the Interior had denied that Mr. and Mrs. Thyssen had been arrested at Cannes.

"If Mr. and Mrs. Thyssen have been obliged to report to the local police station," the spokesman was quoted as saying, "it can only have been for the periodic control required of all foreigners."

"If I know anything about fascist journalism," Marcu said, "that means they have been arrested. Why don't you stop off at Cannes on your way back to Marseille and find out?"

By the time I got to Cannes, night had already fallen. It was Christmas eve. I checked my suitcase at the station and walked down dimly lighted streets to the Carlton, where Thyssen and his wife had been living. But at the Carlton they told me that the Thyssens had moved to the Hotel Montfleury, on the hill back of the town, so I retraced my steps to the station, crossed the tracks, and climbed the hill.

The Hotel Montfleury stands in a park of palms and pines, and from the gravel terrace in front of it you can get a magnificent view of the town below and the bay and mountains beyond. There was a dim light burning under the *porte-cochère* when I went into the lobby and asked for Mr. Thyssen at the desk.

"Mr. Thyssen has left. Are you a friend of his, sir?" the concierge said.

I said I was an American journalist who wanted to interview him.

"Then you haven't heard the news?" the man asked, raising his eyebrows phenomenally.

"What news?" I asked, playing innocent.

"If you haven't heard, I'm afraid I can't tell you," the concierge said, solemnly. "You'd better talk to the boss."

As soon as he had telephoned upstairs for the boss, I moved toward the entrance door.

"I'll wait outside," I said.

"Bien, monsieur," the concierge said.

Outside, the doorman was more communicative. He said that on Friday morning at seven o'clock five plainclothesmen had come to the hotel in two automobiles bearing Vichy license-plates and demanded to be shown up to the Thyssens' suite immediately. As Mr. and Mrs. Thyssen were not in the habit of coming downstairs until eleven o'clock, the manager refused to allow them to be disturbed at that hour, or even to tell the plainclothesmen the numbers of their rooms, and the men had to wait. As soon as the Thyssens came downstairs, however, about eleven o'clock, the plainclothesmen placed them under arrest, ordered them to pack a few clothes in two small suitcases, and drove them off in the cars, in the direction of Vichy.

"They wouldn't even let them have lunch before they left," the doorman said, "so the boss had box lunches prepared and we put them in the cars with the suitcases."

"Where do you think they were taking them?" I asked.

"To Vichy and the Boches," he said.

Just then the concierge called me inside.

"The boss is waiting for you in the office," he said.

The "boss" was short and fat and very bourgeois. Very pleasantly, unctuously even, he asked me what he could do for me. I think he must have expected me to ask the price of a suite of rooms. When I told him I had come to find out about the Thyssens, his whole manner changed abruptly.

"I regret," he said coldly, "that I can give you no information whatever about that. I have given my word of honor not to speak of it to anyone."

"To whom did you give your word of honor?" I asked.

"To the agents who arrested them," he said.

"The local agents?" I asked.

"No, agents from Vichy," he said. "The local police knew nothing about the affair."

"Oh," I said, "then it's true that they came all the way down from Vichy to get them?"

"I can say nothing, absolutely nothing," the owner said, irritated at having been trapped into admitting even that much. "I tell you I have given my word of honor not to speak about it."

"But this is important," I said. "Don't you realize that lives may be at stake?"

"I realize only," he said, "that I have given my word of honor not to talk, and I intend to keep it."

"Don't you realize," I said, "that there is a higher honor than your word to the police, the honor of France?"

"Come, come," he said, officiously, "you are an agreeable young man. Come to my bar and have as many drinks as you like at my expense. Be my guest at dinner. Spend the night in my hotel if you please. You are very welcome. But don't ask me any questions about Mr. and Mrs. Thyssen. I can't answer them."

"I have not come for free drinks or a meal," I said, righteously. "I have come to find out what became of the Thyssens."

"That," he said, growing visibly excited, "you will never learn from me. Now get out. Get out of my hotel, I tell you, before I throw you out."

He was advancing toward me menacingly.

"By refusing to talk you are doing the work of the Nazis," I said.

"Don't you dare come here and tell me what to do and what not to do," he shouted. "Why don't you go back where you came from, anyway, and leave us French alone? If we want to collaborate with the Germans we will collaborate with the Germans, and nothing you pigs of Americans say will influence us in the slightest. Now get out, I tell you! Get out!"

I got out.

While waiting for my train. I went to a café and wrote a report of what I had learned and mailed it to Archambault at the *New York Times* office at Vichy.

When I got back to Marseille I found the city under a blanket of wet slush. But, in spite of the cold and the damp, an old woman was selling tracts on the corner of the boulevard Dugommier-Garibaldi and the Canebière.

"Lisez 'La fin du monde,' " she kept crying. "Read 'The End of the World.' "

## XI. *Delivery to Death*

FOR us and our work it really looked like the end of the world. Not that Fritz Thyssen and his wife were people I was likely to waste any sympathy on. No, it wasn't so much of the Thyssens I was thinking that night as it was of the others who would now soon be following them on the long road north. Here, for the first time, we had a verified case of an extradition by the French police, without prior warning to the victims, and with every precaution to catch them unawares and spirit them off with a minimum of publicity. It was virtually an official kidnapping.

I passed a restless night wondering where the Gestapo would strike next, and how we could possibly get the rest of our people out before they too were caught and carried off to

Germany. I think I must have had nightmares all night, for I remember waking up again and again with my heart pounding in my chest and the sound of a knock at the door ringing in my ears. But when I went to the door, still trembling with the fear of the dream, there was no one there.

-2-

Christmas and the days immediately following I spent trying to find ways of getting large numbers of the refugees out of France without waiting any longer for United States or other overseas visas. Treacy was getting ready to leave and had already appointed Captain Murphy his successor.

The first time I met Murphy, he was dressed in a leather jacket and was standing in a dimly lighted corner of Treacy's narrow room on the top floor of the Hotel Nautique. Jean Gemahling and I had gone up together to see him. Treacy was in bed with a bad case of the mumps, and we all kept a safe distance from him—all, that is, except his girl friend, who was nursing him. But Murphy behaved as though it were just as important for him to keep a safe distance from us.

Perhaps it was his experiences with the Germans which accounted for Murphy's extreme caution in the first days of our acquaintance. Not only would he not go in or out of the hotel with me (which was wise), but he wouldn't even come out of his dark corner, as though my seeing his features would somehow endanger him, or me. But he had a conspiratorial air which I didn't like; it was altogether too melodramatic. Later it gave place to a lack of caution which was even more dangerous.

Unlike Treacy, Murphy felt that even a few weeks in a Spanish concentration camp was more than the British soldiers ought to be asked to endure. He wanted, if possible, to find ways of sending them to Africa and the Near East, whence they could somehow make their way to Gibraltar by sea or to Palestine or Egypt overland.

After Treacy left—he went through Spain to Lisbon and

was killed in a crack-up a few days after getting back to England—Murphy, Jean and I used to meet late at night in a
back room of the Sept Petits Pêcheurs. Jean and I would go
there for dinner and linger on until all the other guests had
left. Then Jacques would let down the iron shutters and
lock them. Presently Murphy would come in by the back door,
and we would all sit down with Jacques at a stone-top table
and talk. Jacques invariably drank bicarbonate of soda; the
rest of us drank cognac.

Jacques' smuggling had made him thoroughly familiar with
the port and its ways. He knew most of the dock workers and
at least some of the members of the crew of every ship, and
he said it would be an easy matter for him to smuggle refugees
and British soldiers onto ships bound for Beyrouth, Algiers,
Oran and Casablanca, and off again when the ships arrived at
their destinations. For each passenger he wanted from 3,000
to 8,000 francs, depending on the length of the voyage and
the risks involved.

We used the British for guinea pigs first because they ran
smaller risks than most refugees. At worst, they could only
be interned for the duration of the war, whereas the refugees
could be tortured and killed, and no one would have the right
even to complain. We sent the British all over the Mediterranean: to Syria, North Africa, Gibraltar, Rabat and Casablanca; even, I think, to Dakar. Those who got to Gibraltar
jumped off the French ships as they passed the Rock and
swam ashore; but most went on to the French ports, and most,
I am afraid, were arrested there. At least they were released
when the American troops invaded North and West Africa;
if they had stayed in Marseille they would have been taken to
Germany.

From the experience gained with the British, it was evident
that Jacques could perform what he promised. There was
never a slip in Marseille, and never, unless I am greatly mistaken, a slip at the other end either—so far as getting off the
ships was concerned. What we lacked was organization in the
ports of destination. When the British were arrested, it was

because they had nowhere to go when they left the ships. Although Jacques always provided them with crew cards and clothes, he could not provide hiding places in cities other than Marseille. For the British this was unfortunate, but it did not matter so much to the refugees. We could give them false identity cards and, since most of them could speak some French, they ran little risk of being arrested once they arrived. To give the British false identity cards would have been to court double disaster—for them and for us.

-3-

One of our principal difficulties came from the fact that we still had no way of knowing who was really in danger. Georg Bernhard was the only person in France we definitely knew to be wanted by the Gestapo. I urged him to go to Africa, but he refused to go without his wife. When I asked Jacques if he could take care of a woman, he served himself a glass of bicarbonate of soda and said that he had no way of smuggling a woman on board one of the cargo ships, and didn't want to have anything to do with women anyway; they always caused trouble. So the Bernhards had to wait in their *hôtel de passe* until I found some other way of getting them out of France.

If we had been almost completely in the dark before, the arrest of Largo Caballero and the extradition of Mr. and Mrs. Thyssen gave us some basis for evaluating relative danger. It looked as though Berlin and Madrid were determined to strike from the top and get their hands on the leaders of their exiled nationals.

The problem then was to see who were the next most prominent Germans after the Thyssens. The answer was Rudolph Breitscheid and Rudolph Hilferding. Both of them were still living in *résidence forcée* in the Hotel Forum at Arles.

But saving Breitscheid and Hilferding was bound to be extremely difficult, even if they were willing. In the first place, both men were very well known; and, in their different ways, they were rather conspicuous. With his height and snow-white hair, Breitscheid would stand out in any crowd; and Hilferding, though shorter and less striking-looking, would also risk being recognized by the average German, Gestapo agent or otherwise. Yet if we could get them to Marseille, we could disguise them with makeup and hair dye and put them on one of the cargo ships to Africa. The real problem was to get them out of Arles without attracting the attention of the police, and onto a ship and away before they were missed and the alarm was spread.

Obviously, they couldn't travel on a train, and the only available automobiles belonged either to the French police or to members of the German and Italian armistice commissions. No taxi was allowed outside the city limits, and most of the few private cars allowed to pass the *octroi* belonged to manufacturers who were collaborationists.

But when I took the problem to Jacques, he said it was easy. One of his gangster friends had a big limousine licensed for driving in the Bouches-du-Rhône and neighboring departments any time of the day or night, seven days a week. This was an unheard-of privilege. Even the busiest Marseille manufacturer could drive his car only on alternate weekdays, and then only during the daylight hours. But Jacques showed me the *carte grise* and *permis de circulation*, and what he said proved to be perfectly true.

-4-

The next problem was to find a place to hide the men in case something went wrong at the last minute and they weren't able to get on the ship. For hiding places in Marseille I also consulted Jacques, and again Jacques had a solution.

One night after dark, one of his men led me down a narrow street of the Vieux Port district until we came to a small opening in the façade of a house. We entered the opening and went through a long low tunnel between two buildings.

Coming out in a back alley, we crossed it and went through a door of the rear building, walked down a long, dimly lighted corridor, up two flights of stairs, returned half the distance we had come in the corridor below, went down another half flight of stairs and followed another corridor at right angles to the first. Then, when we were in a building far removed from the one we had first entered, we stopped before an obscure door and the man gave a special knock. After a few moments a small round hole opened and an eye looked out at us. The man gave the password and the door opened.

Inside, there was a large room full of boxes and bundles piled from floor to ceiling, as in a warehouse. We entered the room and the door closed behind us; another man came forward and the two men had a whispered conversation. The second man then took us to a room in the far corner, already half-hidden by boxes. It was a small room with a dirty double bed and no window. After looking it over, we went out into the larger room again and the second man showed us how, if necessary, the whole corner could be hidden by piling up the merchandise outside to make it look like a corner solidly filled with boxes.

-5-

When everything was ready, Heine sent word of our plans to Arles and, to our great relief, he got word that the two men were willing to take the risk. We had false identity cards made for them which turned them into Alsatians, so they could safely register at hotels in Algeria, and we arranged a place and time for the car to meet them on a night when a cargo ship was leaving for Oran.

I had dinner at Jacques' restaurant that night and sat late at my table afterward waiting for news. To my annoyance, Dimitru, the little Russian money changer, was there when Murphy came in by the back door. It was obvious that Murphy had a rendezvous with him, for he went straight over to Dimitru's table, shook hands with him and then brought him over to my table and asked me if I knew him. Dimitru gave me his Mazda-light smile and his empty-glove hand and we all sat down and had a drink.

I tried to confine the conversation to banalities, but after he had had several cognacs, Murphy began to talk about the British soldiers we were smuggling on the ship to Oran that night. I pretended not to have the slightest idea what he was talking about, and he soon shut up.

Later, when he went into the washroom, I followed him and told him I thought he was a fool to talk before strangers.

"Don't you worry about little Boris," Murphy said. "He's all right."

By eleven o'clock he had reached the limerick stage.

"D'you know the one about the young girl from Mauritius?" he asked.

"No."

*"There was a young girl from Mauritius*
*Who said, I think . . ."*

Just then the driver of the gangster's car appeared in the doorway. He was obviously furious.

*"——delicious,"* Murphy went on.

*"But if you don't mind . . ."*

The driver advanced toward the zinc.

*"I'll put off this——"*

Jacques, who was sitting behind the cash register, looked up from his account books.

*"Those spots——"* Murphy continued.

I pretended not to be interested in anything but the limerick.

*"——look suspicious,"* Murphy concluded, triumphantly, and Dimitru and I both laughed.

"*Allez!* What's up?" Jacques asked.

"They've changed their minds," I could hear the driver answer.

"What?" Jacques asked, incredulous.

Murphy was starting on another limerick.

"They don't want to leave," the driver said.

"What do you mean, they don't want to leave?" Jacques asked.

The driver shrugged.

"*C'est à se les prendre et à se les mordre,*" he said. "Here I go all the way out to Arles to get two men who are supposed to be in danger of their lives, and when I get there they tell me they've changed their minds and don't want to leave after all! *Je me fous de ces gars-là! C'est des couillons!*"

Murphy had just finished his second limerick, and I had to laugh again. Over my left shoulder I could see Jacques stirring himself a bicarbonate of soda. He said nothing at all.

-6-

We didn't have to wait long for the explanation. Heine received it by mail the next day. We knew that Breitscheid and Hilferding had for some time been making efforts to obtain exit visas through friends in the United States. In his letter from Arles, Hilferding wrote that he had just had a cable from America saying that the exit visas had been granted.

I was extremely skeptical about this piece of news, and strongly inclined to deprecate it. I had sent nearly 350 human beings out of France by that time, most of them without any exit visas at all, and not one with an exit visa which would stand up under careful scrutiny, and I had come to think of illegal emigration as the normal, if not the only way to go.

But I was just a simple American, with only as much authority as my moderate success at arranging escapes had given me, whereas Breitscheid and Hilferding thought of themselves as great statesmen, and were unaccustomed to taking orders from anybody, and not very favorably disposed to accept even polite suggestions, at least when they came from me.

Thus, although I asked Heine to tell them I thought they were unwise to pursue the chimera of exit visas any longer, my advice was not taken. Instead, the two men now dropped all thought of leaving France illegally and began to devote all their attention to getting legal permission to go.

As soon as Hilferding got the cable from America, Breitscheid called on the Sub-Prefect of Arles and asked him whether he thought it would be safe for them to make formal applications for exit visas, and whether the applications would be submitted to the German authorities if they did. The Sub-Prefect said he couldn't answer the question himself but would make inquiries at Vichy.

Two days later he told Breitscheid that there would be no danger at all. Later the same day he appeared at the hotel in a pouring rainstorm and announced that it was no longer necessary for them even to apply for the exit visas: he had just had a telegram from Vichy saying that the visas had been authorized. All they had to do now was to go to the Prefecture at Marseille and pick them up.

About the time this was happening, Heinz Oppenheimer was working a *combine* of his own in Aix and Marseille. One day—it was the 22nd or 23rd of January, I think— he appeared at the office and created a small sensation by announcing rather mysteriously that he had just received exit visas for himself and his family. They were all leaving for Martinique on the *Winnipeg* on the 24th, he said.

This was the first we had heard of the *Winnipeg*, or the Martinique route, and Oppy asked us not to talk about it for fear the German armistice commission would get wind of his success and revoke the visas. He explained that the *Winnipeg* was taking French army officers and civil officials to the capital of Martinique, Fort de France, and said that one of the officers was a friend of his and had somehow managed to persuade the Prefecture to give him the visas, on the solemn promise that he wouldn't tell a soul about it. So we said good-bye and wished him good luck, and he went away, taking his secret with him. As he didn't come back, we knew his *combine* had worked.

-7-

Thus, when Heine brought Breitscheid and Hilferding into my office on the morning of Monday, the 27th, and they told me what the Sub-Prefect had told them, I was no longer quite as incredulous as I would have been if it hadn't been for Oppy's experience. And when they showed me the exit visas on their American "affidavits in lieu of passport," I was properly embarrassed at my pigheaded insistence on extralegal and illegal methods, and dismayed to think of the unnecessary and even foolish risks I had been persuading them to take. Hilferding was beaming, and the wax mask of Breitscheid's face came alive for the first time since I had known him. Mrs. Breitscheid and Breitscheid's secretary, Erika Bierman, seemed even more pleased than the men, if that was possible. But the happiest of all was certainly Bedrich Heine. He had worried like a mother about the two men ever since they were sent to Arles, and now that they were on their way to safety at last he could hardly contain his joy.

Their exit visas specified that they should go via Martinique. With the visas, the Prefecture had given them a letter of introduction to a steamship company which was supposed to have a ship sailing for Fort de France on February 4th. Breitscheid and Mrs. Bierman went down the Canebière to the office of the company to make their reservations. There they were told that all first- second- and third-class cabins had already been sold, and that the only things left were bunks in a dormitory in the hold. The clerk said he thought it would be too much of a strain for Breitscheid and his wife to spend thirty days in the hold and strongly advised them to wait for a later sailing. As Breitscheid suffered from insomnia, and his wife wasn't at all well, they decided against the dormitory and left without making any reservations after all.

The next day Heine and I tried to persuade them to take any accommodations they could get, even if it meant unpleasantness and discomfort. But Breitscheid firmly refused to consider the dormitory for his wife, Mrs. Breitscheid as firmly refused to consider it for her husband, and Mrs. Bierman declared it equally impossible for both.

This time Hilferding did not submit to Breitscheid's moral authority, but decided for himself. He went down to the steamship company's office with Heine that morning to make a reservation in the dormitory and, while he was there, he also tried to get places for the three others, in the hope that Breitscheid would change his mind before the boat sailed. The clerk said he would see what he could do and told Hilferding to come back for the answer the next day.

By now it was Tuesday evening. They had all had their safe conducts prolonged a day, but could not get them prolonged any further at Marseille and had to return to Arles that night or break the law. When I saw them for the last time, Breitscheid was still determined not to sail if he had to bunk in the dormitory, and Hilferding was equally decided to take anything he could get.

On Wednesday Heine went back to the steamship company, where the clerk told him he had been able to find a place for Hilferding in the dormitory but could do nothing for Mr. and Mrs. Breitscheid and Mrs. Bierman, as it was now too late.

Early Friday morning Heine had four letters from Arles. The first one he opened contained Hilferding's final plans for the trip. He said he would come to Marseille on the morning of Saturday, February 1st, and listed the things he wanted Heine to do for him meanwhile. Breitscheid's first letter also contained instructions and seemed to indicate he had changed his mind—too late—and had decided to go with Hilferding after all.

The other two letters were very brief. Both explained that on the afternoon of Thursday, January 30th, the Sub-Prefect at Arles had informed the two men that Vichy had ordered him to cancel their exit visas.

The ship for Martinique sailed on Tuesday, but of all our protégés it was only little Walter Mehring who sailed with it. He got the bunk which had been reserved for Hilferding.

When he went down to board the ship, he was questioned, like all the other passengers, by a representative of the *Sûreté Nationale*. After examining his papers, the detective took a card out of a box and showed it to him. The card ran something like this: Forbidden to leave France, Decision of the Kundt Commission.

"I'm afraid you'll have to wait a few minutes," the man said. "I'll have to look into this."

Mehring sank onto a bench, convinced that once again his life was hanging in the balance. The detective went into another room to telephone the Prefecture. Ten minutes later he came back and handed Mehring his papers.

"I guess it must be another Walter Mehring," he said with a wink. "You can go."

A month later Mehring was in New York.

-8-

What happened next has been told by Mrs. Breitscheid in a memorandum she wrote at my request less than two weeks after the event. Rather than try to reconstruct the story myself, I am going to give excerpts from it in her own words— or rather in a literal translation of her words, for her memorandum is in German.

"On Saturday evening, February 8th, shortly before eleven o'clock, if I remember rightly," her memo runs, "there was a loud knocking on our door, and officials of the local police told us excitedly that we should immediately pack a couple of bags, as my husband must get away at once, in order to avoid a German commission which was looking for him. The same thing happened to Hilferding. I was not, under any circumstances, to be allowed to go with him; it was a strict order . . .

"At the police station the Chief of Police said he knew nothing beyond the fact that an automobile was coming from Marseille to take us away . . .

"We finally set out, and, in spite of the protests of the officials, I went along. We arrived at Vichy. On the way my husband complained, 'Why do you torture us this way if you only want to extradite us in the end?'

"Whereupon the official said, 'Vous pensez bien bas de la

France, monsieur. You have a very low opinion of France, sir.'

"In Vichy we were taken to a hotel. There was no sign to identify it, but there is no doubt that it was the Sûreté. I now had to separate from the two men. I was told I could inquire after my husband at two o'clock. But it was not until seven o'clock that I was able to talk to my husband. He told me that they were to be extradited.

"I was able to be with him a quarter of an hour, always in the presence of officials. Neither Hilferding nor my husband had any kind of hearing; there had been no formal proceedings of any sort. But the police had taken away their razors, their medicines and a book opener.

"After collecting myself a little, I ran to the American Embassy. It was Sunday evening, and already past eight o'clock, and there were only two porters, but one of them finally gave me a pad of paper, on which I wrote down everything that was necessary and stressed that the message was to be given to the Ambassador as soon as possible . . .

"From five until seven o'clock the following morning I walked up and down in front of the hotel which housed the Sûreté, in order not to miss my husband.

"At seven o'clock, finding the door unlocked, I went in, and was able to speak with both men until eight o'clock. I then went to the American Embassy again, though it was naturally much too early. But now I listed on the other side of the piece of paper what it was I begged them to do: intervene with the Marshal's Cabinet, and also with the Sûreté, to try and have the extraditions postponed; cable to Washington to bring pressure on the French. I begged the Ambassador or the Chargé d'Affaires to receive me, and promised to return.

"Then to the Ministry of the Interior. There the public was not permitted to ask for interviews until half-past nine. Back to the American Embassy, where the porter explained that the Secretary of Embassy had asked him to tell me that there was unfortunately nothing to be done. Under the armistice the Germans had the right to demand the extraditions, and the French could only yield to this demand.

"Back at the Ministry of the Interior I wrote out a slip asking to be received. Reason: extradition of my husband. The *huissier* refused to take my request to the Minister. It was forbidden.

"Hurried to the *Sûreté*. It was a quarter to eleven. At eleven o'clock Hilferding and my husband were taken away. I left them a couple of minutes before, because my husband insisted on it. Again I could speak to both of them only in the presence of the officials. They had taken Hilferding's poison away from him, but they had not found my husband's. He planned to take it only in the last extremity, but I am afraid the Germans will find it.

"From my hotel I watched the two autos drive away . . ."

-9-

It all happened so quickly that I knew nothing about it until I got to the office Monday morning. By that time it was already too late to do anything but get the news to America. My emotion overcoming my caution, I telephoned the *New York Times* office at Vichy and gave them the story over the phone.

In the afternoon Alfred Apfel called on me. Apfel was a German anti-Nazi lawyer with a good heart in the metaphorical sense and a very bad one in the medical. Like many criminal lawyers, he had a flair for striking up acquaintances with the police wherever he happened to be. At Marseille one of his police friends was a certain Monsieur Mercury, of the *Police Mobile*. Apfel had taken an *apéritif* with Mercury that morning and had found him in a rather depressed mood. They talked about the weather and one thing and another. Suddenly Mercury asked Apfel a question.

"What do you suppose would happen to two very prominent German political refugees," Mercury said, "if they should fall into the hands of the Nazis?"

"Do you mean Breitscheid and Hilferding?" Apfel asked.

"For instance," Mercury said.

"They would certainly be killed," Apfel said.

For several minutes Mercury was silent. Then he drank his *apéritif* in one gulp.

"You know," he said, "the life of a policeman isn't always a pleasant one."

Apfel and I talked about the outlook and tried to guess who would be next. I suggested that Apfel ought to look out for himself.

"You've been a pretty outspoken anti-Nazi yourself," I said. "Don't you think you ought to be careful?"

A shadow passed over his face, and I could see the color draining out of it.

"I—I—I don't know," he said.

He shifted in his chair.

"I think I'm having a heart attack," he said.

I jumped up and caught him just in time to prevent him from falling on the floor. Within half an hour he was dead.

-10-

Mrs. Hilferding arrived in the unoccupied zone in the middle of February. She had sold the few jewels she had left and, with the money she had got for them, she had bought her way to Arles, paying a high fee to the man who conducted her across the demarcation line, and walking through twelve kilometers of bog and swamp.

When she reached Arles she still did not know what had happened. She was looking forward to seeing her husband again after a separation of nine months, and fully expected to be able to leave France with him immediately. She was happy to have been able to escape from Paris without accident.

When she got to Arles, in the early morning, she went direct to the Hotel du Forum, told the clerk who she was and asked him not to wake her husband. He often slept late, she said, and she didn't want to disturb him. She would just wait until he rang for his breakfast.

It was then that she learned for the first time of the extraditions.

But what she did not learn even then was that her husband was already dead. Months later, when I was in Lisbon, I received a postcard from France announcing his death. His body, suspended from a hook in the ceiling by his necktie or belt, was found in a cell of the Santé Prison at Paris the day after Vichy handed him over to the Germans. Was it suicide, or murder? I suppose nobody will ever know.

Three and a half years after the extraditions, the Germans announced that Breitscheid and Ernst Thaelmann, leader of the German communists, had been killed by American bombs during an attack on the concentration camp of Buchenwald. But the American military authorities denied that there had been a raid at or near the camp on that day, and it was generally believed that the two men had been murdered by order of Heinrich Himmler, as part of a widespread purge to eliminate all possible leaders of any government which might succeed Hitler's.

## XII. *Spring in Provence*

SPRING came early to Provence. You knew that winter was over when in every city and village, and along many a country road, men climbed the plane trees to cut the previous year's growth from the knotted stumps of the branches, and gathered up the twigs and made them into bundles of faggots and carried them home to light the last fires of the dying season. At the Villa Air-Bel Dr. Thumin directed the operations himself, and we were awakened early one morning by the noise he made shouting directions to two good-natured peasants who had climbed the two great trees in front of the house and were clipping away at the twigs, wholly oblivious of the little old man calling up at them from the terrace below. Later, when we gathered up the twigs which had been left behind, with the intention of using them to start our fires, Dr. Thumin, discovering what we had done, made us pay him one franc a bundle for them.

Then, imperceptibly, the days lengthened, and the sun grew warmer, and little lizards came out and ran along the garden wall. Spring powdered the trees with green, covered the tracery of the plum trees with a veil of coral pink, made the lilacs swell with sap and brought sharp swords of iris up through the rotting leaves of the previous fall. Magpies flew over the carpet-green meadows, their black-and-white wing feathers flashing in the sun. And in the woods yellow fuchsias blossomed, and there were golden showers of mimosa in the hedges.

Then a nightingale sang in the medlar and the toads croaked their love songs around the ogival fish pool. When we walked on the terrace at night we risked stepping on pairs of them, each great fat female carrying a ridiculous little male on her back; and in the morning we found the females lying, white bellies up, in the fish pool, dead, with long strings of eggs trailing behind them—proving, as André said, that life feeds on death.

And later still the snails came out, to eat the fresh green foliage and perform their complicated bisexual amours, and André got out the butterfly nets, and the gardener dug in the earth and planted vegetables in the beds around the fish pool, and we opened the doors and windows of the house and let the world of scent and sound come in and stir us with its pulsing.

-2-

Jean was the first to succumb to it. He fell in love, had a sort of nervous breakdown, and spent several weeks in bed, reading Verlaine and Baudelaire and André's *Soluble Fish*. He was far too wan to blush, and even his blue eyes seemed faded.

When he had recovered enough to be up and around again, he would sit on a bench in the garden every evening after dinner, holding hands with his girl friend, and sighing heavily from time to time. Later, when it was quite dark, they would come into the house and read poetry to one another.

Jean got so moony about this "affair" that I was afraid he was going to have another nervous breakdown. One night I tried to argue him into a more Gallic frame of mind. I said, among other things, how sensible and matter-of-fact I thought the typical French attitude toward love was.

"Yes," Jean said solemnly, "you Americans take love much too seriously."

The gardener was more successful. He won the affections of the cook and slept with her regularly every night—to the scandalization of Theo, who never ceased to talk about it.

"I'm sure I don't see what she sees in him," she said one night at dinner.

"I hope you don't," Danny laughed.

Dr. Thumin reacted to spring in ways peculiarly his own. We called on him one Sunday to discuss renewing the lease, which had been signed for six months and was about to expire. We knocked and rang, but no one answered, and we were starting away again when a second-floor window opened and Dr. Thumin thrust his head out, clad in a white night cap.

"*Qu'est-ce qu'il y a?*" he called, in a more than usually crotchety voice.

"*C'est nous, vos locataires,*" we called back. "It's us, your tenants."

"*Mais non, mais non,*" he whined. "Go away. I am very ill."

"But Dr. Thumin," we said, "we have come to talk about renewing the lease."

"What's that you say?" he called, cupping his hand over his ear.

"*Le bail!*" we shouted. "The lease!"

"Oh, ah. The lease, you say? Very well, I'll be right down." "I thought you were strangers," he said, when he opened the door. "Come in. I have been very sick, very sick."

We said we were sorry to hear that and asked him what it was.

"The spring sickness," he said. "Everything I eat goes right through me. Last night I took some carrots and potatoes, and just now I was called. It went *broo-ah-ah, broo-ah-ah*. Such a terrible waste! And potatoes so scarce, too. I have tried everything but there is no stopping it. It's the spring."

-3-

But spring did not affect all the French as it affected Jean, the gardener, or Dr. Thumin. When people began coming out of their damp unheated houses to greet the sun and the returning warmth, they began to write on the walls. And while small boys sometimes wrote slogans like "*Vive les pineurs*" and even simply "*Vive moi*," others painted V's in bright red or indelible black on the walls of the houses and the fronts of movies and public buildings. Then still others came along and wrote or painted P's after the V's, to make the combination "*Vive Pétain*" instead of "*Victoire*." And when, one night, the B.B.C. called on the French to write H's after the V's, for "*Vive l'honneur*," VH's appeared all over Marseille the next morning. It was called "the battle of the walls," and it went on for months and years, always taking new forms, never ceasing.

There was also a new attitude toward the Germans now. Instead of referring to them respectfully as the "occupying authorities," people began calling them *ces messieurs, nos bons maîtres*, and even the *doryphores*—potato bugs—because they wore green and ate so greedily, and the "vacuum cleaners," because they cleaned up everything in their path.

-4-

With the coming of spring, we began worrying about food in earnest. Our rations were cut again, and people said there was real danger that there would be no bread at all before the wheat harvest began. The queues in front of the food stores grew longer and longer. I have seen them, two abreast, two blocks long, kept in order by half a dozen *gendarmes,* before a single butcher's shop. And more and more frequently those who had to stand in them for hours a day found by the time their turns came that everything had been sold. So many people lived on rutabagas, and very little else, that there was a kind of grim joke about them: whenever anyone asked what's the matter with you, you answered "rutabagatism."

Already our bread ration was so small that Madame Nouguet had to buy a kitchen scale and weigh it out in even slices, so that each person would get his fair share. We found our rations for the day at our places at breakfast in the morning, and, if we had enough self-restraint not to eat them all at once, we wrapped up what was left in our napkins and saved it for dinner. For several days toward the end of April we had no bread at all, and practically no meat—just Jerusalem artichokes boiled in water, boiled squash and, as a rare treat, a little macaroni or spaghetti without butter or sauce, or a wrinkled, brown-spotted apple for dessert. We were so hungry that we ate the goldfish in the pool, and, however unappetizing our meal, we always wiped our plates clean.

Toward the end of May they began the distribution of the American Red Cross flour, in the form of bread. The bread was handed out at the bakeries on several successive Sundays. It was good, white bread, all right—dazzlingly white compared to what we had been eating. But the funny thing about it was that you had to give ration tickets for it—no money, just ration tickets. Thus we got no more bread than we would have had if the Red Cross hadn't sent the flour; only we got white bread instead of gray, and we got it free. Everyone was mystified.

But at least it was good propaganda for America. Everywhere the bakeries displayed American flags and the empty flour sacks, with the words "Gift of the people of the United States to the people of France" printed on them—until the members of Pétain's Legion of War Veterans went around and made them take them down.

Danny and I spent our Sundays hunting snails on the garden wall, and when they had been dried out in a burlap bag we boiled them and ate them with all the relish we would have felt for a juicy beefsteak the year before. As a kind of bitter jest, we kept a copy of *Le Boeuf Clandestin* in the cupboard where the meat would have hung, if there had been any. Madame Nouguet locked the cupboard where the bread was kept, but sometimes when we were too hungry to sleep we took the pins out of the hinges and stole a little of the next day's rations before going to bed. And we regularly ate the larger part of our month's sugar rations on the day they arrived, so that in the second half of every month we were wholly without sugar.

Once I made a trip to the country and bought a pair of young rabbits, for breeding. I got back just as the people in the house were beginning their meager dinner, and it took all the persuasive powers I could muster to prevent them from killing the rabbits and cooking and eating them that night.

Necessity overcoming our scruples, we patronized the black market freely and bought some of the counterfeit bread tickets which were circulating in Marseille's gangster circles. On the black market we were able to get such things as a real Yorkshire ham, but we had to pay 3,500 francs for it— more than $85.00 at the official rate of exchange.

Like everybody else, we began to develop signs of malnutrition. I lost twenty pounds and was hungry all the time, but the hungriest were the young, for they had the biggest appetites. We gave up drinking the milk from our clandestine cow, giving it instead to the children of Dr. Thumin's tenant farmers. They came up to the house every morning after their own breakfasts of dry bread to get it, seizing the bowls and drinking down the milk like little savages—until the cow was discovered, and her milk had to be turned over to the municipal authorities.

The worst of it was that it also became harder and harder to find wine. And even cigarettes began to run out. Jean, who was a chain smoker, manufactured his own from a recipe he found in a newspaper, using the dried leaves of eucalyptus, sage, and I don't know what, and spraying some of the gardener's nicotine over the mixture with an old perfume atomizer.

Yet, with all its privations, life at the villa was immensely pleasant that spring. Before long we were supplementing our poor meals with string beans, tomatoes, radishes and lettuce fresh from our garden around the fish pool. For a while the Surrealists continued to come to the house on Sunday afternoons, holding auctions of their pictures on the terrace and drinking tea with us in the library at the end of the day, or helping us to empty magnums of cognac and Armagnac. When the weather got really warm we had three or four Spaniards come and clean the muck out of the bottom of one of Dr. Thumin's irrigation basins, and then we had a beautiful tile-lined pool to swim in. We even had a Spanish refugee barber who came every morning to shave us.

When some of those who lived in the house gave up their rooms and left, others took their places. White-haired Max Ernst came down to Marseille from St. Martin d'Ardèche, wearing a white sheepskin coat and bringing with him a great roll of his pictures, which he tacked up in the drawing room, so that we had a show which people came all the way from Marseille to see. Consuelo, Antoine de St. Exupéry's wife, arrived from nowhere one night and stayed for several weeks, climbing the plane trees, laughing and talking, and scattering her money liberally among the impecunious artists. Kay Boyle visited us on her periodic trips from Mégève in the French

Alps to help an Austrian refugee friend get his visas and prepare her own. She was like her books: intense, emotional and very finely wrought. She always wore small white-bone earrings cut in the form of the many-petaled flowers of the edelweiss, and her blue eyes seemed like lapis lazuli. Peggy Guggenheim closed her museum of modern art at Grenoble and took Mary Jayne's room when Mary Jayne left for Lisbon and New York. Peggy's earrings were long crescents from the ends of which hung tiny framed pictures by Max Ernst. Her conversation was a series of rapid, nervous questions. Charles Wolff, a former feature writer for the *Lumière*, installed himself in a room on the top floor and consoled himself with much wine. He had had a large collection of phonograph records in Paris, including some very rare ones of *"les soupirs des femmes dans l'amour."* When the Germans came he had had to abandon them. Whenever he thought of the Boches listening to the sighs, which was often, he took another drink.

## XIII.  *Underground Through Spain*

AT THE end of December we had moved our office from the rue Grignan to much lighter and larger quarters on the boulevard Garibaldi. We moved in as the beauty parlor which had been occupying the premises moved out. Whereas in the first days at the rue Grignan we had been surrounded by pocketbooks, we were surrounded now by hairdriers, permanent-waving machines, white-cloth screens and full-length mirrors.

But the beauty shop was much quicker than the pocketbook merchant in getting its property moved, and we were able to start the new year in quarters every bit as respectable as those of the Quakers or the Red Cross. The police, we felt, might continue to suspect us, but they could no longer call our office a *boîte louche*. To the world at large we now presented an appearance so respectable that it would be difficult, we thought, for the police to suppress us.

To make it still more difficult, we bought a large American flag, put it on a six-foot flagpole, and set it up in the interviewing room. We also tried to borrow a photograph of President Roosevelt from the Consulate and have it copied, but the Consulate had portraits only of Washington, Lincoln and Hoover.

-2-

At the end of January many of the refugees discovered they could get exit visas. I don't know for certain what the explanation of the sudden change of policy was, but from what I learned later it seems it meant that the Gestapo and the other secret-police organizations had completed the task of going over the lists of the political and intellectual refugees in France and had decided which of them they wanted and which they would allow to slip through their net. Anyway, the immediate result for us was that from having been ostensibly a modest relief organization, paying small weekly allowances to keep men, women and children from starving to death, ours now quickly became a kind of travel bureau, rivaling in its sense of rush and bustle the office of the American Express Company on the Canebière. For we could now openly engage in what had all along been our *raison d'être*— emigration.

It took us a little while to get used to the change, but by the end of the first week we had already adjusted to it, and for the first time since we began work, more than five months before, we were soon sending refugees down to the Spanish frontier to leave France legally.

Many people passed through our offices on their way to

Lisbon that spring, among them Siegfried Kracauer, the film critic; Max Ernst and Marc Chagall; Jacques Lipchitz, the sculptor; Professor Boris Mirkine-Guetzévitch, of the Sorbonne; the singer, Lotte Leonard; Valeriu Marcu, the Rumanian historian; the physicist, Peter Pringsheim; the German poet, Hans Sahl; the writer, Hans Siemsen; the motion-picture producer, Hans Aufricht; the theatrical producer, Poliakoff-Litovzeff; Professor de Castro, secretary of the Faculty of Science at the University of Madrid; the mathematical physicist, Jacques Hadamard, the Einstein of France; and one of the innumerable Princes Obolensky.

Still more would have gone if it hadn't been so infernally difficult to get the transit visas. It could be done, but only just.

-3-

It was the ships to Martinique which really kept us busy. We couldn't have thought up anything better if we had had the power to arrange the route ourselves. They not only eliminated the trouble with the transit visas—they also removed the danger of the trip through Spain. For they went directly from Marseille to Martinique, and from there it was possible to go straight to New York. They were almost as good as the much-advertised but never-realized "rescue ship," which was to have come to Marseille to take refugees to New York, but wouldn't have been able to take a single refugee on board at the time it was proposed, for at that time literally no one was able to get an exit visa.

The route started slowly, but expanded miraculously as time went by. On February 18th we were able to start nine of our clients to Martinique and toward the end of March forty more, including André, Jacqueline and Aube Breton; Victor Serge and his son, Vladi; Oscar Goldberg, the Hebraic scholar; and, most remarkable of all, two of the four men who had set out on the ill-fated *Bouline* the previous fall.

To our surprise, the Administration transferred these men to the embarkation camp at Les Milles, near Aix-en-Provence, at our request, granted them exit visas and permitted them to leave, despite the fact that they had already been convicted of the crime of trying to leave (on the *Bouline*) without permission. But although we made exactly the same request in behalf of the other two, and they were in exactly the same legal situation, so far as French law was concerned, our request was refused without explanation—proof, we thought, that the Gestapo must have spoken.

In April still another ship sailed, and among the passengers were twelve of our refugees, including André Masson and his family.

By May the stream had become a river, with ships leaving for Martinique every four or five days. Among those who took them were Mrs. Hilferding and Mrs. Bierman; the Paris photographers, Ylla and Lipnitski; the German anti-fascist writer, Wilhelm Herzog; the orchestra leader, Eduard Fendler; the pianist, Erich Itor-Kahn; an Italian anti-fascist writer named Aurelio Natoli; Jacques Schiffrin, publisher of the Pleiade editions of the French classics; and many former workers in the German and Austrian underground, whose identity was apparently not known to the Gestapo.

In fact, those days of the ships to Martinique were the busiest days in our history, and the most fruitful. Our small staff quickly grew to impressive proportions. For a while we had more than twenty people working in the office, and we all worked so hard that when a ship finally sailed we were exhausted. But we never got a chance to rest and recover, for the next week there would be another ship leaving, and we had to begin all over again.

At the end of May, when we came to tally our work, we found that in less than eight months over 15,000 people had come to us or written to us. We had had to consider every one of their cases and take a decision on it. We had decided that 1,800 of the cases fell within the scope of our activities. In other words, that they were genuine cases of intellectual or political refugees with a good chance of emigrating soon. Of these 1,800 cases, representing, in all, some 4,000 human beings, we had paid weekly living allowances to 560 and had sent more than 1,000 out of France. For the rest we had made every kind of effort, from getting them liberated from concentration camps to finding them a dentist.

-4-

But it was not everyone who could get an exit visa and leave France legally, even then. As usual, the regulations were shrouded in mystery, but we were told that every prefecture in the unoccupied zone had been provided with lists of persons to whom the visas were to be refused.

It was several weeks before we could get copies of those lists—one of Bedrich Heine's friends finally got them for us by bribing a clerk at the prefecture at Pau to copy them down for him—but when we did we found that there were a number of our protégés on them, including some who had already left France illegally and more who had not yet found a way to go.

Those who had, or could get, Portuguese and Spanish transit visas we immediately sent to Lisbon. They crossed the frontier via the "F" route, or in other ways. They included Heine himself and another of our collaborators, a former worker in the German underground named Heinrich Mueller.

But many still had no overseas visas, and so no possibility of obtaining transit visas. To get them out of Continental France as quickly as possible we used the method we had originally planned for Breitscheid and Hilferding—smuggling them to North Africa. From our experience with the British we had learned that it could be done. What had been lacking were places to hide in once the refugees had arrived in Africa, and some way of moving them on to Lisbon or Gibraltar from there.

For these, we turned to the two Italians, Lussu and Pacciardi. Since most of the Italians felt they couldn't go through Spain safely, no matter what papers or disguises they had, Lussu and Pacciardi had been working on schemes to get their men across to Africa, and thence to Gibraltar or Lisbon. Their ideas on how to do this differed radically. Lussu, the more cautious of the two, sought and found genuine safe conducts from Marseille to Oran or Algiers, and then sent his people on to Casablanca by an underground railway which he had built up by remote control from Marseille. Pacciardi stowed his people away for the Mediterranean crossing, hid them in Oran, and was planning to put them all on a big fishing boat which was to take them to Gibraltar.

Although Lussu's program seemed to be working very smoothly, he quite properly reserved it for the members of his own *Giustizia e Libertà* group. Our role in it was merely to supply the money. Lussu had solved everything but the question of how the people were to go from Casablanca to Lisbon. When he got the last of them to Casablanca, he was planning to go to Lisbon via Spain and solve that problem there. He promised that when he had moved his people on from Casablanca he would give me all his leads. But that would not be for some time yet.

Pacciardi was more generous. He had already sent his group down to Algiers and Oran, and he was willing to have us send others and include them among the passengers of his fishing boat when it left for Gibraltar.

As a matter of fact, we had sent a few refugees down to North Africa even before Breitscheid and Hilferding were arrested and extradited. After that alarming event we sent more. By the end of February, we had, between us, fifty or sixty persons (including the Italians) waiting in Algiers, Oran and Casablanca for word of what they were to do next.

But Pacciardi never succeeded in sending a single one of them to Gibraltar, and his attempt to do so came very close to ending in disaster. He finally found a fishing boat, but when the people in his group assembled at a point on the shore to the west of Oran, expecting to get on it, they found that the police were already there, and they had to make their way back to Oran as best they could. It took us months to spirit them, one by one, from Africa and get them to Lisbon and New York, and the details are too complicated to report. No two cases were handled alike, but they were all handled successfully. Eventually everyone got out.

-5-

Long before we realized how the North African venture was going to end, we stopped sending any more people down to Algiers and Oran. But the news of the extradition of Breitscheid and Hilferding spread a new wave of panic among the refugees. Many of them gave up their rooms and moved to *maisons de rendezvous,* where they were not obliged to make out police reports. We had not yet obtained a copy of the Gestapo's blacklist, but one man who seemed pretty certain to be in danger was Arthur Wolff. Before Hitler came to power he had been one of Berlin's leading criminal lawyers, and had defended many of the victims of Nazi street fights. After Hitler's triumph he was one of the first to lose his German citizenship. As he and his wife had been sent to Arles, along with Breitscheid and Hilferding, the previous autumn, he was convinced he was being held for the same fate as they. When he came to see me, white with terror, a few days after they were extradited, I agreed immediately to do what I could to help him.

While they were waiting for me to find a way to get them out of France, Mr. and Mrs. Wolff went to live in the room behind the packing boxes we had originally reserved for Breitscheid and Hilferding. The great difficulty in Wolff's case was that he was very lame, so lame that he could walk only with crutches. Hence he could neither cross the frontier on foot nor be smuggled on a ship as a member of the crew.

There were also Mr. and Mrs. Georg Bernhard. They had been living quietly in their *maison de passe* for five months, but when they heard about the extraditions they too became impatient to leave.

And then, when we got the copy of the Gestapo's list, there were many others.

For all these people the only way out seemed to be through Spain. But we didn't dare cable their names to New York to get them steamship reservations, and we couldn't make the reservations in Marseille because of the depreciation of the franc. Yet without reservations it was impossible for them to get Spanish and Portuguese transit visas.

One day Murphy told Jean he had met a man in the Vieux Port who claimed he could buy Portuguese and Spanish transit visas from employees at the Consulates, without steamship reservations and without telegraphing to Lisbon and Madrid. The price was 6,000 francs a visa. We tried it out for the Wolffs and the Bernhards and it seemed to work; their papers were returned in a few days with both transit visas on them. But there was still the problem of getting Wolff over the frontier with his lame leg.

-6-

Just about the time we got the "special" transit visas, through Murphy's tip, Jean met a Marseille gangster who claimed he was in league with an official of the Spanish Embassy at Vichy. The official said he would take five passengers to Lisbon in his diplomatic car, at 100,000 francs the trip.

It looked like the answer to our prayers. Though the price was high, we snatched at it eagerly, the more so as the man asked for only half the money in advance; he was willing to wait for the balance until the passengers had arrived in Lisbon, Jean said.

We decided at once to send the Wolffs, the Bernhards and a fifth man named Caspari. Caspari's exit visa had been refused, and as he had fought on the republican side during the Spanish Civil War, and had adopted Spanish citizenship, he felt he could never go through Spain in the ordinary way. But he was willing to risk the trip in the diplomatic car.

Because his crutches made him conspicuous, Wolff was afraid of being recognized if he took the train at Marseille, and he was afraid of passing through Arles on the train for fear the police would be looking for him there. So we agreed to take him to Les Baux by car at night, and put him on the train at Tarascon, the first stop beyond Arles, the next morning. Meanwhile Jean was to put the others on the train at Marseille. They would all meet at Tarascon, and go on together to Ax-les-Thermes, a watering place in the high Pyrenees, near Andorra. There the diplomatic car would pick them up and take them to Lisbon.

One moonlight night in early March, Mr. and Mrs. Wolff, Maurice and I set out in a gangster's limousine from Marseille to Les Baux. It was the same car we had sent to Arles to get Breitscheid and Hilferding two months before. But it was not the same driver. This one's head had been shaved close to the skull, and it was obvious that he had only just been let out of prison. Wolff was very nervous, and the sight of the shaved skull on the front seat didn't make him any less so.

We hadn't gone far before we had a resounding blowout, and we all had to get out and stand by the side of the road while the driver changed the tire. The delay made Wolff even more nervous than before, and his nervousness infected the rest of us. When he saw a car coming toward us from the direction of Marseille, he clutched my arm, convinced it was the police. But the car drove by without stopping, and we didn't see another sign of life until we climbed the hill to Les Baux and stopped in front of the Hotel de la Reyne Jeanne.

Les Baux is an eagle's nest perched high on a crest of the Alpilles, a range of barren, weather-beaten limestone hills stretching from Tarascon, on the Rhone, almost to Salon, halfway between Arles and Marseille. It was founded in the Middle Ages by the feudal lords of the neighborhood—a band of pirates who used to descend from their mountain fastness from time to time and plunder the outlying districts. Today it is a ruined and abandoned town, its 6,000 inhabitants reduced to some sixty-odd. I had visited it the previous autumn on one of my weekends in the country and had found it an ideal hideout, especially because its only hotel was kept by an American who was already sheltering an English soldier and a French pilot, and who seemed perfectly willing to take in a few fugitives from Vichy and Gestapo "justice" as well. His name was Donald Purslow, and he came, originally, from Boston.

Purslow met us at the door of his inn that night and welcomed us as I knew he would. There was a roaring fire in the great stone fireplace, and we all sat around it on comfortable Provençal chairs and drank warm red wine and talked and listened to the B.B.C. Wolff was worried about being so near Arles, but Maurice and I kept telling him he was safer at Les Baux than he had been at Marseille. The police would certainly look for him there, we said, but they would never guess he was hiding so near the town he had just escaped from. Whether it was our argument, or the wine, or Purslow's kind and reassuring nature, he gradually relaxed, and seemed in quite good spirits by the time we went to bed.

The next morning, while we were having breakfast, the telephone rang. It was Jean, calling from a café in Marseille. He said there had been a slight delay, and began to explain; but I broke in and told him I'd call him back later. I didn't want to talk to him from the hotel, for fear the police might be listening. Wolff sensed that something had gone wrong, and he was close to collapse when I left him.

I drove to Arles in the gangster's car and telephoned Jean from the post office. He told me again that there would be a slight delay, and said he thought I ought to go back to Marseille. It was obvious he felt he couldn't say any more than that on the phone, and I didn't press him.

I drove back to Les Baux in the car and told Maurice and the Wolffs what Jean had said. Wolff was terribly upset at the idea of being left alone at Les Baux, but we had lots of wine at lunch and spent the afternoon reassuring him. As soon as it was dark Maurice and I left for Marseille in the car, promising to be back in a few days.

We found Jean waiting for us at the Villa Air-Bel. He

explained that the man who arranged the trip to Lisbon in the diplomatic car had some business or other in Marseille, probably connected with smuggling, which he insisted on finishing before he would leave. He expected to be ready in about a week, Jean said.

Some days later Caspari came to the office with the news that the diplomatic car was a hoax. Our clients would have to walk through the mountains to Andorra, and from there would be taken by bus and train to Barcelona. What would happen after Barcelona wasn't made clear, but it didn't matter much, because the climb to Andorra would take from eighteen to twenty hours, part of it through ice and snow, and the Wolffs and the Bernhards obviously could never manage it. Caspari, who was younger and more able-bodied, might have; but he had decided not to take the chance, and we couldn't say for sure that he was wrong. He eventually found a way of his own to escape from France.

Jean and Danny were both in my office when Caspari arrived with the news about the diplomatic car. As he told his story, Jean began to blush until his face was fiery red, and, although he said nothing, Danny, who had maintained all along that Maurice and Jean and I were making a serious mistake in dealing with gangsters and smugglers, assumed the self-satisfied look he always had when he was proved right. Jean went to bed early that night and didn't get up again for a week.

I sent Maurice and Danny down to Ax-les-Thermes to investigate. They came back a few days later and reported that all that Caspari had said was perfectly true: there was no trace of a car, and no further pretense that there ever had been one. The climb to Andorra involved going through a mountain pass more than 5,000 feet above sea level. And the frontier was closely guarded; in trying out the route to see whether it would do for younger men, and perhaps for the British, Maurice and Danny were fired on by French *douaniers*, and only escaped arrest by giving the impression that they were young de Gaullists, trying to get to London.

-7-

With the diplomatic car gone up in smoke, we had to find something else, and find it fast. One evening when we were discussing it for the hundredth time I suddenly remembered I had seen on the walls of Barcelona and Port-Bou the letters CNT-FAI, initials of the Catalan labor movement and party.

"*Ecoutez*," I said, "there's an active underground movement in Spain. I saw signs of it on my way back from Lisbon last fall. If we could only get in touch with it, and get it to work for us, our problem would be solved."

"I know a man in Toulouse who says he's a member of the CNT," Maurice said. "He even claims to have some connection with the underground movement in Spain."

"Well, for God's sake, get out there and see him," I said. "See whether his comrades in Spain can't arrange something for us."

Maurice left for Toulouse that evening, and when he got back to Marseille, a couple of days later, he looked like the proverbial cat.

"I saw Carlos," he said, when Danny had locked the doors of our private office and had pulled out the telephone plug. "He's a member of the CNT, all right, and he says his organization can take people all the way through Spain to Lisbon. They provide the transit visas themselves, and they know all the inspectors on the trains, so there won't be any trouble that way. And they've got good hiding places in Barcelona and Madrid."

"Are you sure?" I asked.

"Absolutely," Maurice said. "Carlos is a serious type. He's not one of these gangsters. He's a political refugee himself. He wouldn't lie."

"What does he charge?" I asked.

"Fifteen thousand francs a person," Maurice said.

Danny whistled.

"And you say he's a serious political type?" he asked.

"I know it sounds high," Maurice said, "but think of the risks they have to take, and the palms they have to grease."

"You feel sure of Carlos, do you, Maurice?" I asked.

"Absolutely sure," Maurice said.

"Do you think he can handle the Wolffs and the Bernhards?"

"I told him about Wolff," Maurice said. "He said he has strong guides who can carry him over the frontier. His men cross near Cerbère, so it ought to be possible."

"What do you think, Danny?" I said.

"I don't know," Danny said. "If it's really a CNT group Maurice has stumbled on, it's probably all right. But I'm against using gangsters, as you know, and the price makes it sound like a gangster outfit to me."

"I don't think it's a question of gangsters," Maurice said. "These men are smugglers, *bien sûr*, but only on the side. After all, they have to live, like everybody else. They're also expert forgers. They not only forge the transit visas but also the French exit visa, the *cachet* of the Bank of France, and the rubber stamps of the French and Spanish border officials. The French visas can't be used in France, of course, because they can't have the confirmations telegraphed to the border from Vichy, but they fool the Spanish police, and the Spanish *entrada* stamp convinces them that everything is absolutely regular."

"You mean they don't go to the border post in Spain?" I asked.

"No," Maurice said. "You see, with the forged transit visas it wouldn't do. There wouldn't be any confirmations from Madrid. So they go around the border post and get on the train several stations down the line, toward Figueras. Carlos swears his *entrada* stamp is an exact duplicate of the real thing. He says it's never failed."

After a good deal more discussion we decided to entrust the Bernhards and the Wolffs to Carlos' organization. At the frontier, they found only one guide and, though he was a very husky fellow, especially for a Spaniard, it was out of the ques-

tion for him to carry Wolff. Wolff, of course, was surprised
and disappointed to learn that he wasn't going to be carried,
but he decided to try to make it anyway, rather than stay any
longer in France.

As soon as it was completely dark, they all set out into
the foothills of the Pyrenees, the Bernhards, the Wolffs and
their Spanish guide. But they had not gone far when Wolff
realized he would have to give it up. Leaving the Bernhards
crouched under a low railway culvert, the guide brought the
Wolffs back to Banyuls and then set off into the mountains
to look for the Bernhards again. It was more than a week before
we heard anything more of them.

Meanwhile Maurice stayed on at Banyuls, investigating the
possibilities of sending the Wolffs around the point to Port-
Bou in a motorboat, and we sent Mr. and Mrs. Berthold
Jacob into Spain via the "F" route.

Jacob was a German journalist and a lifelong pacifist.
After the First World War he founded the German pacifist
group called "No More War" and devoted himself to exposing
the secret rearmament of the Reichswehr and its notorious
"Feme" murders of democrats and pacifists. He was an outspoken anti-Nazi long before Hitler came to power. In 1932,
shortly after von Papen became Chancellor, he was cited as
a co-defendant in the trial of Germany's great pacifist leader,
Carl von Ossietzky. Realizing which way the wind was blowing, Jacob escaped to France.

After the extradition of Breitscheid and Hilferding I decided
not to let the Jacobs wait in France any longer. I bought them
Venezuelan visas and travel documents, under false names,
had Murphy's man get them Portuguese and Spanish transit
visas and sent them down to Banyuls in the company of Jean.

Maurice was still in Banyuls when Jean arrived with the
Jacobs, but he came back to Marseille with him the next day
and reported that F—— had taken them safely over the frontier. He had also completed the arrangements for sending the
Wolffs around the point in a motorboat, Maurice said; they
would be leaving in a few days.

The day after Maurice's return we had word of the Bernhards. It came in the form of a telegram from Madrid. There had been so many delays that their Portuguese visas had already expired by the time they crossed the frontier, but Carlos had assured them his organization could easily get them renewed at Madrid. In the telegram, however, Bernhard said that he and his wife were stuck in Madrid, unable to get the visas renewed, after all.

As the Bernhards were traveling under their own names, I didn't dare wire Lisbon. Instead, I sent Maurice off to Toulouse to find Carlos, and, as soon as I had a chance, I sent a toothpaste-tube message to Lisbon with one of the rare refugees who was leaving France legally via Spain. In it I told the Unitarians who Bernhard was and why he was in special danger, and urged them to do everything they could to get him out of Spain as quickly as possible.

Maurice returned from Toulouse a day or so later to say that Carlos was sending a man down to Madrid to fix up the Bernhards; everything would be all right.

Lussu had got the last of his group to Casablanca by that time and was preparing to leave for Lisbon, traveling on a Lithuanian passport left over from the days of the Honorary Consul at Aix-en-Provence. So I wasn't surprised when the office boy told me he was waiting for me. But the minute he crossed the threshold I could see that something was seriously wrong. He looked distressed, and was tugging on his goatee even more nervously than usual.

It was a couple of days after Maurice got back from Toulouse. Danny, thank God, was away at the time, and I was alone in the inner office. As soon as I locked the door and made sure that the telephone plug had been pulled out, Lussu took his Lithuanian passport out of his pocket and showed me the transit visas we had gotten for him from Murphy's useful friend.

"These visas are crude forgeries," he said indignantly.

"But I'm sure you're mistaken," I said. "They can't be forgeries. They came straight from the Consulates."

"Huh!" he said, throwing up his chin, like a Greek saying no. "Straight from the Consulates, you say? Look!"

And, holding the passport in his left hand and tapping it vigorously with the index finger of his right, he pushed it to within a few inches of my nose.

"Look!" he said, "you can see that the signatures have been traced with a pencil, and then haltingly inked in. You can even see some of the pencil lines, which they have been too careless to erase. And there are mistakes in the spelling of some of the Portuguese words! Crude, useless forgeries!"

And he laid the passport on my desk with a flourish, as much as to say, "You know what you can do with it!"

I sat down and got out a magnifying glass and examined the visas. As I studied them I began to feel a terrible dread. The Jacobs and the Wolffs had identical visas. Had the Jacobs already crossed the frontier? Had the Wolffs already left for Port-Bou in the motorboat? Or were they all still waiting in Banyuls? If they were still at Banyuls, I had to stop them at all costs.

I got up and unlocked the door to the outer office and called for Maurice. When he came in, and I had locked the door again, Lussu showed him the visas. Like me, he at first insisted they were genuine, but when Lussu pointed out the faults he finally admitted that they looked like forgeries.

We talked it over and decided there was no time to be lost. No time for messengers now. We had to telephone to Banyuls and stop the Wolffs.

But it was dangerous to telephone from the office. So Maurice ran across the Canebière to the Café Noailles and telephoned from there. Somehow he managed to make F—— understand. F—— told him that the Wolffs were still there, but that the Jacobs had already left.

I had a telegram from the Jacobs a few days later. It said they had been arrested at the Portuguese border and sent back to Madrid, where they were in the Model Prison. They evidently still thought their visas were genuine, for they were obviously highly indignant at the Spanish frontier police.

That day was one of the worst I spent in France. I now had four people in Spain, two of them caught in Madrid, unable to get visas for Portugal, and two of them already arrested. And of the four, one was wanted by the Gestapo, and another was almost certain to be.

But there was almost nothing I could do. I telegraphed the Unitarians, asking them to overturn heaven and earth to get the Jacobs out of prison, and Maurice and I decided to go to Toulouse to see Carlos and find out what he could do to help.

Just before we left, we had a telegram from Lisbon saying that the Bernhards had arrived. How it had been managed, of course, the telegram didn't say. But the Jacobs were still in prison.

Lussu went with us to Toulouse. We all caught the noon train at the Gare St. Charles, changing at Tarascon and again at Narbonne. We had to stand up in the corridors all the way, but we didn't mind much, for it was a beautiful day, and we could watch the view. It was particularly fine at Carcassonne, with the sun setting behind the old city as we approached it from the east.

We reached Toulouse at a quarter after ten, and after registering at the Hotel de l'Opéra, under false names, we went straight to bed.

The next day, which was a Sunday, we had two long talks with Carlos, both of them at the hotel. I didn't like him at all. He was an oily little creature who lied quite unashamedly and shifted nervously in his chair as he talked. We tried to find out what had happened to the Bernhards at Madrid, whether he could get the Jacobs out of jail, what he could do for the Wolffs, and what he could do for all the other people on the Gestapo's blacklist.

For a long time he insisted it was his organization which got the Bernhards' Portuguese transit visas renewed. But, under Lussu's careful questioning, he was finally forced to admit that the only kind of visas his organization could get were what he called "extra-official" ones—apparently a euphemism for counterfeit—and that the Bernhards had refused to accept for-

geries, insisting instead on having real visas and being sure they
were real. He didn't know how they had finally gotten them.

He also said he could get the Jacobs released for 50,000
francs, but he was so vague about the method that I decided to
wait a while and see what the Unitarians could do.

For the Wolffs he began by saying he could provide a
diplomatic car which would take them all the way through to
Lisbon, for 100,000 francs. But when we told him of our
experience with that same phantom car he merely shrugged,
and immediately changed the subject.

Seriously, he said, he could get them real French exit visas
and have them taken all the way through from Cerbère to
Lisbon by train. We discussed this prospect a long time. We
showed him the Wolffs' false transit visas, and after examining them carefully with a watchmaker's glass he said he
thought they would get by. His men had such good connections with the police inspectors on the trains that almost
anything would pass, he said.

We had a third talk with him the next morning, and tried
to impress on his mind the importance of improving his
service, if he wanted any more business from us. He promised
to take his responsibilities more seriously in the future, and,
when he left, I had already half decided to use his organization again if he succeeded in getting exit visas for the Wolffs.
At least he hadn't gotten anybody arrested in Spain, as we had
when we had acted without his help.

I returned to Marseille that afternoon. When I told Danny
about our conversation with Carlos, he snorted.

"He's obviously just a gangster, like all the rest of Jean's
and Maurice's friends," he said. "Look out, or you'll find
you've sent still more people into the concentration camp at
Miranda."

But when I asked him what he would do if he were in my
place, he made no answer.

-8-

A week later we had a telegram from Lisbon saying that the
Jacobs had been released from prison and were living in a

Madrid hotel. The telegram removed my last doubts about Carlos and his underground organization. If the Jacobs had succeeded in persuading the Spanish authorities that their forged visas were genuine, then surely it would be safe to entrust more refugees to Carlos' care, I thought.

My decision to let Carlos try again was strengthened a few days later by the arrival of F—— from Banyuls with the news that he had decided to give up smuggling refugees over the frontier. He said that as the Spaniards had started to arrest all travelers from France who didn't have French exit visas, and the stamps showing they had left France in the legal way, it was useless for him to continue. But only Carlos could provide them with French exit visas and the stamps of the frontier officials. Good or bad, careful or careless, devout Marxist or common smuggler, Carlos was the only thing we had left for what we called our "special" cases.

The next to go were a French de Gaullist named Vatroslav Reich (he had been recommended to us by the British) and two men whose names had appeared on the Gestapo's blacklist, a German social democrat friend of Heine's named Walter Benninghaus and a Hungarian anti-fascist named Ladislas Dobos. Carlos provided all the visas, and his men took them over the frontier into Spain.

It was nearly three weeks before we had any further word of them. We knew that if they had reached Lisbon we would have heard, because we had given each of them a code name to telegraph back. But no telegram arrived.

As day followed day with no news from Lisbon, we began to grow nervous again. Finally Maurice went to Toulouse to see Carlos and find out what had happened.

He came back a few days later with the news that Benninghaus and Dobos had been arrested in Madrid. Only Reich had reached Lisbon, and so long after he left France that he had evidently forgotten his promise to wire.

The arrests of Dobos and Benninghaus looked like the end of our underground railroad through Spain. It also looked like the end of the hopes of the refugees who couldn't get steamship reservations, legal transit visas, and legal exit visas.

Danny had been right: Carlos was irresponsible and we would have to give him and his underground railroad up for good.

But when we talked it over with Lussu, he wasn't so sure. He pointed out that Reich and the Bernhards had been taken through all right, even if there had been delays. What was needed, he thought, was not to abandon the route but to make it better—eliminate the accidents, and make it foolproof.

So Maurice and Lussu went back to Toulouse and had another talk with Carlos, and once again Carlos promised to be more careful. A few days later Lussu announced that he had decided to try the route himself.

Maurice and I had a farewell lunch with him and his wife at a little outdoor restaurant on the promenade de la Plage. We sat in a garden on the edge of the Mediterranean, with the sun on our backs and a gentle breeze blowing off the water, drank Mercurey and ate our meager meal and talked about all the things that had happened since we had first met and all the things we hoped would happen before we met again.

"When we meet again," Lussu said, "it will be in Rome. I will be a member of the government, and you will come as an official guest."

When we had finished our lunch, and were ready to say good-bye, we wished Lussu and his wife the best of luck on their dangerous journey. Lussu tugged at his goatee a moment. Then he looked up at the sky.

"Enfin, within a week I shall either be in Lisbon, or back on Lipari!" he said.

-9-

It was some time before we had any word of Lussu, and during those days we almost literally held our breaths. He had promised to wire as soon as he arrived. He had also promised to write a long report on the route and smuggle it back to us, so we could do whatever was necessary from our end to improve it. But nothing came—neither telegram nor report. Spain had swallowed the Lussus as it had swallowed so many others.

Meanwhile there was a showdown between Danny and

Maurice. The whole business was getting very badly on our nerves, there was no doubt of that. We were as jumpy as rabbits, and utterly confused.

One night Danny let the storm loose. He accused Maurice of being incorrigibly careless, of treating human beings as though they were so much merchandise, of sending them into prison in Spain. He said that Maurice didn't seem to realize the seriousness of what he had done, that it was criminal to act so, that we were all playing at conspiracy, Jean and Maurice and I, that it had better stop.

"You've often reproached me for my fixed opinions," he said to me. "Well, I reproach myself now for not having imposed them on you. If Jean and Maurice, with their conspiratorial airs, have any other business between them more serious than sending refugees into the camp of Miranda, then I feel sorry for all of us. You don't fool the police by using conspiratorial names, talking in low voices, and slinking along walls dressed in coats the color of old stone, you know."

Although the attack was really directed at me, I tried to act as arbiter and smooth the ruffled feathers. I promised Danny that we would be more careful in the future. And I told Maurice that I didn't agree with Danny either, that he didn't seem to realize we had to take chances if we were going to accomplish anything, and that accidents were unavoidable. But I asked him to be doubly careful in future, and to impress on Carlos the extreme importance of avoiding any further arrests. Maurice defended himself at first, but in the end he promised to be more cautious.

The next morning he came to me before breakfast and said he had been thinking it over and had decided that Danny was right—he had been inexcusably careless, and he wanted to resign. It took a good deal of coaxing to get him to agree to go on at all.

The telegram from Lisbon came a few days after that. Two words: DUPONT ARRIVED. "Dupont" was Lussu.

We showed it to Danny, but he only shrugged.

"Through no merit of Maurice's," he said.

And then we sent an Austrian named Johannes Schnek. And he got through. Our underground railroad was working at last.

## XIV. *"Because You Have Protected Jews and Anti-Nazis"*

ALTHOUGH we had more successes than failures that spring, and sent people out of France legally in wholesale lots, and illegally in retail, I shall always think of it as a period of growing difficulties culminating in a series of crises and disasters.

In the first place, despite the new policy on exit visas, the attitude of the police toward the refugees became increasingly menacing as time passed. In March, Vichy issued a decree forbidding all Spanish males between the ages of eighteen and forty-eight to leave the country, and began sending them down to the Sahara Desert, for forced labor on the Trans-Saharan Railroad. Early in April they arrested all the Jews who were staying at Marseille's hotels and took them to the police stations for "control of situation."

Among those who were arrested was Marc Chagall. He and his wife had come down from Gordes a few days before to get ready to leave France. They took a room at the Hotel Moderne. Early one morning the police arrived and arrested everybody in the hotel who seemed likely to be Jewish. They took Chagall away in the Black Maria.

Mrs. Chagall called me about it almost as soon as I got to the office, and I telephoned a police official at the *Evêché*.

"You have just arrested Monsieur Marc Chagall," I said.

"So?"

"Do you know who Monsieur Chagall is?"

"No."

"He is one of the world's greatest living artists."

"Oh."

"If, by any chance, the news of his arrest should leak out," I went on, tingling with suppressed excitement at what I was saying, "the whole world would be shocked, Vichy would be gravely embarrassed, and you would probably be severely reprimanded."

"Thank you very much for calling me. I shall look into the case at once," the wretched policeman said.

Danny was standing beside me as I talked. As soon as I had finished he put his arm around my shoulders and squeezed me.

"That's the way to talk to them, boss!" he said, with a broad grin on his face and a tremor in his voice. "Now you're talking!"

"If he isn't out in half an hour," I said, "we'll call up the *New York Times* and give them the news."

Half an hour later the telephone rang. It was Mrs. Chagall. She said that Chagall had just returned to the hotel.

Others were not so lucky. They were expelled from the department and placed in *résidence forcée,* or, if they had no visible means of support, were sent to concentration camps or forced-labor battalions.

In May this delightful system was extended to foreigners of other faiths. One morning the father of our Spanish scullery maid set out for market with the family's food tickets in his pocket. He was arrested and sent off to work in a labor battalion. It was a week before we could find out where he was or get the food tickets back.

When the British and the Free French launched their attack on Syria, the police began rounding up Frenchmen suspected of pro-British and pro-de Gaulle sympathies and putting them in concentration camps. A few days later it was announced that every person in France with two or more Jewish grandparents, whether French or foreigner, would have to fill out a long questionnaire, listing, among other things, his bank accounts, securities and real estate. When Germany attacked Russia, all Russian émigrés were arrested, the Whites along with the Reds, and not all of them were subsequently released. And in late June and early July a *numerus clausus* of Jews was introduced in the high schools and universities and the learned professions.

-2-

The police also paid closer attention to us as time went by. When Lena left for Lisbon, early in February, she was stripped to the skin at Cerbère. In March the court released Freier, the little Austrian cartoonist who had forged the identity cards for us in the early days, but the Administration immediately interned him in the concentration camp at Vernet.

Later, in flagrant violation of his *exequatur*, they arrested the Czech Consul, Vladimir Vochoč, and placed him in *résidence forcée* at Lubersac, near the demarcation line. We were convinced that he was being held for extradition, but two months later he managed to escape and get to Lisbon.

The day after Vochoč's arrest, we learned that Jay Allen had been caught by the Germans in an attempt to cross the demarcation line without permission. The Consul said he felt sure Jay's arrest had nothing to do with us, but it was an uncomfortable feeling to have one of our band in the hands of the Germans just the same. It wasn't until the end of the summer that he was finally sent to Lisbon, to be exchanged for a German journalist arrested in the United States.

In April, Captain Dubois, our friend and protector in the *Service de la Surveillance du Territoire*, was suddenly ordered to Rabat, in French Morocco. He made no effort to conceal the fact that it was a kind of punishment for his pro-British and pro-American feelings.

Early in May I was warned that the Jeunesse de France et d'Outre Mer, Vichy's fascist youth organization, which used the Marshal's baton as its emblem, and seemed to have Pétain's blessing, was planning to raid our offices and smash them up—because we helped "Jews and dirty de Gaullists." I told Danny to have all the locks changed and put new and heavier bolts on all the doors. To make doubly sure, we hired a husky Spanish Republican refugee to be our night watchman. His name was Alfonso Diaz, and he was full of a doglike affection, which he expressed by giving us big Spanish hugs that nearly cracked our ribs.

-3-

The $10,000 Sir Samuel Hoare had authorized me to spend in evacuating the British was almost gone by the time Lena left Marseille. As Murphy had no money to work with, he asked me to get more, and I sent a message to the British by Lena asking for $50,000. With the first $10,000 we had gotten out about 125 officers and men, including at least one secret agent and a handful of veteran pilots. At that rate, $50,000 would have been enough to take care of the remaining 300 members of the B.E.F. in Southern France and the next 200 R.A.F. men to come down from the occupied zone.

I never got any answer to my request. But as I learned early the next month that Admiral Darlan had agreed to have the *Deuxième Bureau* collaborate with the Gestapo and the German armistice commissions in tracking down British espionage and all pro-British activities, I wasn't very sorry.

Early in April Murphy got tired of waiting for Sir Samuel's decision and made an exchange transaction with Dimitru which yielded him 600,000 francs in cash. The next day his apartment was robbed, and every franc of the money was taken.

The strange thing about it was the way it happened. For some time Murphy had been living with the pretty Corsican girl cashier who worked at the Sept Petits Pêcheurs. Her story was that on her way home from work she was held up by a couple of gunmen and forced to show them where she lived. To save her life she went to the room, and the gunmen broke open Murphy's trunk and found the money inside.

Murphy insisted the girl was straight. He said she not only didn't know where the money was but didn't even know he had it. The only people who knew anything about it at all were himself and Dimitru, he said.

Then who were the gunmen, and how did they know? Could Dimitru have been careless and told Jacques? And could Jacques have double-crossed Murphy, using the girl as a blind?

There was no way of finding out. Jacques wouldn't talk. He just sat behind his cash register, drinking bicarbonate of soda, and shrugged. I made up my mind to be extremely wary of him after that, but I didn't think much more about it until May, when everything became quite clear.

Meanwhile, Murphy had decided that the time had come for him to go. As his successor in charge of evacuating the British he appointed a Captain Garrow. Then he left for Spain. He was arrested there, on charges of espionage. When I last heard of him he was still in prison. The British Embassy at Madrid had refused to intervene for him.

Garrow was a quiet and sober fellow, without the extravagant, movie-thriller caution or the flamboyant recklessness of Murphy. I met him a few times at the Sept Petits Pêcheurs, and Jean kept in touch with him for many months, exchanging information on sources of false passports and visas, escape routes, and so forth. But from now on our relations with the British were casual rather than official.

-4-

Some time in March or April Dimitru had given me an opportunity to buy $8,000 in U. S. gold dollars, worth about $15,000 in paper currency. The deal seemed particularly advantageous because gold was the most desirable form of wealth in Europe then, and those five bags of gold gave us a very handy backlog in case of emergency. At first we kept them in the safe, but when we heard about Murphy's experience we buried them in the pinède behind the house.

We didn't bury them any too soon, for one morning early in May the police arrived at the house before breakfast with a warrant to search the safe for gold and foreign currency. They found only a small number of franc notes, which it was perfectly legal to have, and a few harmless papers, like our lease, and they went away manifestly disappointed.

But how did they know we had gold?

A week later, Dimitru pointed out that gold dollars were selling at the very high price of 268 francs, and advised me to sell out half of mine and take the profit. I said yes right away. We agreed that I would bring the coins to his hotel the next day.

But the next day I was so busy that instead of meeting Dimitru myself I sent Danny. He went up to the house after lunch and, as the gold was too heavy to carry all at once, he took $2,000 to town and delivered it safely to Dimitru. Then he went back to the house to get the second $2,000.

As he neared Dimitru's hotel with the second load of gold coins in his briefcase, he saw Dimitru standing on the steps, and three suspicious-looking men loitering across the street. Suspecting a trap, he decided to walk right by without speaking to Dimitru or seeming to recognize him. But as he passed the door of the hotel Dimitru came down the steps and spoke to him.

"I don't like the looks of things just now," Dimitru said, with one of his Mazda-light smiles. "Better not bring that stuff in now. Take it back to the house. I'll see you later."

He took Danny's hand in his own empty-glove hand and shook it limply. Then he turned back to the hotel.

Immediately the three men who had been loitering on the other side of the street crossed over and showed their badges.

"Let's see what you have in that briefcase," one of them said.

Obediently, Danny opened the briefcase. When they saw what was in it, they arrested him and took him to the *douane*. There they asked him how he got the gold and where he was taking it, and wrote out his answers in the form of a *procès verbal*.

Danny took all the responsibility on himself. He said that Max Ernst had offered me the gold as a gift to the committee and that I had refused it because it was illegal to dispose of gold; that Max Ernst had then offered it to him, and that, knowing how badly the committee needed the money, he had accepted it without my knowledge, with the intention of changing it into francs and giving the francs to the committee.

When they had taken the *procès verbal*, the detectives let him go. But they made him promise to return for more questioning the next day.

Danny was convinced that Dimitru had deliberately betrayed him, and insisted that he came down the steps of the hotel and spoke to him only to show the detectives whom to arrest.

"*Il m'a donné*," he kept saying, over and over again. "*Il m'a donné! Je te jure, il m'a donné!* He turned me in! He turned me in! I swear, he turned me in!*"

The next morning he went down to the *douane* to report, as he had promised to, and he didn't come back. By the end of the afternoon I had grown sufficiently anxious to consult a lawyer. The lawyer made inquiries, and then telephoned to say that Danny had been indicted on four counts and locked up in the Prison Chave. He was charged with illegal possession of gold, transporting gold illegally, intention of changing it illegally, and presumptive intention of diverting it to his own use. The total penalties might amount to four or five years in prison, the lawyer said.

For a long time I hadn't made any important decision without first consulting Danny, and, though I frequently acted against his advice, I always considered it carefully and respected it even when I didn't follow it. We had breakfast together in the morning, went to the office together, went home again together, dined together—did almost everything, in fact, but sleep together. It was about as close a companionship as I have ever had with anybody. To a large extent Danny had become the new Beamish, and, despite his highly critical attitude toward a part of my work, I was very fond of him.

The worst of it was that if Danny had told the truth, I would have been arrested too. It was that I found the hardest of all to accept. Twice a day, on my way to and from the office, I passed the Prison Chave, and I thought of Danny, down there at the bottom of one of the narrow shafts of light the long prison windows must let through. And, knowing that it was I who had put him there, I wanted to go to the police and tell them to arrest me instead. But I knew that if I did the committee would immediately be closed, and hundreds of poor devils would lose their last chance to escape from the Nazis. But it would have been much easier to do that than what I had to do.

-5-

After making further inquiries, the lawyer told us he thought the Ministry of Finance at Vichy might be persuaded to let Danny off with a heavy fine if the American Embassy would intervene for him. Knowing the Embassy, and its attitude toward "aliens" in general, and us in particular, I had no hope whatever, but I went to the Consul at Marseille to ask him what he thought about the chances. I told him exactly what had happened, and exactly how I felt about it. Without consciously trying to, I think I must have touched something very deep in him, because he did an extraordinary thing: he went down to the *douane* and told them that as Danny was the employee of an American relief organization the Consulate was following his case closely and was surprised that he had not yet been brought before a magistrate.

The next day, when I again saw the lawyer, his attitude had changed. He said that the *douane* had been greatly impressed by the Consul's visit, and that the case looked much better than it had before. A few days later he got a court to issue an order to the Administration to produce Danny for a hearing, and, thanks very probably to the Consul's visit, the *douane* obeyed the order. Until that time Danny had simply been arrested "administratively," without any court hearing at all.

When the court heard the charges, it decided at once to release Danny on bail, pending the trial. But under Vichy's methods, the *douane* was free to ignore the decision and keep him in prison anyway.

All that day we waited to learn what the *douane* would do. Toward evening the lawyer phoned and asked me to come to his office. I took Theo and Jean with me. Danny arrived about six o'clock, in a police car. He was dirty and unshaven, and he looked very thin and pale. But he was free, at least until the trial. I knew I was behaving like a sentimental fool, but when he came into the room I couldn't help throwing my arms around him and hugging him. And I couldn't help crying.

I felt like an awful fool, with Jean and Theo and the lawyer all watching, but I couldn't help it.

-6-

Dimitru never paid us for the $2,000 in gold Danny delivered to him. When I sent Jean down to get the money for it, Dimitru told him the *douane* had searched his room and confiscated it. The lawyer, inquiring at the *douane*, could find no record of any search. But he came back with the conviction that Dimitru was a police agent, and a few days later he told us he had learned he was also a Gestapo agent.

After that everything was clear. We not only knew who had betrayed Danny. We also knew who had kept the police informed of all our illegal financial transactions, and who had robbed Murphy.

But what else did Dimitru know, and hence the Vichy police and the German Gestapo? How much had Murphy told him?

"Don't you worry about little Boris. Little Boris is all right . . . "

Did Dimitru know we had been smuggling out British soldiers? Had he told the Gestapo?

I would willingly have given another $2,000 to find out. But I didn't have to wait long for the answer, and I didn't have to pay for it. I got it free.

-7-

After Danny's arrest, everything seemed to go to pieces at once. The British seized one of the Martinique ships and took her to Trinidad as a prize of war, and Vichy immediately canceled all future sailings and ordered two ships which had already left Marseille to put in at Casablanca. All the passengers were disembarked and placed in concentration camps, and it took months of hard work to get them released and send them on to Spain and Portugal, where they could get passage for New York, Havana or Vera Cruz. Meanwhile, Portugal had again become congested, so that virtually no one was able to leave Marseille for Lisbon.

Then Harry Bingham was recalled, and his place at the head of the visa service at the American Consulate was taken by a vice-consul who seemed to delight in making autocratic decisions and refusing as many visas as he possibly could. He was also very weak on modern European history, but very strong on defending America against refugees he regarded as radicals.

One day I went to see him about a visa for Largo Caballero. The court at Aix had refused to grant his extradition, but he had been placed in "forced residence" in a small town in Southern France. I thought that if I could get him an American visa I might be able to smuggle him to Casablanca, via Lussu's route, and put him on a boat for America. When I mentioned Caballero's name to the Vice-Consul he looked puzzled.

"Who's Caballero?" he asked.

I told him he had been Prime Minister of Spain during the Civil War.

"Oh," the Vice-Consul said, "one of those Reds."

I explained that Caballero had resigned the Premiership rather than continue to co-operate with the communists.

"Well," the Vice-Consul said, "it doesn't make any difference to me what his politics are. If he has any political views at all, we don't want him. We don't want any agitators in the United States. We've got too many already."

By the end of June, the American Consulates in France received new instructions forbidding them to grant any visas at all except on specific authorization from the State Department. Even transit visas had to be authorized by the Department, and all the refugees who had been patiently building up immigration-visa *dossiers* at the Consulates now had to begin all over again in Washington. No one with a close relative in Italy, Germany or any of the occupied countries, including the occupied part of France, could get a visa under any circumstances.

The police also became bolder in their attitude toward us.

One day I picked up the telephone and dialed a number, and when I got it I could hear a regular click, click, click in the receiver. The sound was unmistakable—it was the sound of a cracked dictaphone cylinder.

The following week three detectives arrived at the office with a warrant to look for false passports, false visas, false identity cards, and the machines and material for fabricating them. They made a thorough search, spending more than an hour at it, but they found nothing, because there was nothing to find. We may have been naive—we probably were—but had never been quite stupid enough to make or keep false documents in the office.

Two days later, at the Villa Air-Bel, I was awakened at about half-past five in the morning by the sound of tires on the gravel, and I knew at once that at that hour it could mean only one thing—the police. They surrounded the house and ordered everyone to get up and come downstairs. When we were all assembled in the hall they searched the house from top to bottom for a clandestine radio-sending set, and seemed surprised and disappointed not to find it.

Early the next week I accepted $6,000 from a French-woman who was leaving for New York, giving her a written promise that she would be repaid there. The following afternoon six detectives from the *douane* arrived at the office and turned it upside down in an effort to find the money.

The man in charge was a big bruiser who bellowed and bullied and did his best to terrorize us. When he saw me reaching for the telephone—I wanted to cancel an appointment at the Consulate—he sneered.

"If you're trying to warn your colleagues at the house, it won't do you any good," he said. "Your phone is already on the *table d'écoute!*"

He seemed to take delight in yanking the drawers out of the tables and desks and dumping their contents on the floor. He even looked up the chimney, where, as Dimitru knew, until Danny's arrest we had kept a supply of dollar bills.

When they had made a shambles of the office, without finding any trace of the money, they went out to the house to look there. But the money was already buried in the *pinède*, and they didn't find it.

Aside from the fact that it clearly revealed the mounting exasperation of the police, the thing which disturbed me most about this incident was the leak. The detectives not only knew I had received some money the day before, they also knew from whom, and exactly how much.

The Frenchwoman was above suspicion. I had had many dealings with her before, without the slightest difficulty. Besides, the *douane* had also raided her room, and likewise found nothing.

When I talked to her about it the next morning, she at first insisted that she and I were the only two people in the world who knew anything about the transaction at all. Then she said quite casually that of course Mr. Dimitru also knew about it. He got a commission on it, as usual.

It was that evening, I think, that I decided to give Dimitru the scare of his life. Jacques had frequently boasted that his price for murdering a man was 5,000 francs, with a twenty-per-cent discount if the victim were a policeman. I said nothing about it to Danny, but I talked it over with Jean, and he agreed to be the intermediary. He went down to the Sept Petits Pêcheurs and had several talks with Jacques about it. At first Jacques agreed to do it for the regular price. But as usual there was a delay. Then he said there was a difficulty. Later he explained that Dimitru had disappeared, and, in fact, we found he was no longer in Marseille. Later still we learned that he had gone down to Cavallaire, on the Côte d'Azur. When we told Jacques this, he said he would send a man down to deal with him there.

Weeks passed, and still nothing happened. Finally, pressed for a definite answer, Jacques said that Dimitru was very well protected. Murdering him would be exceedingly dangerous; it couldn't be done for less than 100,000 francs. Of course I knew it wouldn't be done even for that huge sum, for I had not forgotten that Jacques and Dimitru were partners. But I thought that by that time we had given Dimitru enough of a scare to make him transfer his attentions elsewhere, and I was evidently right. He never bothered us again. We didn't even have to play the comedy through to the end.

-8-

On the basis of his experience at the *Préfecture de Police* in Paris, Danny kept assuring me that his own arrest and the whole series of searches which followed it were part of a campaign to frighten me into leaving France of my own free will.

"They can't expel an American without proof," he said, "and they haven't found any proof. So they're trying to scare you out. It's a classic maneuver."

He was so positive about it that I was half persuaded he was right. As search followed search, my nerves got more and more on edge, but I tried to behave with all the calm I thought I would have shown if I had been conscious of untarnished innocence.

I also tried to bolster up the committee. As the police had reproached us with helping only Jews and foreigners, we added a department, under the direction of Charles Wolff, to assist intellectual refugees from Alsace and Lorraine, and we sent notices of the new service to the papers. The notices were widely printed; even Vichy's official news bulletin picked them up.

We also announced our Committee of Patrons. It included, among others, three members of Marshal Pétain's *Conseil National*, the President of the French Red Cross, Georges Duhamel, André Gide, Aristide Maillol and Henri Matisse. This, too, the newspapers faithfully reported. Inspired by our good works, one influential paper even ventured to editorialize on the generosity of America and its undying friendship for France.

The weakest thing about our position was the fact that we could get no support at all from the American Embassy or the Department of State. The Department continued to take the attitude that I should go home, and the Embassy co-operated with the French police in bringing pressure on me to go.

In January, when my passport expired, and I went to the Consulate to have it renewed, the Consul put on a very solemn face.

"I'm sorry," he said, "but I have instructions not to renew your passport until I've consulted the Department. If you'll leave it with me, I'll cable the Department and see what they say."

When I went back a few days later, he told me that instead of being renewed, my passport had been confiscated.

"I've had a reply from the Department about your passport," he said. "My instructions are to renew it only for immediate return to the United States, and then only for a period of two weeks. So I'm afraid I'll have to keep it here until you're ready to go. When you are, let me know, and I'll get it ready for you."

I tried again in May, with exactly the same result.

As a matter of fact, I would have been glad to go if there had been anybody to take my place. I tried to get one or two of the other American relief workers to step into my shoes, but with the exception of Howard Brooks of the Unitarian Service Committee, no one would, and Brooks could do so only for a very short time—after that he had to return to the States. I cabled the committee in New York to send someone over to replace me, but they never did. Instead, they kept telling me to stay; and I apparently never succeeded in making them realize that I could stay only for a very limited time.

It was a question of hanging on by grim determination until a substitute arrived; and the substitute never arrived. Meanwhile everyone on the staff was more than ever convinced that if I left before the successor showed up, the committee would immediately collapse, and everybody connected with it be arrested.

After Danny's arrest the Consul told me the police had informed him that unless I left France voluntarily they would have to arrest me or expel me. He said he had sent the State Department a coded cablegram asking the Department to ask the Emergency Rescue Committee to recall me.

A few weeks later he said he had had an answer. He wouldn't show it to me, on the grounds that it was an official communication and therefore not to be seen by anyone outside the Foreign Service. But he claimed that in substance it said the Emergency Rescue Committee had agreed that I should return to the United States "without delay."

As I had been getting cables from the committee almost daily telling me to stay, I found this difficult to believe. But I cabled New York once again, and promptly received the reply that they had never agreed to my recall and had done everything they could to make it possible for me to stay. The Consul, they said, had "acted entirely on his own responsibility."

By this time I was completely confused, and very, very tired of the whole business. If it hadn't been for Danny's pleading, I think I would have thrown everything over and gone. Danny, and the thought of what would happen to so many of the refugees if I did, kept me in Marseille.

Even the Villa Air-Bel was no longer what it had been: it was strangely solemn and silent now. After he left for Martinique, I moved up to André's room on the top floor. There were still some of his queer colored-paper cutouts on the sides of the window recess and the inside of one of the doors, and a few of his shells and butterflies on the mantel. But that was all that was left of him, that, and the memory of his laughter. The Surrealists came up to the house a few more times, but they seemed lost without their leader, and, after a few awkward hours, they went away again. The days of the games and drawing competitions were over. Sometimes, in that barnlike old house, I felt as though I were living in a painting by Louis David.

Then the people who were still living at the house quarreled, and most of them—including Jean and Maurice—moved away. In the end the only ones left were the Bénédites, Charles Wolff, the journalist, and I. Then I learned that Danny was taking part in underground meetings of the Socialist Party and, while I could hardly disapprove, the information made me uneasy. A little later Jean told me he had joined a de Gaullist group called Libération, and asked me if I thought the British would help him get arms. It was a thrilling, but also a rather disturbing, idea.

About the same time I discovered that our *Ministre aux Affaires Étrangères*, Marcel Chaminade, was contributing a weekly column to a rabidly pro-German and anti-Semitic newspaper. Although his column was straight reporting, I had no choice but to give him notice. The discovery was a rude shock to my self-confidence. First Dimitru, then Chaminade. How many more enemies had I naively welcomed into camp?

-9-

Shortly after the episode of the $6,000, the American Consul called me in and warned me that the Gestapo was bringing pressure on the French police to arrest me immediately. A few days later, at about six o'clock in the evening, a motorcycle dispatch rider arrived at the office from the Prefecture with a summons from the *Intendant de la Police de la Région Marseillaise, le Capitaine de Frégate* de Rodellec du Porzic. I was prayed to present myself at the *locale* of the *intendant* the following morning at eleven o'clock sharp. Failure to accept the invitation would result in my immediate arrest, the summons said.

I saw de Rodellec du Porzic the next morning. As a matter of fact, I was curious to meet him. I knew that he was a Breton naval officer from an old and aristocratic family; that he was a close friend of Admiral Darlan; that he had been appointed to his unpleasant post by the Admiral; and that all the search warrants which had been waved in my face during the previous month had been signed by him or his *chef de cabinet.*

I arrived at his office promptly at eleven o'clock, and he kept me waiting on a bench outside for three-quarters of an hour—a subtle form of torture. When the buzzer finally sounded, I was shown into a large office, with a desk at one end of it, in front of a big window. De Rodellec du Porzic was sitting behind the desk, but the light from the window was so bright that I couldn't see his face clearly for several minutes.

He motioned to me to sit down in a chair opposite him. Then he opened a big *dossier,* and I could see the blue stationery of my committee from time to time as he slowly turned over the papers.

Finally he looked up.

"You have caused my good friend the Consul-General of the United States much annoyance," he said.

"I guess the Consul can take care of his own problems," I said.

"My friend the Consul-General tells me that your government and the American committee you represent have both asked you to return to the United States without delay," he continued.

"There's some mistake," I said. "My instructions are to stay."

"This affair of your secretary," de Rodellec du Porzic went on, obviously referring to Danny, "will have very serious consequences for you."

"I can't see how," I said. "One of my employees has committed an indiscretion. But he acted entirely on his own responsibility. There is no proof that I was involved in any way."

"In the new France, we do not need proof," de Rodellec du Porzic said. "In the days of the Republic, it used to be believed that it was better to let a hundred criminals escape than to arrest one innocent man. We have done away with all that. We believe that it is better to arrest a hundred innocent men than to let one criminal escape."

"I see," I said, "that we are very far apart in our ideas of the rights of man."

"Yes," de Rodellec du Porzic said, "I know that in the United States you still adhere to the old idea of human rights. But you will come to our view in the end. It is merely a question of time. We have realized that society is more important than the individual. You will come to see that, too."

He paused to close the *dossier.*

"When are you leaving France?" he asked.

I said I had no definite plans.

"Unless you leave France of your own free will," he said, "I shall be obliged to arrest you and place you in *résidence forcée* in some small town far from Marseille, where you can do no harm."

I had to play for time.

"I see," I said. "Can you give me a little time to arrange my affairs and get someone over from America to take my place as president of the committee before I go? I'm willing to go myself, since you insist; but I want to make sure the committee will go on after I leave."

"Why are you so much interested in your committee?" he asked.

"Because it is the only hope of many of the refugees," I said.

"I see," he said. "How much time do you need?"

"Well," I said, "I'll cable New York today. It will take them a little time to find someone to replace me, and some more time for him to get his passport and visas and get here. Can you give me until the 15th of August?"

"That will be satisfactory," he said.

I got up to go. Then I turned back and asked a final question.

"Tell me," I said, "frankly, why are you so much opposed to me?"

"*Parce que vous avez trop protégé des juifs et des anti-Nazis,*" he said. "Because you have protected Jews and anti-Nazis."

## XV. *Good-bye to All That*

A DAY or so after my talk with de Rodellec du Porzic the Consul handed me my passport, validated for one month, for westbound travel only, and with the Portuguese and Spanish transit visas and the French exit visa already in it. This was a service the American Consulate did not ordinarily render; usually you had to get the transit and exit visas yourself.

I decided to go to Vichy and find out what was behind it. Once again the Consul warned me not to go. This time, he said, the police would surely arrest me. But nothing happened in Vichy at all—that was the trouble with it. I saw everybody;

at least I saw everybody who would see me. Except at the Ministry of the Interior, everyone was very friendly. But no one could do anything for me. The American Embassy refused even to make an inquiry; you ought to have gone home a long time ago, they said.

The best advice came, as usual, from the American newspapermen. They advised me to stay away from Marseille until my successor arrived, on the theory of "out of sight, out of mind."

So from Vichy I went on a little "vacation" on the Côte d'Azur. I stayed a week at Sanary-sur-Mer, and Jean and Maurice came down from Marseille from time to time to consult me about the underground railroad through Spain. Then, because the period of grace he had given me had expired by that time, and I was afraid that de Rodellec du Porzic might arrest me if he knew where I was, I moved slowly along the coast, staying a day or two at Toulon and St. Tropez and St. Raphael, until I reached Cannes.

Danny met me at Cannes, and we went on to Nice by train, and then walked along the Grande Corniche to the Italian demarcation line, just west of Menton. From Menton we took a bus back to Monaco, along the Petite Corniche.

Strange feeling at Monaco: you could sense as soon as you stepped over the line that you were no longer in France. Vichy's propaganda was completely absent; there was not a single portrait of the Marshal, nor even one of the posters which were everywhere in France announcing the first anniversary of the Legion. It was a wonderful relief, and once I got there I didn't want to go away again. For the first time in more than a year I felt safe from arrest.

But Danny persuaded me that my feeling was foolish. The French police were only bluffing, he said; they would never dare arrest me. So, after a day of idleness and good eating, we started back to Nice. While we were waiting in Beausoleil for the bus, I photographed a Vichy propaganda poster. Immediately a plainclothesman appeared as if from nowhere and arrested us. We had to go with him to the police station and show our identity papers and satisfy him we were not spies before he would let us out again.

In Nice I took pictures of the broken windows of Jewish-owned shops, and the entrance of the local office of the Legion, which flaunted a large sign reading *Entrée interdite aux juifs non-combattants*—"Entrance forbidden to non-combatant Jews." I called once again on Matisse and Gide. Finally I gave in to Danny's pleading, and my own real desire, and took the train back to Marseille. My passport and visas had expired by that time, and I thought I couldn't be expelled.

-2-

When I reached the office, I found a cable from New York on my desk.

"Successor appointed making last preparations to send him," it read.

It was Wednesday, August 27th, almost two weeks to the day after my period of grace had expired, and still I hadn't been arrested. Perhaps, after all, I thought, as I settled down to work, de Rodellec du Porzic was only bluffing.

Two days later, just before lunch, two young detectives came to the office with an order signed by de Rodellec. It said they were to take me to the *Evêché* and hold me at his disposal there. No explanation. I was not to be allowed to communicate with anyone. I tried to telephone the Consulate, but even that was forbidden.

At eleven o'clock the next morning, after spending the night on a table in the big room of the *Brigade des Râfles*, I was called into the office of the *commissaire* and shown an *ordre de refoulement*, signed by de Rodellec. It said that the *nommé*, Varian Fry, being an undesirable alien, was to be conducted to the Spanish frontier immediately and there *refoulé*—pushed out.

The *commissaire* was very polite. He pointed out that I was not being expelled, and explained that if you are expelled you may never return, whereas if you are *refoulé* you may come back, if you can get a visa.

When I told him I could be neither *expulsé* nor *refoulé* immediately, as my transit and exit visas had all expired, he called de Rodellec's office, but they ordered him to send me down to the border anyway, saying that my visas would be renewed there. I told the *commissaire* this was impossible, but he only shrugged.

"Orders are orders," he said.

Then he presented me to the man who was to accompany me to the frontier.

"This is Inspector Garandel," he said. "He is going to take you to the border."

"How do you do?" Garandel said, taking my hand. He seemed embarrassed.

"It is my duty to show you that we French are not barbarians," he said.

"I never for a moment thought you were," I said.

He smiled.

"But the way you have been treated . . . ?" he said.

"Oh, that," I said, "that is just some Frenchmen. One might almost say one Frenchman. . . ."

He beamed.

"Yes," he said. "I'm glad you realize."

At half-past three the same two detectives who had arrested me came to get me. Riding in a large police van, we went first to the office. I emptied the contents of my desk into a paper box and said good-bye to the members of the staff who were still there. Danny had gone to Vichy to try and stop the proceedings, and most of the others, profiting from the lull in refugee work which always followed a raid or an arrest, had gone home for the day. But little Anna Gruss was there and helped me get my things together, and Alfonso the night watchman gave me one of his bearlike Spanish hugs.

When all my personal papers had been packed, I took the box down to the car, and we drove out to the house. There I had to pack, in one hour, everything I had accumulated in more than a year: clothing, paintings, maps, books and documents. No time for long farewells; but I said good-bye to the cook, the scullery maid and the gardener, and shook hands with Dr. Thumin, who had come up to see what the excitement was about, and stood on the terrace, holding his dirty bowler hat in his hands, and looking more puzzled than ever as we drove away.

Garandel showed up again at six and took me to the railroad station in a police car. As we drove through back streets, I didn't have a chance to see the Canebière and the Vieux Port again, but when we got to the Gare St. Charles I went to the top of the monumental staircase and looked down the boulevards d'Athènes and Dugommier to the Canebière and the boulevard Garibaldi. The city was golden in the late afternoon sun, and people were hurrying home from work. But it was hushed and silent, nevertheless. There were almost no automobiles anywhere, no sounds of gears grinding, horns honking, policemen blowing their whistles. Everywhere people were wandering down the middle of the streets, as unconcernedly as though they were on the sidewalks, and almost the only sounds you could hear were the distant moans of the trolley cars' horns and the occasional patter of a pair of wooden-soled shoes on the pavement. Even the port was dead.

-3-

We had a hurried dinner at the station restaurant, with most of the members of the staff somehow assembled, and then packed ourselves into a compartment marked *Réservé pour la Sûreté Nationale:* Theo Bénédite, Jean Gemahling, Maurice, three other members of the staff, Garandel and "*le nommé.*"

It was the eve of the celebration of the first anniversary of Pétain's Legion. In true Goebbels' fashion, Vichy had arranged to have relay runners carry the flame from the tomb of the unknown soldier in Paris to every corner of France, to light ceremonial fires in all the principal cities and towns.

As we passed through blacked-out Nîmes we could see the fire burning on the top of the Tour Magne.

Someone had given me a bottle of cognac as a farewell present, and, as the bottle went around, Garandel began to tell stories of Marseille police life. The time passed quickly until we reached Narbonne at one o'clock in the morning.

Danny arrived from Vichy at eight the next morning. He reported that there was nothing to be done at Vichy. My expulsion had been ordered by the Ministry of the Interior, with the approval of the American Embassy, and neither the Embassy nor the Interior had any intention of reversing the verdict.

About eleven o'clock we took the train for Cerbère. We arrived at half-past one and had lunch in the station restaurant, a rather doleful lunch, because I thought it was to be my last in France.

After lunch Garandel took me through to the desk where they visa the passports. The *commissaire* took one look at mine and announced that I had no valid transit visas on it. Garandel told him what the Prefecture had said about getting the visas renewed at the border, but the *commissaire* only made a grimace.

"What's the matter with them up there at Marseille?" he asked. "They don't seem to know their heads from their tails! You can't get any visas here. There aren't any Consulates."

I thought Garandel looked pleased at that. We went back to the station buffet, where the others were waiting, and he put in a call to Marseille to ask for instructions. It wasn't until half-past eight that evening that he was able to reach the Prefecture. Meanwhile the rest of us spent the afternoon talking and swimming.

When Garandel had made his call he told us the Prefecture had instructed him to take me back to Perpignan and hand me over to the local police, to be locked up in the Perpignan jail until the visas had been renewed.

"Don't you worry," he said, looking me straight in the eye, "you'll stay in a hotel."

-4-

Thanks to the enthusiastic co-operation of the American Consulate in Marseille, it took only five days to renew my passport and get new transit and exit visas on it.

The week passed quickly—too quickly. Garandel spent the days visiting old cronies who had retired from the police force on their pensions and had bought farms in the neighborhood of Perpignan. But he always returned to the city just before dark, and stuck close beside me from then until it was time to go to bed.

One evening at dinner I asked him why he felt he could safely leave me alone with my colleagues in the daytime but guarded mc like a hawk at night.

"After all," I teased, "I could just as easily escape during the daytime as at night."

"*Il n'y en a pas question*," Garandel said with an impatient snort. "But the town is full of Boches. [As a matter of fact, it was; they had come to supervise the gathering of the grapes.] You can never tell what they might do to you on one of these dark streets if you should go out alone at night."

Garandel's absences gave us a welcome opportunity to talk over the problems created by my sudden departure. We decided to make Jean the executive director of the committee, pending the arrival of my successor from New York, for he was the only non-Jewish male member of the staff who had never had any trouble with the police. Danny was to continue to direct the *marche du bureau*, as he called it, but from behind the scenes. And Maurice would have charge of the illegal departures as before.

As for the Villa Air-Bel, it was to be turned into a *centre d'accueil* for Alsatian intellectuals, in the hope that this would strengthen the position of the committee. Our greatest fear was that as soon as there was no longer an American at its head, the police would suppress the committee and intern the whole staff in a concentration camp.

Saturday turned out to be a gray and rainy day. We took

the eleven-o'clock train to Cerbère, and had our second and final farewell lunch in the station restaurant. It was a depressed and awkward ceremony, in which there were many long silences.

After lunch, we went into the station waiting room, and there, surrounded by travel posters and trunks in transit, we took leave of one another. Everybody seemed very much moved, and everybody kissed me good-bye. But it was Danny who seemed the most deeply affected. He put his arms around me and hugged me, and I could feel his muscles, young and hard, under the thin material of his coat.

"You can't leave us, mon vieux," he whispered. "You've become almost more French than American."

Just then the conductor blew his whistle.

"En voiture!" the guard cried.

It was time for the train to leave. I stood on the bottom step and waved my handkerchief as it pulled slowly out of the station. They waved back.

They were still standing there, in a stiff row, waving, as the train entered the international tunnel.

At Port-Bou all the passengers had to line up for the examination of passports. I took my place in the line and Garandel stood beside me, making conversation. I was afraid he would tell the Spanish police I had been expelled from France, but he simply showed his badge.

"I am accompanying this gentleman," he said.

After my passport had been stamped, he helped me open my bags for the customs inspection. He was very solicitous of my things and packed them back carefully after the inspector had passed me.

When everything was finished, and I was ready to get into the Barcelona train, he shook my hand.

"I hope you will not think ill of France," he said.

"Of France, never," I said. "Of certain Frenchmen, yes. You understand?"

"I understand," he said.

And he stood on the platform, waving to me, as the train started toward Barcelona.

-5-

It was also raining in Spain, and the trees and fields were wet and sad. I got down my bag and took out the copy of St. Exupéry's *Terre des Hommes* Danny had given me in Perpignan. On the fly leaf, in his round, full hand, was a dedication:

".... *et celui-ci, qui doit se relire de temps à autre et qui rend optimiste. Nous en avons eu besoin parfois et il en faudra encore souvent.*"

During the rest of the trip I alternately looked out the window at the muddy Mediterranean and the glistening Catalan landscape and read *Terre des Hommes*. But it did not make me optimistic, or do very much to lessen my gloom. Innumerable images crowded my mind and filled me with a melancholy nostalgia. I thought of the office first, of course, and of my colleagues there. Then of the Villa Air-Bel and of the good company which used to fill it. Then of countless weekend trips: of Les Baux in the golden autumn sun, of Nice, and its roses in the snow in December. Of Sanary and St. Tropez and Cannes and Nice, and the day I spent walking along the Grande Corniche with Danny. Of the Allier at Vichy, flowing silent at night beneath its weeping willows. Of the days on the *Sinaïa*, and the songs we sang, and the tricks we played to get more wine, and the deep anger I felt at being held against my will. Of letters and reports and cables. Of passports and visas, real and false. Of the concentration camps, and the people in them. Of the faces of the thousand refugees I had sent out of France, and the faces of a thousand more I had had to leave behind.

Oh, let's admit it—I was very sad. It was partly the land—one grows attached to a place very easily, especially when the place is a country as beautiful as France. But it was much more my friends, French and refugee, and that spirit of intimate companionship and devotion to a common cause we had all shared.

*"Liés à nos frères par un but commun et qui se situe en dehors de nous, alors seulement nous respirons et l'expérience nous montre qu'aimer ce n'est point nous regarder l'un l'autre mais regarder ensemble dans la même direction. Il n'est de camarades que s'ils s'unissent dans la même cordée, vers le même sommet en quoi il se retrouvent . . ."*

St. Exupéry was writing of a crack-up in the desert, but the same words, I found, applied with equal force to my own experience in those thirteen months now past—an experience none the less intense for being more protracted. We too— my friends and I—had been bound together by a common cause, and we too had stood shoulder to shoulder with our eyes fixed on a common goal. Thus we too had become comrades.

-6-

One of the first things I did in Lisbon was to look up Lussu. He and his wife were living, entirely illegally, in a private house far from the center of town. From him I got, for the first time, a clear picture of the underground railroad over which I had sent so many men and women that spring and summer—some to prison, to be sure, but most to safety. Lussu not only had his own experience to report, but he had also interviewed the grateful Schnek before Schnek sailed for America.

Lussu was enthusiastic about the route. He said that all the guides were excellent. There were good resting places on the Spanish side of the French frontier, in old churches, abandoned barns, and tool sheds; the guide from Barcelona met the guide from France at the appointed place, and almost on schedule (punctuality has never been a Spanish virtue).

In Barcelona the underground travelers were hidden in the house of a waiter, where they were treated beautifully and even had their clothes washed and pressed by the waiter's wife. The guide from Barcelona to Madrid got the travelers through the control by pulling out of his pocket the visiting card of Serano Suñer, General Franco's brother-in-law. On it was written the Spanish equivalent of "Please show every courtesy to the bearer." In Madrid the travelers were put up in small hotels where they didn't have to register.

It was only on the last lap that the route began to break down. The guide responsible for the stretch from Madrid to the town where the route crossed the Portuguese frontier was less successful than the others with the police control on the train. Both Schnek and Lussu had had difficulties with it, though both had managed to keep out of serious trouble by paying bribes. As for the Portuguese guide who was supposed to conduct the travelers from the Portuguese border to Lisbon, he never showed up at all. Lussu somehow managed for himself, and Schnek was actually arrested by the Portuguese police, only to be saved from prison by some Portuguese soldiers, who took him for a French de Gaullist and sent him to the capital in a truck, hidden under a load of cabbages!

I spent six weeks in Lisbon trying to improve the route. Before I left, Maurice arrived from Marseille and set to work on it too. Lussu made frequent trips to the border to find better guides for the Portuguese end. He even went into Spain to see about replacing the guide between Madrid and the Portuguese frontier. He was interested in the underground railroad not only as a means of getting people out of France, but primarily as a means of sending underground workers into Italy. Some months later he used the route to go back to France, and from there he went to Italy, to direct the underground work of the Action Party. He was in Rome throughout the period of the German occupation, and he was there when the Allied troops liberated the city from the Nazis. How many others used our route to go back and carry on the underground struggle I have no idea. But I am sure that many more used it to get out of Europe.

Carlos never succeeded in getting exit visas for the Wolffs. Instead Maurice bought Danish passports for them from

Drach, got them Cuban immigration visas, and moved them from place to place in Southern France, until, with the help of the Abbé Glasberg, assistant to Cardinal Gerlier of Lyon, they were able to get exit visas at the Lyon Prefecture and board a Spanish ship at Cadiz. When they reached Cuba, one of our hardest problems was solved.

Among the very few refugees left in Lisbon were Mr. and Mrs. Berthold Jacob. The Unitarians had persuaded an influential Spanish businessman to get them released from prison and bring them to Portugal in his limousine—without visas. Like the Lussus, the Jacobs were living illegally, waiting for overseas visas, which never arrived.

One day Jacob called at the Unitarian office, and was told, as usual, that there was still no news of his visa. That night he did not return to his room. His wife came to us the next morning, in great anxiety, to report his disappearance. We made inquiries, and learned that on leaving the office the previous day he had been stopped by two detectives, accompanied by a man speaking Portuguese with an accent, who pointed him out to them. It was ten days before we could get any further information about him; and then we were told that he was in the Model Prison in Madrid, at the disposition of the Ministry of Foreign Affairs. We hired Spanish lawyers, but they were helpless. Jacob was incommunicado. So far as I know, no one has ever heard of him since. He has simply disappeared. It is not difficult to guess where he went.

# XVI. *After Much Suffering*

WHEN I arrived in New York, I learned that the State Department had devised a new and cruelly difficult form of visa application, which made it almost impossible for refugees to enter this country. Fortunately, Mexico and Cuba were more humane, and our office in Marseille (which still continued to function) sent out nearly three hundred more people between the time I left and the time it was raided and closed by the police, on June 2, 1942.

Among the refugees to cross the Atlantic were the pianist, Heinz Jolles; the Catholic writer, Edgar Alexander-Emmerich; the sculptor, Bernard Reder; Wanda Landowska, the harpsichordist; the psychiatrist, Dr. Bruno Strauss; the German art critic, Paul Westheim; the Sicilian novelist, Giuseppe Garetto; the Surrealist poet, Benjamin Péret; Otto Klepper, a former liberal Prime Minister of Prussia, and one of the most endangered men in France; Charles Stirling, formerly director of the Ingres Museum at Montauban, and now an assistant curator at the Metropolitan Museum of Art in New York City; Marcel Duchamp, the Surrealist painter; Jean Malaquais, the French novelist; Alfredo Mendizabel, formerly professor of philosophy at the University of Madrid; and Dr. Gustavo Pittaluga, once vice-president of the Health Commission of the League of Nations.

Almost immediately after the closing of the office on the boulevard Garibaldi there began one of the most horrible man-hunts in all history. First in the occupied zone of France and then in the unoccupied, men, women and children of

Jewish ancestry were rounded up by the police, packed into cattle cars, and sent off to Poland to be exterminated.

Meanwhile, Danny and one or two other members of the staff had gone into hiding. But the committee was able to send them funds via Switzerland from time to time, and somehow they managed to pass the money along to the refugees, most of whom had also gone into hiding. Thus they kept them alive even after the occupation of the unoccupied zone, or enabled them to escape over the border to Switzerland. Even old Modigliani finally gave in to his wife's insistence and fled, though he took his beard and his fur coat with him.

I would like to be able to end this book like a Victorian novel, by telling you what finally happened to all the characters. But I can't do that, not only because there are far too many characters, but also because I don't know myself what has happened to many of them.

We have now accounted for all the members of the staff who remained in France, and for most of our co-conspirators. Jean was arrested for his underground activities only three months after I left—apparently the police had been observing him for a long time—but he was released on bail a few months later, and immediately disappeared. He was arrested once and perhaps twice subsequently, but both times he got away. He is back in Paris now with his wife. For he has married a girl he met in the underground.

Danny, too, is back in Paris, though it is only by a miracle that he is still alive. Some time in 1942 he joined a *maquis*, becoming the leader of the group. In May, 1944, he was arrested by the Gestapo. Luckily, the Germans didn't find the arms his group had been receiving by parachute, so he was not immediately shot, as he would have been if they had. Instead he was kept in prison, as a hostage. In August, however, a member of his *maquis* confessed, under torture, and Danny was about to be led before a firing squad when the American troops landed in Southern France and he was saved. He is now business manager of the daily newspaper, *Franc-Tireur*, organ of the moderate wing of the Resistance.

Theo, too, has come through all right, and she and Danny now have a baby daughter.

Mrs. Gruss, my gnome-like secretary, turned out to be a heroine. Throughout the long years of the total occupation she worked in our underground, helping to get money to the refugees or guide them to the frontier.

But Bill Freier, the little Austrian cartoonist, will never draw another cartoon, or forge another identity card: he was one of the many thousands who were sent to Poland to be destroyed. Nor will Charles Wolff, the journalist, ever listen to his phonograph records again or ever take another drink of wine: the sighs of women in love were drowned out forever by his own screams. For he was tortured to death by the French fascist militia.

The body of Frederic Drach, the purveyor of false passports, was found in his hotel room, riddled by bullets, a few hours after the Germans occupied the southern zone. Still another of our collaborators, a Frenchman by the name of Jacques Weisslitz, was sent to Poland, like Freier. His wife was sent with him. The State Department had refused them visas.

Of our clients who remained in France we know that some were arrested by the Gestapo and taken to Germany, presumably to be murdered. We know that Largo Caballero is in the hands of the Germans, if he is still alive. But many of the refugees, including many of the German social democrats, joined the maquis, and some of them are still within its ranks. One, a former Reichstag deputy, is Adjutant-Chief of the famous Maquis of Savoy, a position any Frenchman would be proud of. But of most of our old clients we have still heard nothing at all.

Of those who came to America, on the other hand, I could tell you much. You already know about the famous ones—about the success of Franz Werfel's *Song of Bernadette*, and Konrad Heiden's *Der Fuehrer*, for instance; about Wanda Landowska's concerts and Max Ernst's and André Masson's exhibitions. Marc Chagall is well satisfied with American trees and American cows and finds Connecticut just as good to paint in as Southern France. Jacques Lipchitz is delighted with New York and says it is an ideal place to work. Some of the writers, and particularly the poets, have had a harder time adjusting. But Walter Mehring has published a volume of poems, and I think that he intends to stay. In fact I have a whole shelf full of books published since they got here by men and women I sent to America.

Many of the refugees are, of course, in the United States Army. Beamish is attached to the Office of Strategic Services, and is now in Italy. Maurice is a lieutenant in the Army Medical Corps. He is also in Italy. Others are privates or corporals or sergeants in Italy, France, Belgium, Holland.

At least one, Heinz Behrendt, has given his life for America. He was killed in the attack on Biak, in the South Pacific.

Scores are working in various government offices. Among them are Franzi and Lena and André Breton. Still others are doing jobs in defense plants. Some have already returned to their own countries, to resume the battle for democracy there: Randolfo Pacciardi, of the Italian Republican Party, Giuseppe Modigliani, of the Socialist Party, and Emilio Lussu and Alberto Ciana, of the Action Party, to mention only a few. Others are planning to leave as soon as they can get the visas. Among them is Bedrich Heine. Like many another German social democrat, he is waiting impatiently for the day when he can go back to Germany to help rebuild democracy there.

Not all, perhaps, have justified the efforts we made for them. Some have died, and, in a very real sense, some have been crippled for life by what they have been through. But, as Beamish said, we had to bring them *all* back. At least we had to try.

None, I need hardly add, has ever had his loyalty questioned. All of them know, perhaps even better than we, the true value of democracy. For they once lost it, and only after much suffering found it again.

# ORIGINAL, UNPUBLISHED FOREWORD

This is the story of the most intense experience of my life. I have been told that I can't tell it now; that I can never tell it. But I think I can tell it now, and what's more I think I must. That is what I am going to do. I am going to tell it as honestly and as completely as I can, changing names and details only when to give the true names and details might compromise someone still in Nazi Europe and get him arrested and imprisoned—or worse.

I think I can tell the story if I do it that way. And I think I must tell it. Not only because it is difficult for me to keep it to myself any longer. Not only because it is struggling in me to be told. Also because if, by telling it, I can make even a few other Americans understand, then I shall have fulfilled a duty to my friends in Europe which nothing can make me forget or shirk.

I have tried—God knows I have tried—to get back again into the mood of American life since I left France for the last time. But it doesn't work. There is only one way left to try, and that is the way I am going to try now. If I can get it all out, put it all down just as it happened, if I can make others see it and feel it as I did, then maybe I can sleep soundly again at night, the way I used to before I took the Clipper to Lisbon. Maybe I can become a normal human being again, exorcize the ghosts which haunt me, stop living in another world, come back to the world of America. But I know now that I can't do that until I have told the story—all of it.

Those ghosts won't stop haunting me until I have done

241

their bidding. They are the ghosts of the living who do not want to die. Go, they said, go back and make America understand, make Americans understand and help before it is too late.

I have tried to do their bidding in other and easier ways. By lecturing, writing articles, talking to friends. But it doesn't work. That doesn't work either. People don't understand. Because they don't see the whole thing, or because what they see they see distantly, impersonally. It doesn't touch them, any more than a table of statistics touches them—even when the statistics represent the strangling death of children by diphtheria or the violent deaths of women and children under Stuka dive bombers. They haven't seen it, heard it, smelt it, so it doesn't move them.

But if I put it all down, the little things with the big, the joys as well as the pains and sorrows, the successes and the failures, the country, the people, the things they ate and what they couldn't find to eat, the fear . . . then maybe others will understand and be moved and want to do something to help. That is really why I have decided I must tell the story now.

It is a story of horror. Not the horror of sudden death on the battlefields, but a slow horror which is none the less terrible for being protracted and invisible. The horror of men, women and children shut up in concentration camps. Of a man-hunt by the Gestapo. Of arrests, extraditions, kidnappings. Of suicide, murder, death in a Gestapo prison.

It is a story of gangsters, smugglers and spies. Of baseness and heroism, treachery and devotion. Of escapes which succeeded, and some which didn't. Of bureaucracy and indifference which cost men their lives. Of human solidarity and the warmth of human sympathy. Of the anguish of human suffering. Of hope and despair.

When I think about it, and I think about it all the time, there emerges from the confused jumble of images in my mind the look on Helen's face when I left France for the last time, left leaving behind me so many refugees who had come to identify me with their only hope of being rescued from the hell Hitler has made of Europe. Helen, standing there on the platform of the railway station at Cerbère, and waving her handkerchief as my train drew out of the station, bore on her face the sadness of all the refugees who have been left behind.

I wish I could forget that look. If only for five minutes. I deserve that much respite from the strain. But I can't. I wonder if I ever shall be able to. For I left her, knowing that she would go back to Sanary and her crippled son and realize slowly—only slowly—that for her there is no hope.

I think of Bill Freier, the cheerful little cartoonist, in the prison camp at Vernet, and of his friend Mina, already expecting a baby when he was taken away. They gave him 24 hours leave to marry her just before the baby was born. Then they took him back to camp, probably to spend the rest of the war there.

I think of Franz Boegler, also in Vernet. His wife and son are here. I tried to get him out of France. I put him on a sailboat bound for Gibraltar. But the boat sprang a leak in a storm and had to turn back, and Boegler was arrested and taken back to the camp. He never hopes to see his baby again. He is on the Gestapo's blacklist.

I think of Limot, the photographer, living, with his wife, his two children and his aged mother, in a one-room housekeeping apartment in Marseilles, still hoping—vainly, I am afraid—that their visas will come before the Germans come, or they all die of hunger, or Limot kills himself because he can't stand seeing his children growing up to be slaves.

I think of Vladimir, the boy with the tumor on the brain which will kill him some day if it isn't operated, and who can't go to Paris to have it removed there because he is Jewish and can't come to New York to have it operated here because he has no friends in the United States who will fill out the yards and yards of State Department visa forms.

I think of Rudolph Breitscheid and Rudolph Hilferding as they were the last time I saw them, just before the French police arrested them and handed them over to the Gestapo, and Hilferding was found dead in his Gestapo cell a few days later.

I think of the ash-grey color of Alfred Apfel's face as he lay dying of a heart attack in my office, after I had told him what had happened to Breitscheid and Hilferding.

I think of a certain German anti-Nazi novelist when fear got the better of him and he came to my room in the Hotel Splendide at Marseilles and refused to go out again unless I went with him—believing, pathetically, that the mere presence of an American beside him would protect him from Hitler's hangmen.

I think of Berthold Jacob, who managed to get to Lisbon, with the help of a false passport, only to be kidnapped by the Gestapo there before he could get a visa to go on.

I think of Hermann Richard Wagner, who also got to Lisbon and was also kidnapped there, for the same reason.

Of those two young men who were brought through Marseilles from a concentration camp in Africa and handed over to the Gestapo to be shot because they had had the courage to defy Hitler when they were members of the seamen's union at Hamburg, years ago.

Of all the other men who have been dragged out of the French concentration camps and handed over to the Nazis to be tortured, hanged, beheaded or shot.

When I think of all this, it seems incredible, macabre, even, that I should have spent some of my last few hours in New York worrying about not having a new dress shirt, and actually going over to Brooks Brothers and buying one.

But that only shows, I guess, what a novice I was at the sort of work I was setting out to do, and how little I really understood what it means to a country like France to be defeated by the Nazis. Or what it means to the refugees in France to have no place to flee to.

Now I know, and I want others to know before it is too late. That is why I have decided to write a book.

# AFTERWORD

Varian Fry's completed version of *Surrender on Demand* appeared shortly before VE day, some three and a half years after Fry was forced to leave France. Despite the passage of time, Fry—a foreign-affairs journalist by profession—chose to bring out *Surrender on Demand* as a personal odyssey. In all respects, Fry offered the account of his experiences as a story of naive courage in the face of great odds.

At this moment in world events, Fry could not have done otherwise. The war in Europe was ending. *Surrender on Demand* had to appeal to a particular audience: post-war readers seeking to learn not about America's short-comings, but about its valiant efforts. The book was presented, according to the published foreword, as a thrilling story of how Europe's cultural elite were rescued through the daring initiatives of an unsuspecting and inexperienced reporter. It was issued with a dramatic and eyecatching book jacket, designed to appeal to eager book buyers.

Fry had always intended that the account of his underground activities would be told from a personal point of view. The original draft foreword, written early in 1942, and never published until now, also expresses without reservation Fry's desire to present a confidential memoir. However, *Surrender on Demand* could not stand totally outside the larger political arena. Fry's background as a journalist and as a critic of current world affairs did not permit that.

Fry in the end chose to close his story with a commentary not on the success of his mission, but on the reluctance of

America to embrace Europe's refugees. In his final words, Fry muses that not one of his "clients" was ever accused of being disloyal. None became a "public charge," or a "fifth columnist"—the feared character traits, identified by the State Department, that barred thousands of would-be émigrés. As he did so often in *Surrender on Demand*, Fry presented his remarks with elegant subtlety, with great dignity, and with tremendous restraint.

Nevertheless, State Department documents in the National Archives reveal that Fry's actions both in Marseille and after his return were hardly restrained. Nor were they naive. From the very first days of his arrival in Marseille, Fry challenged local consuls and openly criticized their slow and bureaucratic methods of processing visa applications. Within weeks, the American diplomatic corps in France had launched a serious campaign to have him leave. In Washington, State Department officials pressed his home committee, the Emergency Rescue Committee, to recall him. All the while, Fry continued to write countless protest letters, to send distress telegrams, and to file detailed reports. Fry's prolonged stay in Marseille was not so much in contempt of German and French authorities as in opposition to American officials, the very persons whose aid and assistance he sought during his first hours there. He maintained his stance long after he was expelled and throughout the war's duration.

Fry's behavior in Marseille is indeed surprising given his background. Varian Mackey Fry was born on October 15, 1907, and grew up in Ridgewood, New Jersey. He attended several prep schools, including Hotchkiss in Connecticut. At Harvard, he chose the prestigious but austere concentration, Classics. By tradition, his classical education would have sent him directly into the foreign service, a world requiring knowledge of history and culture, and excellence in languages. Harvard also nurtured his literary interests. As an undergraduate, he, together with his classmate, Lincoln Kirstein, was a founding editor of the journal *Hound & Horn,* an innovative and creative quarterly containing prose, poetry, and critical essays. One summer he set out on a tour of Europe, visiting major museums and surveying remote classical sites in Greece. Fry's exposure to Europe's contemporary scene, as well as to its past heritage, influenced him. After graduation he returned to New York and began studies at Columbia University in the field of international affairs and journalism. By 1935, he established himself as a writer, succeeding the respected Quincy Howe as editor for *The Living Age*, a well-established monthly magazine that reprinted articles and stories from the foreign press. Three years later, he was appointed editor of Headline Books, an educational series of the Foreign Policy Association. He wrote position papers and policy pamphlets, intended by this educational "think tank" to influence American foreign policy in Europe and the Far East.

His travel to Germany in 1935, on behalf of *The Living Age*, made him an eyewitness to the brutal acts of Hitler's anti-Jewish policies. Fry returned to write his first news report describing a pogrom he had witnessed on the streets of Berlin. Shortly thereafter, he met Karl Frank (a.k.a Paul Hagen), a young leader of Germany's ousted Social Democratic party. Taken by Frank's ardent and persuasive ideas, Fry agreed to help raise funds in the United States to support the anti-Hitler resistance activities of some of Frank's colleagues in Czechoslovakia. Eventually, Frank founded the American Friends of German Freedom, with the influential educators Dr. Frank Kingdon (then president of the University of Newark) and Reinhold Niebuhr (head of Union Theological Seminary, New York) as its principal spokespersons.

Fry's involvement with the American Friends of German Freedom intensified when Germany began to extend control over Europe. In June 1940, Fry was instrumental in organizing a luncheon held to raise funds to support the emigration of the young Social Democrats (the very ones Fry names in *Surrender on Demand* as his first clients at the Hotel Splendide). At the luncheon, held three days after France's capitulation to Germany on June 22, 1940, guests such as Erica

Mann, daughter of Thomas Mann, argued that writers, artists, and intellectuals who opposed Hitler through their works were also threatened by Article XIX, the so-called "surrender on demand" clause of the Franco-German Armistice. On that day the Emergency Rescue Committee was formed.

In the weeks following the luncheon, the new committee solicited names of endangered intellectual and political refugees from a wide spectrum of prominent leaders in the United States. The German writer Thomas Mann and the French Theologian Jacques Maritain joined with other celebrated academic and political exiles to draw up lists of persons caught up, as Fry put it, "in the most gigantic man-trap in history." Max Ascoli provided the names of at-risk anti-fascist Italians; Czech leader Jan Masaryk provided names of stateless Czechs; Alvarez del Vayo and Joseph Buttinger compiled names of Spanish and Austrian anti-Nazis, respectively. Other cultural and academic figures, including Alvin Johnson of the New School for Social Research and Alfred H. Barr, Jr., of the Museum of Modern Art, also sent in names of persons thought to be on the Nazis' "blacklist." These names were sent to the State Department for consideration of special emergency visitors visas. When no one came forward to go to France to help these individuals, Fry volunteered. He expected to contact each one, probably in relaxed, social circumstances, and hand out the money collected. He also assumed that it would be a routine matter to inquire about their individual visa cases at the American Consulate. Fry took a brief leave of absence from his post at the Foreign Policy Association. He suspected that it would take just three weeks to contact the few hundred people on the committee's lists.

Undoubtedly, it was Fry's dismal reception at the American Consulate during his first day in Marseille that influenced his future actions. This encounter must have had such a lingering effect on Fry that he chose to begin *Surrender on Demand* with an elaborate account of it. Obviously offended and outraged at the indifference he witnessed, Fry then opted, quite unexpectedly, to depart from the original goals of the newly formed Emergency Rescue Committee. *Surrender on Demand* imparts one reason: Fry was genuinely moved by the human suffering he witnessed from his window in the Hotel Splendide.

Beyond this, Fry was, at age 32, a seasoned observer of foreign affairs. He correctly perceived inconsistencies regarding the issuance of French exit visas by Vichy officials. Particularly fond of following French politics, Fry was skeptical of the extent to which the French authorities would carry out extraditions according to Article XIX's "surrender on demand" clause. Fry also observed, especially during his first days in Marseille, disarray in the political stances of neighboring Spain and Portugal. He noted that the neighboring governments were hardly coordinated in their attitudes toward the refugees. Fry and his colleagues thus took full advantage of this timely situation, acting with surprising fearlessness in their exploitation of the current political confusion.

Fry, of course, was writing *Surrender on Demand* with the benefit of hindsight. Yet, there is little in Fry's writing to suggest that his actions were anything but spontaneous and acutely perceptive. His reconstruction of events, his descriptions of encounters, and his intricate story-telling faithfully unfold the process by which he found the "inner courage" to step outside of his commissioned assignment. Motivating Fry was his own doubt regarding the reach of Article XIX. Fry persisted without assured funding and lacking home support, because he believed that all refugees who opposed Hitler, regardless of their political or intellectual status, were at risk of the "surrender on demand" clause.

In January 1941, Fry was reassured of the validity of his operations, although the methods were sometimes unorthodox and exotic for a man of his upbringing. It became obvious to him that Germany was not interested in having masses of refugees returned. Fry was convinced that each of the great powers—Germany, France, and the United States—was handling the refugee crisis according to its own particular interests. As a result, he was acting defiantly and with great insight when he described the sudden turn of events in his work:

> At the end of January many of the refugees discovered they could get exit visas. I don't know for certain what the explanation of the sudden change of policy was, but from what I learned later, it seems it meant that the Gestapo and the other secret-police organizations had completed the task of going over the lists of the political and intellectual refugees in France and decided which of them they wanted and which they would allow to slip through their net. . . . [N]ow we could openly engage in what had all along been our *raison d'etre*—emigration. [*pg. 186*]

In stressing emigration rather than simply handing out relief, as the Red Cross and other relief organizations were doing, Fry saved thousands of persons who would have been interned. Even as he tried to determine who was "blacklisted," for political and cultural reasons, Fry regarded with much concern the increase in anti-Jewish statutes appearing in Vichy France. The first was issued in October 1940, a little more than a month after his arrival in Marseille. Fry wrote of the fate of his most famous Jewish client, the artist Marc Chagall, who was apprehended in late spring, as an example of the application of the anti-Jewish laws. Fry learned that Chagall was arrested not because he was known by the authorities as an esteemed painter whose art had been declared "degenerate," but because he was Jewish.

Fry continued to act deliberately, although his tenure in Marseille was coming to an end. He lobbied on all fronts, to the extent that he angered his original supporters and alienated himself from them. Independent of his home committee, he solicited new support, largely through the efforts of his wife, Eileen Hughes Fry, who volunteered for the New York office of the Emergency Rescue Committee. She launched an aggressive appeal among a prestigious circle of American intellectual figures. They sent a barrage of telegrams and letters to top State Department personnel, pleading for the extension of Fry's work on behalf of refugees. In France, Fry sought support for his mission, engaging leading French cultural and intellectual figures who did not choose to emigrate, including André Malraux, André Gide and Henri Matisse. Ultimately, this effort was unable to help him. The United States Government finally prevailed. The brief letter Eleanor Roosevelt wrote to Eileen Fry on May 13, 1941, accurately describes the situation:

> Dear Mrs. Fry:
>
> Miss Thompson gave me your message and I am sorry to say that there is nothing I can do for your husband.
>
> I think he will have to come home because he has done things which the government does not feel it can stand behind. I am sure they will issue him a passport to come home even though it means that someone else will have to be sent to take over the work which he is doing.
>
> Very sincerely yours,
> Eleanor Roosevelt
> [*Varian Fry Papers, Rare Book and*
> *Manuscript Library, Columbia University*]

Even with his expulsion, disgraceful and undignified as it was, Fry made efforts to contrive ways for refugees to escape. As Fry notes in the closing chapter of *Surrender on Demand*, he tried to resume his operation from the Unitarian Service Committee in Lisbon, then the center of relief organizations for refugees. Realizing that he was unable to remain in Europe, he returned to the United States. In New York, Fry still refused to consider his mission closed. Upon his arrival, he held an impromptu news conference, picked up by *The Washington Post* of November 3, 1941:

> An American engaged in aiding refugees to reach the United States . . . criticized as a "stupid policy" the State Department's method of handling visas for refugees. . . . [S]ince July 1, when

new visa regulations were imposed, only 6 of 150 refugees who had previously met former visas requirements were able to obtain them.

Ever headstrong and confrontational, Fry had alerted other colleague journalists of his return, hoping to gain momentum and support for the work, now left in the hands of his trusted coworkers, Danny Bénédite, Theo Bénédite, Jean Gemähling, Maurice Verzeanu, and others.

In New York, Fry once again faced opposition, and once again it came from those who were thought to be his chief supports. While Fry was in France, the Emergency Rescue Committee had actively organized exclusive fund-raising dinners, auctions, and lectures. But they failed to gather money to support the wide-ranging rescue effort Fry had championed. The Emergency Rescue Committee found that it could raise money for the likes of Franz Werfel, Lion Feuchtwanger, Konrad Heiden, and Marc Chagall. However, finding public funds for uncelebrated refugees, such as those who sought Fry's aid in Marseille, was difficult indeed. The paperwork required by the United States was overwhelming for the Emergency Rescue Committee's limited staff. As Fry learned, the committee, mirroring other organizations such as the Unitarian Service Committee, the American Friends Service Committee, and the American Red Cross, was reluctant to support unorthodox relief work like Fry's. None were willing to take the risks he had taken. Fry's own expulsion and discredit offered sure evidence of the result of such inappropriate actions.

In vain, Fry sought to convince his home committee to continue aiding clandestine operations in Marseille. He met with no success. Unfortunate timing was also to play a role in the ultimate demise of his work. Just weeks after Fry's return, and coinciding with the Japanese attack on Pearl Harbor and America's formal entry into the war, the Emergency Rescue Committee decided to merge with the International Relief and Rescue Committee. Fry was left out of the merger; he was without a home base from which to continue his style of relief efforts.

Facing the certain end to his work, Fry also experienced deep personal upheaval. Within less than a year he separated from Eileen. Their correspondence over the tense year of Fry's work in Marseille reveals that Fry persisted in his mission at great personal sacrifice. In a letter written on the train across Spain, when Fry found himself following the refugees' exact route, he warned Eileen that the intensity of his *ad hoc* rescue effort had transformed him in peculiar ways. He wrote, as if to prepare her for the inevitable:

I have just reached the end of the most intense twelve months I have ever lived through. When I left New York on August 4, 1940, I had no idea at all of what lay ahead of me. (Such ideas as I had proved to be fantastic.) Even during the first days and weeks in Marseille, I was so far from realizing the true nature of the situation I faced. Today I think I understand as well as anyone else what is happening to France. And yet I still don't quite know what happened to me. Perhaps I have been too busy to give much thought to that question. Perhaps in the coming weeks, as the confused details of a crowded year fade from my memory, the important facts will emerge, like the stones left on the beach by ebbing tide.

What I do know is that I have lived far more intensely in this last year, far more objectively, actively, really, if you like, than I ever have before. And that experience has changed me profoundly. Shall I gradually return to my old self in the familiar surroundings of New York? Doubtless I shall lose some of my new qualities; doubtless some of the old, now dormant, will be reawakened by the resumption of a normal, American life. But I do not think that I shall ever be quite the same person I was when I kissed you good-bye at the airport and went down the gangplank to the waiting Clipper. For the experiences of ten, fifteen, and even twenty years have been pressed into one. Sometimes I feel as if I've lived a whole life (and one to which I have no right) since I first walked down the monumental stairway of the Gare St. Charles in Marseille and timidly took a small back room at the Hotel Splendide. . . . I don't know whether you will like the change or not: I rather suspect you won't. But it is there, and it is there to stay. It is the indelible mark that a year spent in fighting my own little war has left on me. . . . I just want to tell you that you are going to find your husband a changed man.

Barcelona, September 7, 1941
[*Varian Fry Papers, Rare Book and
Manuscript Library, Columbia University*]

It was in the wake of personal and professional turmoil that Varian Fry began *Surrender on Demand*. From the impassioned words of the original first draft of his foreword, written just months after his return, Fry set out to articulate the utter despair he felt when he realized that he was rendered powerless to come to the aid of those still stranded in Europe. Letters to colleagues suggest that he saw in the writing of *Surrender on Demand* a way to come to understand the emotional drama in which he had become the principal actor. Alone and without a job (while still in France, he had been relieved of his post with the Foreign Policy Association), he immersed himself in letters written home to Eileen and to his other trusted correspondent, his mother Lilian Mackey Fry.

Fry kept no diary while in France; he was compulsive about destroying lists and papers. His work, therefore, was retrospective. Fry's cover organization, the Marseille-based *Centre Américain de Secours*, had codes for keeping financial documents and cables. As Fry had always feared censorship and confiscation, he never recorded specific underground operations. The task of writing his memoirs was monumental. He had to reconstruct exact scenes, sequences, character studies, and conversations.

Letters to Albert Hirschman (Beamish) and Danny Bénédite reveal not only Fry's intention to write his account as a first-person chronicle, but also his dedication to withholding publication until world events changed. Fry was discreet about the on-going work of his colleagues. He knew that Danny Bénédite and Jean Gemähling were engaged in resistance activities. He was reluctant, with good reason, to reveal information about contacts within the Marseille police and other "friendly" sources. Fry was also painfully aware that many of his clients were still waiting for precious American visas and for their cases to be painstakingly reviewed. Fry's personal devotion to his clients and his colleagues never ceased, and his consideration for them superseded his own ambitions.

However, while writing his personal essay, Fry did not stop speaking out on world affairs. He particularly focused his rhetoric on America's cumbersome and obstructive visa review process. As actively as he was able, he continued to write critically and passionately about refugees caught up in a wall of paper and bureaucratic red tape. At first, he concentrated on writing a series of articles publicly revealing the disarray evident in American visa policy. In such magazines as *The Nation* and *The New Leader*, he used as examples some of his cases, although abridged to protect his clients.

As the first draft of *Surrender on Demand* neared completion, Fry also took up a post as Executive Secretary of the American Labor Conference on International Affairs, a loosely structured committee to influence post-war policy for a consortium of American labor groups. More significantly, Fry became a contributing editor to *The New Republic*, writing articles principally about the situation in France. His most vehement article, entitled "The Massacre of the Jews," published in December 1942, was clearly prophetic in its scope. In it he announced shocking reports he had received from his clients in France, regarding the deportations of Jews. As a means to save thousands of Jews in France, Fry called for the relaxation of the lengthy visa review process, a process that forced thousands of applicants to give up for lack of progress. Fry proposed instead that the United States set up camps in America for the purpose of examining the loyalties of applicants. By January 1944, the only tangible action on American soil of Roosevelt's War Refugee Board was the establishment of an internment camp at Oswego (Fort Ontario), New York, for some 1,000 people, most from southeastern Europe. But it was far too little and too late.

Though Fry was determined to focus on his personal experiences in *Surrender on Demand*, his narrative was timely and instructive. In it Fry unhesitatingly speaks to an important point lost on many Americans during the war, but perhaps on the minds of many as the war drew to a close: that true valor was an individual choice. With *Surrender on Demand*'s publication, Fry was able to find a degree of satisfaction.

Despite the array of hurdles—and they were formidable—Fry managed to set in motion an extraordinary rescue effort, rare during World War II. The results were remarkable. Though Fry never took time to count actual cases, he and his coworkers estimate that he was able to offer aid to some 4,000 people. Of these, between 1,200 to 1,800 persons found their way to safety, clandestinely or legally, as a result of his direct efforts. Fry himself claims that he reviewed the cases of 15,000 persons, an astounding number, considering the minimal support and financial backing he had at his disposal and also considering the slow process of issuing visas that the United States consuls had adopted after the fall of France in June 1940.

What Fry did, given his position and his prior experiences, was indeed scandalous, adventurous, and, in the end, blatantly courageous. Fry's escapade was a rare episode of civilian valor worthy of attention, particularly at that time in history. While not a soldier or political leader (Fry was turned down by his draft board due to a history of duodenal ulcers), he did what was completely extraordinary for an American civilian. He engaged black-marketers, organized a network of smugglers, rescued British soldiers from Occupied France, reported on internment camps, set up routes, and arranged illegal escapes across the mountains. All this he did with the aid and collaboration of inexperienced relief workers, wealthy socialites, American students, and with the refugees themselves.

His contributions to the cultural and intellectual climate in New York were hardly less significant than his spontaneous acts of valor. New York was well on its way to becoming the world's center of the modern art world, now that Marcel Duchamp, André Breton, André Masson, and Max Ernst were exhibiting there, publishing their journals and gathering younger American artists to them. The writers to whom Fry had especially tended—Franz Werfel, Heinrich Mann, and Lion Feuchtwanger—were comfortably settled in Los Angeles at the time of the Golden Age of American cinema. Other writers in New York such as Konrad Heiden, Hans Sahl, Walter Mehring, Ivan Heilbut, Arthur Koestler, Hans Habe, Hans Natonek, Leo Lania, and Hertha Pauli, were trying to establish themselves. Exiled academics were seeking appointments to faculties in the United States, including scientists such as Nobel Prize–winning physicist Otto Meyerhof, and social philosopher Hannah Arendt. Fry's contributions, measured by any scale, are concrete.

Though well received in reviews, including an enthusiastic notice in *The New York Times Book Review, Surrender on Demand* was hardly a best seller. Its reception was modest. Popular opinion again controlled Fry's success, or lack of it. Post-war Americans remained ambivalent toward the achievements of French Surrealist artists and foreboding German writers. Very few of the people Fry actually saved had an immediate, direct impact on America's popular culture, save Franz Werfel with his screen play of the widely popular *The Song of Bernadette.* After the war, many of those Fry rescued chose to return to a more familiar Europe, rather than to remain, unpublished and jobless, in a post-war America.

As it turned out, with *Surrender on Demand*'s publication, Fry began to distance himself more and more from the political world in which he had once flourished. For him, 1945 was a turbulent year. He publicly resigned his position with *The*

*New Republic* over his open disagreements with the apparent pro-Soviet sentiments of the editorial board. He saw the end of his brief position as editor of *Common Sense*, a political magazine that espoused his anti-Communist views. His work for the American Labor Conference on International Affairs also petered out for lack of funds and sufficient interest. After *Surrender on Demand*, Fry was ever more estranged from the world's political stage.

As the war years faded, Fry's personal life continued on a precipitous path. He devoted himself to Eileen during a long terminal illness. He tried his hand at photography, a talent he had sharpened in Marseille, and also at television.

In the early 1950s, he married Annette Riley and later moved to New York's Upper West Side, finally settling in Connecticut. Surrounded with the art of many of the *Centre Américain de Secours'* exiled clients, their letters and books, the Frys established a home and raised a family. Fry's interests turned to other things: horticulture, birding, and wine tasting. As his colleague, Mary Jayne Gold, wrote in tribute:

> Varian was a creature of contrasts; a preppie who majored in the classics at Harvard; a bird watcher who was an editor and writer on foreign affairs; a volunteer for a dangerous mission who read Greek and Latin poets for relaxation; a Scarlet Pimpernel who saved hundreds of anti-Nazi intellectual and political refugees from the clutches of the Gestapo but whose manner and appearance, as he himself said, "hardly suggested the daredevil."

It was only in the 1960s that the International Rescue Committee, the successor organization to the Emergency Rescue Committee and the International Relief and Rescue Committee, re-recruited him. After twenty years, Fry came full-circle when he was asked to help raise funds for world relief. The assignment was to compile a portfolio of prints to be created by artists who were former refugees, marking the 25th anniversary of their flight from Hitler. This project led to

Fry's first formal contact with many of his clients after a long hiatus. In the midst of travel through France contacting Matisse, Chagall, Ernst, Masson, Arp, and Lam, as well as "exiled artists" displaced by World War II, including Henry Moore, Joan Miro, Oskar Kokoschka, and Pablo Picasso, he suffered a heart attack. In a letter to Max Ernst, he asked:

> Did you have pain in your shoulders, especially your left shoulder, radiating down your arm all the way to your fingers, and all along the clavicle to the neck, after your coronaries? And were your feet cold as ice afterward? These are some of my symptoms now. I am told they eventually go away.
>
> [*Varian Fry Papers, Rare Book and Manuscript Library, Columbia University*]

Less than a year later, Varian Fry died.

The final year of Fry's life was again combined with a disproportionate balance of defeats over triumphs. He separated from Annette and took a modest job teaching Latin at the Joel Barlow High School in Redding, Connecticut. In the midst of renewed isolation, he began a rewrite of *Surrender on Demand*, this time for young readers. The new version, entitled *Assignment: Rescue*, was intended to teach 1960s youngsters about heroism, spontaneous activism, and the necessity to fight against fascism no matter what the cost. In a brief moment of recognition, in April 1967, Fry was nominated a *Chevalier de la Légion d'Honneur*, one of the few Americans Charles de Gaulle agreed to honor for work on behalf of France during the war. Shortly thereafter, Fry died alone, from a cerebral hemorrhage. When he failed to show up for classes, the åschool dispatched the police to investigate. Officer Schwartz found Fry in his bed, his manuscript by his side.

This re-issue of *Surrender on Demand*, after more than fifty years, signals more than an emerging interest in an astonishing story of a "scarlet pimpernel" who was responsible for coming to the rescue of the world's leading cultural and political exiles. Fry's abiding narrative teaches that one person's actions did have consequences during an unprecedented assault on humanity and its culture. It is fitting that Fry, an unsung American who accomplished so much, and who is now recognized as the only American to have saved Jews during the Holocaust by Israel's Yad Vashem, was the subject of the inaugural special exhibition of America's national memorial to victims of the Holocaust. The United States Holocaust Memorial Museum's exhibition, *ASSIGNMENT: RESCUE, The Story of Varian Fry and the Emergency Rescue Committee*, stresses, as Fry did in *Surrender on Demand*, that one person is able to run against the tide of public opinion and inhumane governmental policy. In his letter to Eileen, days after his expulsion, Fry admits that, despite his role in saving thousands of persons, it was the triumph over his own hesitations that made his story exceptional:

> I have had an adventure—there is no other but this good Victorian word—of which I never dreamed. I have learned to live with people and to work with them. I have developed or discovered within me powers of resourcefulness, of imagination, and of courage which I never before knew I possessed. And I have fought a fight against enormous odds, of which, in spite of the final defeat, I think I can always be proud.
>
> Barcelona, September 7, 1941
> [*Varian Fry Papers, Rare Book and Manuscript Library, Columbia University*]

by Elizabeth Kessin Berman, Research Curator
with Susan W. Morgenstein, Curator
and Anita Kassof, Associate Curator
*ASSIGNMENT: RESCUE, The Story of Varian Fry and the Emergency Rescue Committee*
United States Holocaust Memorial Museum

# GLOSSARY OF FOREIGN TERMS

*Page*
3. *bidet*: small bath, used for hygiene
4. *pissotière*: urinal
6. *ja* (German): yes
8. *Genossin* (fem. form) (German): Comrade
8. *Genosse* (masc. form) (German): Comrade
8. *commissaire*: police superintendent
13. *rafles*: roundups, raids, arrests
14. *en règle*: with documents in order
15. 100 francs (refers to French currency; at the time, the rate of exchange was US\$1=40ff)
17. *apatrides*: stateless persons (deprived of their nationality by Nazi decree)
17. *titres de voyage*: refugee passport (not recognized by the Spanish)
20. *maisons closes*: whorehouses
21. *chéchias*: fezzes
21. *képis*: military caps
21. *chasseurs*: light infantry soldiers
21. *pagaille*: complete disorder
21. *se débrouiller*: watch out for one's own interest first; manage; make do
21. *Faut se débrouiller*: you have to shift for yourself however you can
24. *un peu dans la lune*: absentminded
24. *compréhensif*: understanding
25. *livret militaire*: soldier's book
25. *Sauve qui peut, faut se débrouiller*: Save yourself, every man for himself
25. *feuille de démobilisation*: demobilization orders
25. *carte d'identité*: identification card

261

25. *de Philadelphie*: from Philadelphia
25. *Auberges de Jeunesse*: youth hostels
26. *Club des Sans Club*: Club for those Without a Club (tourist association)
27. *né*: born
29. *visas de télégrammes*: visas sent by telegram (which then needed to be stamped to become official)
29. *belote*: game analagous to nap (card game resembling whist)
29. *gendarme*: member of the French national police which is a branch of the armed services (as opposed to an "agent de police"—a policeman); members of the gendarmerie are armed police (Police Militia)
32. *Vorwaerts* (German): Forward
33. *Evéché*: here, refers to the police station which was housed in the old Bishopric
33. *On vous demande en bas*: They're asking for you downstairs
35. *Il ne faut pas exagérer*: You needn't exaggerate
35. *Je n'ai jamais couché avec*: I never slept with (him)
35. *Je fais ma petite beauté*: I am fixing my make-up
36. *Ministère d'Armements*: Ministry of Armament
36. *Centre Américain de Secours*: American Relief Center
36. *Ça fait bien français*: That sounds really French
37. *Comité d'Assistance aux Réfugiés*: Committee for Refugee Assistance
37. *FERMÉ*: closed
38. *dossier*: folder
39. *pipi*: pee pee
40. *camions*: trucks
41. *prime de démobilisation*: discharge bonus
42. *à volonté*: at will
42. *fiche*: registration card
43. *louche*: shady; suspicious
43. *agent provocateur*: someone hired to instigate a riot or cause trouble
43. *Vu; Lu*: Seen; Read
43. *Deuxième Bureau*: French Intelligence Agency
46. *Neue Tagebuch* (German): New Journal
46. *clovisses, crevettes, Portugaises, moules, oursins, violettes*: cockles, shrimp, Portuguese oysters, mussels, sea urchins, violets
46. *coco*: cocaine
47. *Ils ne sont pas réguliers, ces gars-là*: Those guys aren't on the level

47. *Je vous le dis*: I'm telling you
47. *Etes-vous né bordelais ou bourguignon?*: Were you born in Bordeaux or Burgundy?
48. *flic*: cop
49. *commandant*: commander
49. *permis de séjour*: residence permit
49. *chef du service des étrangers*: head of the Foreign Office
49. *souffrant*: ailing
50. *permis*: permit
50. *Pariser Tageszeitung* (German): Paris Times
50. *émigré*: emigrant
50. *filer*: beat it, scram
53. *débrouillard American*: an American who could manage touchy situations
59. *Giustizia e Libertà* (Italian): Justice and Liberty
62. *Ça ne va pas*: It's not going to work
64. *Das ist Unsinn, Franz* (German): That's nonsense, Franz
64. *Verzeihung, Frau Mann, aber vielleicht wissen Sie nicht dass ich Deutsch verstehe* (German): Excuse me, Mrs. Mann, but perhaps you don't know that I understand German
65. *tabac*: tobacco store
65. *Gauloises Bleues, Gitanes Grises, et Vertes*: brands and types of French cigarettes
66. *douanier*: customs agent
66. *douane*: customs office
68. *gardes mobiles*: militia
69. *opéra-bouffe*: comic opera; musical comedy
75. *savon, sapone, Seife, jabón* (in French, Italian, German, Spanish): soap
78. *entrada* (Spanish): entrance
79. *confiture de sucre de raisin*: jelly made with the sugar of pressed grapes
79. *café national*: national coffee (a "coffee" made from burned grain)
80. *Sûreté Nationale*: Criminal Investigation Department
80. *résidence forcée*: forced residence
80. *inquiet*: anxious
83. *cancelado* (Spanish): cancelled
83. *maisons de passe*: brothels
84. *comité de criblage*: screening committee
88. *Bouline*: gauntlet

88. *Je fais ça pour l'honneur de la patrie et pour assurer ma vieillesse*: I am doing that for the honor of my country and to provide for my old age
89. *Je vais me sacrifier*: I'm going to sacrifice myself
90. *C'est de la blague*: That's a joke
97. *habeas corpus* (Latin): writ issued to ensure the right of prompt disposition of a case
97. *résidence assignée*: assigned housing
98. *prestataire*: conscript for military work
101. *chef de cabinet*: principal private secretary
102. *Consul de France*: French Consul
102. *Secrétaire d'État aux Affaires Étrangères*: Secretary of State Foreign Affairs
107. *Toujours dans la lune*: still absentminded
108. *procès-verbal*: police report
108. *rien de suspect*: nothing suspicious
109. *chalutier*: trawler
114. *Mais non, mais non*: But no, but no
114. *Ça y est!*: There it is! (I've got it!)
114. *Maintenant*: Now
114. *Notre plus grand poète*: Our greatest poet
115. *été de la Saint-Martin*: Indian summer
116. *N'en parlons pas*: Let's not talk about it
116. *Ah, les femmes!*: Oh, women!
116. *Quelle sale espèce!*: What a nasty lot!
117. *Formidable! Sensationnel! Invraisemblable!*: Terrific! Sensational! Hard to believe!
118. *Voyez-vous*: Do you see
119. *n'est-ce pas?*: right?
119. *Stupéfiant!*: Astounding!
119. *vivants*: alive
119. *Tenez!*: Well!
119. *Voyons*: Let's see
119. *En tout cas*: In any case
120. *Enfin*: After all
121. *Château Espère-Visa*: Château Hope-Visa
121. *pinède*: pine forest
121. *poêle*: heating stove
122. *Les femmes de France*: Women of France
122. *Nous étions trois jeunes héros*: We were three young heros
122. *Sur les bords de la Loire*: On the banks of the Loire
122. *Passant par Paris*: Passing through Paris

123. *rejoindre leurs foyers*: go home
126. *Intérieur, Affaires Etrangères, Vice-Présidence, A classer*:
     Internal, Foreign Affairs, Vice Presidency, To be Sorted
126. *lavabo*: Wash-basin
126. *armoires*: closets (wardrobes)
126. *Journal Officiel*: Official Newspaper
127. *Vice-Présidence du Conseil*: Office of the Vice-President of the
     Cabinet
127. *Chef de Cabinet*: Secretary of the Cabinet
127. *Entrez sans frapper*: Enter without knocking
127. *Hommes, Dames, Bains*: Men, Women, Bathrooms
128. *Chargé d'Affaires*: Deputy Ambassador, Envoy
130. *ABRI*: SHELTER
131. *Lumière, eh, lumière, là-bas!*: Light, hey, light, over there!
132. *Bon soir*: Good evening
132. *Comment ça va?*: How's it going?
132. *histoire*: trouble (in this context)
132. *Pas de quoi*: Don't mention it
132. *Alors, bon soir et bonne chance*: Well, good evening and good
     luck
134. *Mille pardons*: I'm so sorry
134. *tellement en retard*: so late
134. *Oui*: Yes
134. *en chemises de nuit*: In our nightgowns
134. *Finalement*: Finally
134. *C'est la visite du Maréchal*: It's the Field Marshal's visit
134. *Mon dieu!*: My God!
134. *Il ne faut pas exagérer, quand même*: It isn't necessary to get
     carried away, for goodness' sake
134. *A votre service*: At your service (whatever you say)
135. *Alors, procédez*: Well, proceed
135. *Voilà, monsieur*: There you are, sir
136. *Eh, ben!*: Hah!
137. *Entendu*: OK (agreed)
138. *Voilà, mademoiselle*: There you are, miss
138. *Pas du tout, mademoiselle, Pas du tout*: Not at all, miss, not at
     all
139. *Qu'est-ce qu'il y a?*: What is it?
139. *Le terrible crétin de Pétain*: Pétain's awful dunce
139. *putain*: whore
140. *C'est contestable*: It's debatable
141. *le petit endroit*: the lavatory

142. *le chef d'oeuvre*: the masterpiece
142. *procès-verbaux*: police reports
142. *bistro*: pub
142. *Quand même*: After all
142. *Il ne faut pas exagérer*: This is really going too far
142. *Merde alors*: Oh shit
142. *Brigade des Rafles*: Roundup Brigade
143. *Tiens*: Hey
143. *vive le Président Veelsson!*: Long live President Wilson!
145. *Basler Neueste Nachrichten* (German): Latest News of Basle (newspaper)
147. *Voilà, messieurs, dame*: There you are, ladies and gentlemen
147. *A votre santé*: To your health
148. *Groupe de Protection*: Protection Group
148. *Garde Pétain*: Pétain Guard
148. *casernes*: barracks
149. *Il faut tourner ça à la rigolade*: We need to treat it like a joke
149. *Que ces gars-là sont bêtes!*: Those guys are so stupid!
150. *filature*: being tailed by a detective
150. *Commissariat Spécial*: Office of the Special Police
150. *un nommé Hermant*: Someone named Hermant
152. *maquis*: French Underground movement
156. *Cour d'Assises*: Criminal Court
157. *Berliner Tageblatt*: Berlin Daily (newspaper)
157. *bourgeois*: member of the middle class
157. *doyen*: dean
159. *Symphonie Pastorale*: Pastoral Symphony
159. *Faux-Monnayeurs*: Counterfeiters
159: *Journal*: Diary
159. *comité de patronage*: support committee
160. *Petit Niçois*: (newspaper of Nice)
160. *porte-cochère*: coach's/servant's entrance
161. *Bien, monsieur*: Fine, sir
163. *Lisez 'La fin du monde'*: Read 'The End of the World'
167. *octroi*: toll-house
167. *carte grise*: grey card
167. *permis de circulation*: driver's license
169. *Allez*: Come on
170. *C'est à se les prendre et à se les mordre* (Slang): It's as hard as biting your own balls
170. *Je me fous de ces gars-là!*: I don't give a damn about those guys!

170. *Ces des couillons!* (Slang): They're jerks (Polite version)
171. *combine* (Slang): scheme
174. *Vous pensez bien bas de la France, Monsieur*: You don't think very much of France, sir
176. *huissier*: door-keeper
176. *Police Mobile*: Militia
176. *apéritif*: cocktail
180. *C'est nous, vos locataires*: It's us, your tenants
180. *Mais non, mais non*: No, no
181. *Le bail*: The lease
181. *Vive les pineurs!*: Long live the studs!
181. *Vive moi!*: Long live me!
181. *Vive Pétain!*: Long live Pétain!
181. *Victoire*: Victory
181. *Vive l'honneur*: Long live honor
181. *ces messieurs, nos bons maîtres*: these gentlemen, our good masters
181. *doryphores* (Slang): Jerries, Germans
183. *Le Boeuf Clandestin*: The Underground Beef
185. *Lumière*: Light
185. *les soupirs des femmes dans l'amour*: the sighs of women making love
186. *boîte louche*: suspicious hole
186. *raison d'être*: reason for being
191. *maisons de rendezvous*: meeting places
195. *douaniers*: customs agents
196. *Ecoutez*: Listen
197. *bien sûr*: of course
204. *Enfin*: Well
208. *numerus clausus* (Latin): final division
208. *exequatur* (Latin): In this case, the order of the French government by which a foreigner, the Czech Consul, could exercise his duties in France
208. *Service de la Surveillance du Territoire*: Regional Surveillance Office
212. *Il m'a donné! Je te jure!*: He turned me in, I swear!
216. *dossiers*: files
217. *Your phone is already on the table d'écoute*: Your phone is already being tapped
219. *Conseil National*: National Council
221. *Ministre d'Affaires Etrangères*: Minister of Foreign Affairs
222. *Intendant de la Police de la Région de Marseille*: Police Superintendent of the Marseille region

222. *le Capitaine de Frégate de Rodellec du Porzic*: Commander de Rodellec du Porzic
222. *locale*: quarters
224. *Parce que vous avez trop protégé des juifs et des anti-Nazis*: Because you have protected Jews and anti-Nazis too much
226. *Entrée interdite aux juifs non-combattants*: Entrance forbidden to non-combattant Jews
226. *ordre de refoulement*: order of expulsion
226. *nommé*: person named
226. *refoulé*: expelled
227. *expulsé*: expelled
228. *Réservé pour la Sécurité Nationale*: Reserved for the Dept. of Criminal Investigation
228. *le nommé*: The named
230. *Il n'y en a pas question*: There's no chance of it
230. *marche du bureau*: running of the office
230. *centre d'accueil*: welcome center
231. *mon vieux*: old friend
231. *En voiture!*: Take your seats!
232. French: ... *et celui-ci, qui doit se relire de temps à autre et qui rend optimiste. Nous en avons eu besoin parfois et il en faudra encore souvent.* English: ... this must be read from time to time—it makes one optimistic. We sometimes needed it in the past, and we often will need it in the future.
233. French: *Liés à nos frères par un commun but et qui se situe en dehors de nous, alors seulement nous respirons et l'expérience nous montre qu'aimer ce n'est point nous regarder l'un l'autre mais regarder ensemble dans la même direction. Il n'est de camarades que s'ils s'unissent dans la même cordée, vers le même sommet en quoi il se retrouvent . . .* English: We can only breathe freely when we are linked to our fellow man by a common and disinterested goal, and life shows us that to love is not to gaze upon one another, but to look outward together, in the same direction. Comrades are united only by striving to reach the same high place wherein they can find one another.
237. *Franc-Tireur*: Sniper

# INDEX

Alexander-Emmerich, Edgar, 236
Allen, Jay, 154, 155, 208
Apfel, Alfred, 176, 177, 244
Archambault, G.H., 163
Arendt, Hannah, x, 257
Ascoli, Max, 248
Aufricht, Hans, 187

Ball, Richard, 53, 54, 58, 61–64, 68,
    83, 91, 92, 106, 108–110, 112, 113
Barr, Alfred H. Jr., 248
Barellet, 49–51, 80, 83
"Beamish," Albert Hirschman, 24–30,
    35, 36, 38–48, 79, 80, 82, 87–91,
    103, 104, 107–109, 111, 112, 115,
    122, 125, 131–133, 150–152, 213,
    239, 254
Behrendt, Heinz, 239
Bénédite, Daniel ("Danny"), 100, 101,
    103, 116, 117, 120–122, 124, 125,
    127, 134, 140, 148, 149, 180, 183,
    195–197, 199, 202, 204, 205, 207,
    209, 211–215, 217, 218, 220, 221,
    223, 225–227, 229–232, 237, 238,
    252, 254
Bénédite, Pierre, 117
Bénédite, Theodora ("Theo"), 101,
    116, 117, 180, 214, 221, 228, 238,
    252
Benninghaus, Walter, 203
Bernanos, Georges, 159
Bernhard, Georg, 50, 83, 92, 95, 111,
    166, 191, 192, 195, 197–199, 201,
    204

Bernhard, Mrs. Georg, 83, 92, 111, 166,
    191, 192, 195, 197–199, 201, 204
Bierman, Mrs. Erika, 8, 9, 11, 12, 22,
    172, 173, 188
Bingham, Hiram ("Harry"), 10–12,
    70, 87–90, 147, 215
Blum, Léon, 97
Boegler, Franz, 243
Bohn, Dr. Frank, 7–12, 22, 23, 33, 34,
    51, 54, 55, 56, 59, 80, 81, 92, 93
Boyle, Kay, 184
Braun, Max, 50, 51
Brauner, Victor, 117
Breitscheid, Rudolph, 9, 11, 22, 23,
    40, 50, 51, 55, 58, 59, 80, 93, 166,
    167, 170–178, 189–191, 193, 198,
    243, 244
Breitscheid, Mrs. Rudolph, 22, 80,
    172–176
Breton, André, 115–117, 119, 136,
    137, 139–141, 144, 179, 180, 187,
    221, 239, 257
Breton, Aube, 117, 187
Breton, Jacqueline, 117, 187
Brooks, Howard, 220
Buttinger, Joseph, 248

Caballero, Largo, 59, 156, 166, 215,
    216, 238
Carlos, 196, 197, 199, 201–205, 234
Caspari, 192, 195
Castro, Professor de, 187
Chagall, Marc, x, xiii, 130, 187, 206,
    207, 238, 250, 252, 259

269

Chagall, Mrs. Marc, 130, 206, 207
Chaminade, Marcel, 102, 107, 108, 125, 221
Ciana, Alberto, 239
Compañys, Luis, 13

Darling, 106
Davenport, Miriam, 38, 39, 87, 117
de Gaulle, Charles, 259
del Vayo, Alvarez, 248
Dentas, Sousa, 128
Diaz, Alfonso, 209, 227
Dimitru, 45, 47, 48, 168, 169, 209–212, 214, 215, 217, 218, 221
Dobos, Ladislas, 203
Dohrn, Klaus, 98, 99, 111
Dominguez, Oscar, 117
Drach, Frederic, 43, 44, 82, 235, 238
Dubois, Captain, 89–91, 132, 148, 149, 150, 208
Duchamp, Marcel, 236, 257
Duhamel, Georges, 219

Ehrmann, Heinrich, 32
Einstein, Karl, 31
Ernst, Max, xiii, 184, 185, 187, 212, 238, 257, 259

Fawcett, Charles ("Charlie"), 37, 38, 53, 93, 108, 131, 149, 152, 153
Fendler, Eduard, 188
Feuchtwanger, Lion, xiii, 11, 12, 55, 56-58, 61, 80, 252, 257
Feuchtwanger, Mrs. Lion, 11, 12, 57, 58, 61, 80
Fishman, Lena, 35, 38, 39, 42, 70, 74, 75, 79, 80, 93, 94, 100, 127, 129, 131, 133–135, 137–139, 141, 148, 149, 208, 209, 239
Fitch, Captain, 105, 106, 110, 112, 113, 133
Frank, Karl, see Hagen, Paul
Frank, Leonard, 32
Freier, Bill, 44, 45, 123, 131, 132, 208, 238, 243
Fry, Annette Riley, 258, 259

Fry, Eileen Hughes, 250–251, 253–254, 258, 260
Fry, Lilian Mackey, 254

Garandel, Inspector, 227–231
Garetto, Giuseppe, 236
Garrow, Captain, 210
Gemähling, Jean, 101, 116, 122, 134, 140, 148, 151, 152, 154, 164, 165, 180, 181, 184, 192–195, 198, 202, 205, 210, 214, 218, 221, 225, 228, 230, 237, 252, 255
Gerlier, Cardinal, 235
Gide, André, 156–159, 219, 226, 251
Glasberg, Abbé, 235
Gold, Mary Jayne, 87, 101, 117, 137, 145, 146, 150, 185, 258
Goldberg, Oscar, 187
Graham, 105, 145
Gruss, Mrs. Anna, 100, 107, 149, 227, 238
Grynszpan, Herschel, 52
Guggenheim, Peggy, 185
Gumbel, Professor E. S., 32

Habe, Hans, 257
Hadamard, Jacques, 187
Hagen, Paul, 10, 14, 27, 32, 86, 87, 92, 93, 247
Hasenclever, Walter, 31
Heiden, Konrad, 11, 32, 238, 252, 257
Heilbut, Ivan, 257
Heine, Bedrich, 8, 10–12, 93, 168, 170–173, 189, 203, 239
Hermant, Albert (Hirschman), see "Beamish"
Herzog, Willhelm, 188
Hildebrand, Professor Dietrich von, 27, 28
Hildebrand, Franz von ("Franzi"), 26–28, 30, 35, 38, 39, 73, 74, 102, 239
Hilferding, Rudolph, 9, 11, 22, 23, 40, 50, 51, 55, 58, 59, 80, 93, 166, 167, 170–178, 189–191, 193, 198, 243, 244

Hilferding, Mrs. Rudolph, 22, 177, 178, 188
Himmler, Heinrich, 94, 95, 97, 178
Hirschman, Albert, see "Beamish"
Hoare, Sir Samuel, 72, 76–78, 105, 110, 209
Howe, Quincy, 247
Hull, Cordell, 57

Itor-Kahn, Erich, 124, 188

Jacob, Berthold, 198, 200–203, 235, 244
Jacob, Mrs. Berthold, 198, 200–203, 235
Jacques, 46–48, 165–170, 210, 217, 218
Johannes F——, 122–124, 133, 151, 152, 198, 200, 203
Johnson, Alvin, 248
Jolles, Heinz, 236
Joy, Dr. Charles, 73, 106

Keun, Irmgard, 31
Kingdon, Dr. Frank, 247
Kirstein, Lincoln, 246
Kleber, General, 104, 105
Klepper, Otto, 236
Koestler, Arthur, 257
Kokoschka, Oskar, 259
Kracauer, Siegfried, 187

Lam, Wifredo, 117, 259
Landowska, Wanda, 236, 238
Lania, Leo, 257
Laval, Pierre, 126, 127, 155, 156
Leonard, Lotte, 187
Leslau, Wolf, 125
Lili, 37, 149
Limot, 243
Limousin, Dr., 127
Lipchitz, Jacques, x, xiii, 187, 239
Lipnitski, 188
Llopis, Rodolfo, 59
Lloyd, 105, 145
Lowrie, Donald, 18, 19, 80
Lubienski, Count, 104

Lussu, Emilio, 59, 60, 72, 73, 109, 131, 152, 189, 190, 199–201, 204, 205, 215, 233–235, 239
Lussu, Mrs. Emilio, 204, 233, 235

Mahler, Gustav, 5
Maillol, Aristide, 219
Malandri, 45, 46
Malaquais, Jean, 236
Malraux, André, 157, 159, 251
Mann, Erica, 248
Mann, Golo, 58, 61, 64, 68–71, 73
Mann, Heinrich, 55, 58, 61, 63–66, 68–71, 74–75, 78, 257
Mann, Mrs. Heinrich, 58, 61, 64, 65, 66, 68–71, 74, 75, 78
Mann, Thomas, 58, 69, 124, 248
Marcu, Valeriu, 156, 157, 160, 187
Maritain, Jacques, 248
Masaryk, Jan, 248
Masson, André, 188, 238, 257, 259
Matisse, Henri, 156, 157, 219, 226, 251, 259
"Maurice," see Verzeanu, Marcel
Mehring, Walter ("Baby"), 38, 48–50, 53, 74, 80, 83, 84, 92, 102, 111, 173, 174, 239, 257
Mendizabel, Alfredo, 236
Mercury, M., 176, 177
Meyerhof, Dr. Otto, 32, 257
Mina, 45
Mirkine-Guetzévitch, Professor Boris, 187
Miro, Joan, 259
Modigliani, Giuseppe, 9, 11, 22, 23, 55, 59, 93, 237, 239
Modigliani, Mrs. Giuseppe, 22, 23, 237
Moore, Henry, 259
Mueller, Heinrich, 189
Muenzenberg, Willi, 31
Murphy, Captain, 164, 165, 168–170, 192, 198, 199, 209, 210, 214
Mutzi, Maître, 49

Natoli, Aurelio, 188
Natonek, Hans, 32, 257

Neumann, Alfred, 156, 157
Niebuhr, Reinhold, 247
Niemeyer, 156
Nouguet, Madame, 121, 137, 140, 142, 182, 183

Oppenheimer, Heinz Ernst ("Oppy"), 35, 36, 38, 39, 171, 172

Pacciardi, Colonel Randolfo, 109–112, 189, 190, 239
Palmer, Margaret, 154–156
Pauli, Hertha, 32, 257
Péret, Benjamin, 117–236
Pétain, Marshal, 98, 126, 133, 134, 139, 145, 147, 155
Peyrouton, Marcel, 127, 148
Picasso, Pablo, 259
Pittaluga, Dr. Gustavo, 236
Polgar, Alfred, 32
Poliakoff-Litovzeff, 187
Pringsheim, Peter, 124, 187
Purslow, Donald, 194

Reder, Bernard, 236
Reich, Vatroslav, 203, 204
Reiner, 42–44
Richard, M., see Hildebrand, Franz von
Rodellec du Porzic, de, *Intendant de la Police*, 222–227
Roosevelt, Eleanor, 251

Sahl, Hans, 187, 257
Schiffrin, Jacques, 188
Schnek, Johannes, 206, 233, 234
Séjourné, Laurette, 117
Serge, Victor, 115, 117, 121, 134–137, 146, 187
Serge, Vladi, 117, 187
Siemsen, Hans, 187

Starhemberg, Prince Ernst Rüdiger von, 50, 51
St. Exupéry, Antoine de, 184, 232, 233
St. Exupéry, Consuelo de, 184
Stirling, Charles, 236
Strauss, Dr. Bruno, 236

Thaelmann, Ernst, 178
Thumin, Dr., 114, 118–120, 179–181, 184, 228
Thyssen, Fritz, 160–162, 164, 166
Thyssen, Mrs. Fritz, 160–162, 164, 166
Torr, Major, 71–73, 76–78, 106
Treacy, Captain, 133, 152, 164

Verzeanu, Marcel ("Maurice"), 103, 151, 152, 154, 156, 193–205, 221, 225, 228, 230, 234, 239, 252
Vladimir, 243
Vochoč Vladimir, 18, 19, 80, 82, 208

Wagner, Hermann Richard, 244
Weiss, Ernst, 31
Weisslitz, Jacques, 238
Weisslitz, Mrs. Jacques, 238
Werfel, Franz, xiii, 5–6, 11, 12, 55, 57, 58, 61, 63, 64, 68–71, 75, 78, 98, 238, 252, 257
Werfel, Mrs. Franz, 5–6, 12, 57, 58, 61, 64, 68–71, 75, 78, 98
Westheim, Paul, 125, 236
Wolff, Arthur, 80, 191–195, 197, 198, 200–202, 234
Wolff, Mrs. Arthur, 80–, 191–195, 197, 198, 200–202, 234
Wolff, Charles, 185, 219, 221, 238
Wolff, Theodore, 156, 157

Ylla, 188

11/01